On the *Revival of the Religious Sciences* (*Iḥyāʾ ʿulūm al-dīn*)

"The *Ihyāʾ ʿulūm al-dīn* is the most valuable and most beautiful of books."
—Aḥmad b. Muḥammad Ibn Khallikān (d. 681/1282)

"The *Iḥyāʾ ʿulūm al-dīn* is one of al-Ghazālī's best works."
—Aḥmad b. ʿAbd al-Ḥalīm (d. 728/1328)

"Any seeker of [felicity of] the hereafter cannot do without the *Iḥyāʾ ʿulūm al-dīn*"
—ʿAbd al-Wahhāb b. ʿAlī l-Subkī (d. 771/1370)

"The *Iḥyāʾ ʿulūm al-dīn* is a marvelous book containing a wide variety of Islamic sciences intermixed with many subtle accounts of Sufism and matters of the heart."
—Ismāʿīl b. ʿUmar Ibn Kathīr (d. 774/1373)

"The *Iḥyāʾ ʿulūm al-dīn* is one of best and greatest books on admonition, it was said concerning it, 'if all the books of Islam were lost except for the *Iḥyāʾ* it would suffice what was lost.'"
—Musṭafā b. ʿAbdallāh Ḥājjī Khalīfa Kātib Čelebī (d. 1067/1657)

"The *Iḥyāʾ* [*ʿulūm al-dīn*] is one of [Imām al-Ghazālī's] most noble works, his most famous work, and by far his greatest work'"
—Muḥammad b. Muḥammad Murtaḍā l-Zabīdī (d. 1205/1791)

On Imām al-Ghazālī

"Al-Ghazālī is [like] a deep ocean [of knowledge]."

—ʿAbd al-Malik b. ʿAbdallāh al-Juwaynī (d. 478/1085)

"Abū Ḥāmid al-Ghazālī, the Proof of Islam (Ḥujjat al-Islām) and the Muslims, the Imām of the imāms of religion, [is a man] whose like has not been seen in eloquence and elucidation, in speech and thought, and in acumen and natural ability."

—ʿAbd al-Ghāfir b. Ismāʿīl al-Fārisī (d. 529/1134)

"Al-Ghazālī is the second [Imām] Shāfiʿī."

—Muḥammad b. Yaḥyā l-Janzī (d. 549/1154)

"[He was] the Proof of Islam and Muslims, Imām of the imāms of religious sciences, one of vast knowledge, the wonder of the ages, the author of many works, and [a man] of extreme intelligence and the best of the sincere."

—Muḥammad b. ʿUthmān al-Dhahabī (d. 748/1347)

"Al-Ghazālī is without doubt the most remarkable figure in all Islam."

—T.J. DeBoer (d. 1942)

". . . A man who stands on a level with Augustine and Luther in religious insight and intellectual vigor."

—H.A.R. Gibb (d. 1971)

"I have to some extent found, and I believe others can find, in the words and example of al-Ghazālī a true *iḥyāʾ* . . ."

—Richard J. McCarthy, S.J. (d. 1981)

The Forty Books of the
Revival of the Religious Sciences
(*Iḥyāʾ ʿulūm al-dīn*)

The Quarter of Worship

1 The Book of Knowledge
2 The Principles of the Creed
3 The Mysteries of Purification
4 The Mysteries of the Prayer
5 The Mysteries of Charity
6 The Mysteries of Fasting
7 The Mysteries of the Pilgrimage
8 The Etiquette of the Recitation of the Qurʾān
9 Invocations and Supplications
10 The Arrangement of the Litanies and the Exposition of the Night Vigil

The Quarter of Customs

11 The Proprieties of Eating
12 The Proprieties of Marriage
13 The Proprieties of Acquisition and Earning a Living
14 The Lawful and the Unlawful
15 The Proprieties of Friendship and Brotherhood
16 The Proprieties of Retreat
17 The Proprieties of Travel
18 The Proprieties of the Audition and Ecstasy
19 The Commanding of Right and the Forbidding of Wrong
20 The Proprieties of Living and the Prophetic Mannerisms

The Quarter of Perils

21 The Exposition of the Wonders of the Heart
22 Training the Soul, Refining the Character, and Treating the Ailments of the Heart
23 Overcoming the Two Desires
24 The Bane of the Tongue
25 The Censure of Anger, Malice, and Envy
26 The Censure of This World
27 The Censure of Greed and the Love of Wealth
28 The Censure of Fame and Hypocritical Ostentation
29 The Censure of Pride and Vanity
30 The Censure of Deceit

The Quarter of Deliverance

31 On Repentance
32 On Patience and Thankfulness
33 On Fear and Hope
34 On Poverty and Abstinence
35 On Unity and Trust
36 On Love, Longing, Intimacy, and Contentment
37 On Intention, Sincerity, and Truthfulness
38 On Vigilance and Accounting
39 On Contemplation
40 On the Remembrance of Death and the Hereafter

THE MYSTERIES OF THE PRAYER
AND ITS IMPORTANT ELEMENTS

Kitāb asrār al-ṣalāt wa-muhimmātihā

Book 4 of

The Revival of the Religious Sciences

Iḥyāʾ ʿulūm al-dīn

بِسْمِ ٱللَّهِ ٱلرَّحْمَٰنِ ٱلرَّحِيمِ

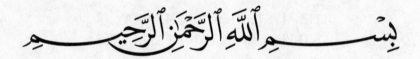

AL-GHAZĀLĪ

Kitāb asrār al-ṣalāt

THE MYSTERIES OF THE PRAYER

BOOK 4 of the *Iḥyāʾ ʿulūm al-dīn*

THE REVIVAL OF THE RELIGIOUS SCIENCES

TRANSLATED *from the* ARABIC
with an INTRODUCTION *and* NOTES
by M. ABDURRAHMAN FITZGERALD

FONS VITAE
2018

The Mysteries of the Prayer and its Important Elements, Book 4 of the *Revival of the Religious Sciences*, first published in 2018 by

Fons Vitae
49 Mockingbird Valley Drive
Louisville, KY 40207 USA

www.fonsvitae.com

The Fons Vitae Ghazali Series
Library of Congress Control Number: 2017916033
ISBN 978-1-94-1610-35-0

Editing and indexing: Valerie Joy Turner
Book design and typesetting: Muhammad Hozien
Text typeface: Adobe Minion Pro 11/13.5

Cover art courtesy of National Library of Egypt, Cairo.
Qurʾānic frontispiece to part 19. Written and illuminated by ʿAbdallāh b. Muḥammad al-Ḥamadānī for Sultan Uljaytu 713/1313. Hamadan.

Printed in Canada

Contents

Editor's Note

THIS is the complete translation of the *Kitāb asrār al-ṣalāh*, *The Mysteries of the Prayer*, book 4 of the *Iḥyāʾ ʿulūm al-dīn* of Ḥujjat al-Islām, Abū Ḥāmid al-Ghazālī. It was translated from the published Arabic text (Jedda: Dār al-Minhāj, 2011; 1:537–773), which utilized additional manuscripts and early printed editions.

Arabic terms that appear in italics follow the transliteration system of the *International Journal of Middle East Studies*. Common era (CE) dates have been added. The blessings on prophets and others, as used by Imām al-Ghazālī, are represented in the original Arabic, as listed below.

Arabic	English	Usage
عَزَّوَجَلَّ	Mighty and majestic is He	On mention of God
سُبْحَانَهُ وَتَعَالَىٰ	Exalted and most high is He	Used together or separately
صَلَّى ٱللَّهُ عَلَيْهِ وَسَلَّمَ	Blessings and peace of God be upon him	On mention of the Prophet Muḥammad
عَلَيْهِ ٱلسَّلَامُ	Peace be upon him	On mention of one
عَلَيْهِمُ ٱلسَّلَامُ	Peace be upon them	or more prophets
رَضِيَ ٱللَّهُ عَنْهُ	God be pleased with him	On mention of one or more
رَضِيَ ٱللَّهُ عَنْهُمْ	God be pleased with them	Companions of the Prophet
رَضِيَ ٱللَّهُ عَنْهَا	God be pleased with her	On mention of a female Companion of the Prophet
رَحِمَهُ ٱللَّهُ	God have mercy on him	On mention of someone who is deceased

The translator has included some of the footnotes and references provided by the editors of the Dār al-Minhāj edition. These footnotes include comments from Murtaḍā l-Zabīdī's *Itḥāf* (a detailed commentary on the *Iḥyāʾ ʿulūm al-dīn*) and identify many of Imām al-Ghazālī's sources. The translator also provided explanatory footnotes where necessary; clarification in the text appears in hard brackets.

In addition, the editors have compiled a short biography of Imām al-Ghazālī with a chronology of important events in his life. This is followed by an extract from Imām al-Ghazālī's introduction to the *Iḥyāʾ ʿulūm al-dīn*; the editors hope this may serve as a guide to the *Revival of the Religious Sciences* for those reading Imām al-Ghazālī for the first time.

Throughout the text we have opted to maintain the Arabic names of the obligatory daily prayers (*ṣalāt*) rather than using English terms that relate to the times of the day and evening. The five prayers are referred to, in order throughout the day, as follows: 1. *fajr* (pre-dawn), 2. *ẓuhr* (noon), 3. *ʿaṣr* (afternoon), 4. *maghrib* (after sunset), and 5. *ʿishāʾ* (night). This eliminates any confusion that would result in discussions of the supererogatory prayers, which are not named, but are referred to by descriptions that when translated into English might be confused with the obligatory prayers.

We would like to thank Annabel Keeler for proofreading the typeset proofs at the last minute in record time.

Biography of Imām al-Ghazālī

He is Abū Ḥāmid Muḥammad b. Muḥammad b. Muḥammad b. Aḥmad al-Ghazālī l-Ṭūsī; he was born in 450/1058 in the village of Ṭābarān near Ṭūs (in northeast Iran) and he died there, at the age of fifty-five, in 505/1111. Muḥammad's father died when he and his younger brother Aḥmad were still young; their father left a little money for their education in the care of a Sufi friend of limited means. When the money ran out, their caretaker suggested that they enroll in a *madrasa*. The *madrasa* system meant they had a stipend, room, and board. Al-Ghazālī studied *fiqh* in his hometown under a Sufi named Aḥmad al-Rādhakānī; he then traveled to Jurjān and studied under Ismāʿīl b. Masʿada al-Ismāʿīlī (d. 477/1084).

On his journey home his caravan was overtaken by highway robbers who took all of their possessions. Al-Ghazālī went to the leader of the bandits and demanded his notebooks. The leader asked, what are these notebooks? Al-Ghazālī answered: "This is the knowledge that I traveled far to acquire," the leader acquiesced to al-Ghazālī's demands after stating: "If you claim that it is knowledge that you have, how can we take it away from you?" This incident left a lasting impression on the young scholar. Thereafter, he returned to Ṭūs for three years, where he committed to memory all that he had learned thus far.

In 469/1077 he traveled to Nīsābūr to study with the leading scholar of his time, Imām al-Ḥaramayn al-Juwaynī (d. 478/1085), at the Niẓāmiyya College; al-Ghazālī remained his student for approximately eight years, until al-Juwaynī died. Al-Ghazālī was one of his most illustrious students, and al-Juwaynī referred to him as "a deep ocean [of knowledge]." As one of al-Juwaynī star pupils, al-Ghazālī used to fill in as a substitute lecturer in his teacher's absence. He also tutored his fellow students in the subjects that al-Juwaynī taught at the Niẓāmiyya. Al-Ghazālī wrote his first book, on the founding principles of legal theory (*uṣūl al-fiqh*), while studying with al-Juwaynī.

Very little is known about al-Ghazālī's family, though some biographers mention that he married while in Nīsābūr; others note that he had married in Ṭūs prior to leaving for Nīsābūr. Some accounts state that he had five children, a son who died early and four daughters. Accounts also indicate that his mother lived to see her son rise to fame and fortune.

After the death of al-Juwaynī, al-Ghazālī went to the camp (*al-muᶜaskar*) of the Saljūq *wazīr* Niẓām al-Mulk (d. 485/1192). He stayed at the camp, which was a gathering place for scholars, and quickly distinguished himself among their illustrious company. Niẓām al-Mulk recognized al-Ghazālī's genius and appointed him professor at the famed Niẓāmiyya College of Baghdad.

Al-Ghazālī left for Baghdad in 484/1091 and stayed there four years—it was a very exciting time to be in the heart of the Islamic empire. At the Niẓāmiyya College he had many students, by some estimates as many as three hundred. In terms of his scholarly output, this was also a prolific period in which he wrote *Maqāṣid al-falāsifa*, *Tahāfut al-falāsifa, al-Mustaẓhirī,* and other works.

Al-Ghazālī was well connected politically and socially; we have evidence that he settled disputes related to the legitimacy of the rule of the ᶜAbbāsid caliph, al-Mustaẓhir (r. 487–512/1094–1118) who assumed his role as caliph when he was just fifteen years old, after the death of his father al-Muqtadī (d. 487/1094). Al-Ghazālī issued a *fatwā* of approval of the appointment of al-Mustaẓhir and was present at the oath-taking ceremony.

In Baghdad, al-Ghazālī underwent a spiritual crisis, during which he was overcome by fear of the punishment of hell. He became convinced that he was destined for hell if he did not change his ways; he feared that he had become too engrossed in worldly affairs, to the detriment of his spiritual being. He began to question his true intentions: was he writing and teaching to serve God, or because he enjoyed the fame and fortune that resulted from his lectures. He experienced much suffering, both inward and outward; one day as he stood before his students to present a lecture, he found himself unable to speak. The physicians were unable to diagnose any physical malady. Al-Ghazālī remained in Baghdad for a time, then left his teaching post for the pilgrimage. He left behind fortune, fame, and influence. He was beloved by his numerous students and had many admirers, including the sultan; he was also envied by many. The presumption is that he left in the manner he did—ostensibly to undertake the pilgrimage—because if he had made public his intention to leave permanently, those around him would have tried to convince him to remain and the temptation might have been too strong to resist.

After leaving Baghdad, he changed direction and headed toward Damascus; according to his autobiography he disappeared from the intellectual scene for ten years. This does not mean that he did not teach, but that he did not want to return to public life and be paid for teaching. This ten-year period can be divided into two phases. First, he spent two years in the East—in greater Syria and on the pilgrimage. We have evidence that while on his return to Ṭūs he appeared at a Sufi lodge opposite the Niẓāmiyya College in Baghdad. He spent the second phase of the ten-year period (the remaining eight years) in Ṭūs, where he wrote the famed *Iḥyāʾ ʿulūm al-dīn*, a work that was inspired by the change in his outlook that resulted from his spiritual crisis.

When he arrived back in his hometown in 490/1097, he established a school and a Sufi lodge, in order to continue teaching and learning. In 499/1106, Niẓām al-Mulk's son, Fakhr al-Mulk, requested that al-Ghazālī accept a teaching position at his old school, the Niẓāmiyya of Nīsābūr. He accepted and taught for a time, but left this position in 500/1106 after Fakhr al-Mulk was assassinated by Ismāʿīlīs. He then returned to Ṭūs and divided his time between teaching and worship. He died in 505/1111 and was buried in a cemetery near the citadel of Ṭābarān.

Legacy and Contributions of al-Ghazālī

Al-Ghazālī's two hundred and seventy-three works span many disciplines and can be grouped under the following headings:

1. Jurisprudence and legal theory. Al-Ghazālī made foundational contributions to Shāfiʿī jurisprudence; his book *al-Wajīz* is a major handbook that has been used in teaching institutions around the world; many commentaries have been written on it, most notably by Abū l-Qāsim ʿAbd al-Karīm al-Rāfiʿī (d. 623/1226). In legal theory, *al-Mustaṣfa min ʿilm al-uṣūl* is considered one of five foundational texts in the discipline.
2. Logic and philosophy. Al-Ghazālī introduced logic in Islamic terms that jurists could understand and utilize. His works on philosophy include the *Tahāfut al-falāsifa*, which has been studied far beyond the Muslim world and has been the subject of numerous commentaries, discussions, and refutations.
3. Theology, including works on heresiography in refutation of Bāṭinī doctrines. He also expounded on the theory of occasionalism.
4. Ethics and educational theory. The *Mīzān al-ʿamal* and other works such as the *Iḥyāʾ ʿulūm al-dīn* mention a great deal on education.
5. Spirituality and Sufism. His magnum opus, the *Iḥyāʾ ʿulūm al-dīn* is a pioneering work in the field of spirituality, in terms of its organization and its comprehensive scope.
6. Various fields. Al-Ghazālī also wrote shorter works in a variety of disciplines, including his autobiography (*al-Munqidh min al-ḍalāl*), works on Qurʾānic studies (*Jawāhir al-Qurʾān*), and political statecraft (*Naṣiḥat al-mūluk*).

Chronology of al-Ghazālī's Life

450/1058	Birth of al-Ghazālī at Ṭūs
c. 461/1069	Began studies at Ṭūs
c. 465/1073	Traveled to Jurjān to study
466–469/1074–1077	Studied at Ṭūs
469/1077	Studied with al-Jūwaynī at the Niẓāmiyya college in Nīsābūr
473/1080	al-Ghazālī composed his first book, *al-Mankhūl fī l-uṣūl*
477/1084	Death of al-Fāramdhī, one of al-Ghazālī's teachers
25 Rabīʿ II 478/ 20 August 1085	Death of al-Jūwaynī; al-Ghazālī left Nīsābūr
Jumāda I 484/ July 1091	Appointed to teach at the Niẓāmiyya college in Baghdad
10 Ramaḍān 485/ 14 October 1092	Niẓām-al-Mulk was assassinated
484–487/1091–1094	Studied philosophy
Muḥarrām 487/ February 1094	Attended the oath-taking of the new caliph, al-Mustaẓhir
487/1094	Finished *Maqāṣid al-falāsifa*
5 Muḥarrām 488/ 21 January 1095	Finished *Tahāfut al-falāsifa*
Rajab 488/ July 1095	Experienced a spiritual crisis
Dhū l-Qaʿda 488/ November 1095	Left Baghdad for Damascus
Dhū l-Qaʿda 489/ November – December 1096	Made pilgrimage and worked on the *Iḥyāʾ ʿulūm al-dīn*
Jumāda II 490/ May 1097	Taught from the *Iḥyāʾ ʿulūm al-dīn* during a brief stop in Baghdad
Rajab 490/June 1097	Seen in Baghdad by Abū Bakr b. al-ʿArabī
Fall 490/1097	Returned to Ṭūs

Dhū l-Ḥijja 490/ November 1097	Established a *madrasa* and a *khānqāh* in Ṭūs
Dhū l-Qaʿda 499/ July 1106	Taught at the Niẓāmiyya college in Nīsābūr
500/1106	Wrote *al-Munqidh min al-ḍalāl*
500/1106	Returned to Ṭūs
28 Dhū l-Ḥijja 502/ 5 August 1109	Finished *al-Mustaṣfā min ʿilm al-uṣūl*
Jumada I 505/ December 1111	Finished *Iljām al-ʿawām ʿan ʿilm al-kalām*
14 Jumada II 505/ 18 December 1111	Imām al-Ghazālī died in Ṭūs

Eulogies in Verse

Because of him the lame walked briskly,
And the songless through him burst into melody.

On the death of Imām al-Ghazālī, Abū l-Muẓaffar Muḥammad al-Abiwardī said of his loss:

He is gone! and the greatest loss which ever afflicted me,
was that of a man who left no one like him among mankind.

About the *Revival of the Religious Sciences*

THE present work is book 4 of Imām al-Ghazālī's forty-volume masterpiece. Below is an extract from al-Ghazālī's introduction that explains the arrangement and purpose of the *Iḥyāʾ ʿulūm al-dīn*.

People have composed books concerning some of these ideas, but this book [the *Iḥyāʾ*] differs from them in five ways, by

1. clarifying what they have obscured and elucidating what they have treated casually;
2. arranging what they have scattered and putting in order what they have separated;
3. abbreviating what they have made lengthy and proving what they have reported;
4. omitting what they have repeated; and
5. establishing the truth of certain obscure matters that are difficult to understand and which have not been presented in books at all.

For although all the scholars follow one course, there is no reason one should not proceed independently and bring to light something unknown, paying special attention to something his colleagues have forgotten. Or they are not heedless about calling attention to it, but they neglect to mention it in books. Or they do not overlook it, but something prevents them from exposing it [and making it clear].

So these are the special properties of this book, besides its inclusion of all these various kinds of knowledge.

Two things induced me to arrange this book in four parts. The first and fundamental motive is that this arrangement in establishing what is true and in making it understandable is, as it were, inevitable because the branch of knowledge by which one approaches the hereafter is divided into the knowledge of [proper] conduct and the knowledge of [spiritual] unveiling.

By the knowledge of [spiritual] unveiling I mean knowledge and only knowledge. By the science of [proper] conduct I mean knowledge as well as action in accordance with that knowledge. This work will deal only with the science of [proper] conduct, and not with [spiritual] unveiling, which one is not permitted to record in writing, although it is the ultimate aim of saints and the ultimate aim of the sincere. The science of [proper] conduct is merely a path that leads to unveiling and only through that path did the prophets of God communicate with the people and lead them to Him. Concerning [spiritual] unveiling, the prophets عَلَيْهِمُ السَّلَامُ spoke only figuratively and briefly through signs and symbols, because they realized the inability of people's minds to comprehend. Therefore since the scholars are heirs of the prophets, they cannot but follow in their footsteps and emulate their way.

The knowledge of [proper] conduct is divided into (1) outward knowledge, by which I mean knowledge of the senses and (2) inward knowledge, by which I mean knowledge of the functions of the heart.

The physical members either perform acts of prescribed worship, or acts that are in accordance with custom, while the heart, because it is removed from the senses and belongs to the world of dominion, is subject to either praiseworthy or blameworthy [influences]. Therefore it is necessary to divide this branch of knowledge into two parts: outward and inward. The outward part, which is connected to the senses, is subdivided into acts of worship and acts that pertain to custom. The inward part, which is connected to the states of the heart and the characteristics of the soul, is subdivided into blameworthy states and praiseworthy states. So the total makes four divisions of the sciences of the practice of religion.

The second motive [for this division] is that I have noticed the sincere interest of students in jurisprudence, which has become popular among those who do not fear God تَعَالَىٰ but who seek to boast and exploit its influence and prestige in arguments. It [jurisprudence] is also divided into four quarters, and he who follows the style of one who is beloved becomes beloved.

Translator's Introduction

بِسْمِ ٱللَّهِ ٱلرَّحْمَٰنِ ٱلرَّحِيمِ

Indeed, prayer has been decreed upon the believers,
a decree of specified times.

Sūrat al-Nisāʾ, 4:103

The verse quoted above, often found carved in decorative calligraphy above the prayer niche (*miḥrāb*) of mosques, is one of the Qurʾānic commandments that make up the particular form of worship called *ṣalāt*; and it is one of the five pillars of Islam.

According to a number of traditional sources, the word itself, which appears in various forms throughout the Qurʾān more than ninety times, is derived from *al-ṣalawayn*, the name of a pair of tendons at the base of the back which bend when someone inclines at the waist.[1] The verbal form *ṣallā* is thus akin to three other verbs—*lāna, ḥanāʾ*, and *ʿaṭafa*—which express both the physical movement of inclination and the affective state of mercy, love, and

1 See the commentaries of al-Zamakhsharī (d. 538/1143), al-Naṣafī (d. 710/1310), Ibn Kathīr (d. 774/1372), and numerous others on Qurʾān 2:3, as well as al-Jawālīqī's (d. 540/1145) commentary on Ibn Qutayba's *Adab al-kitāb*.

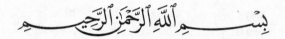

compassion perfectly embodied in the image of a mother leaning down to pick up and comfort her infant.[2]

In the Qur'ān, the verb *ṣalla* may have as its subject God, the angels, or human beings. The verse *God is the One who sends blessings upon you* (yuṣallī ʿalaykum) *as do His angels, to bring you forth from the darkness into the light* [33:43], expresses the mystery of the transcendant divinity and angels on high drawing near to creation in mercy, while the verse *Verily God and His angels bless the Prophet* (yuṣallūna ʿalā l-nabī); *O you who believe, invoke blessings upon him* (ṣallū ʿalayhi) *and salutations of peace* [33:56], indicates that a portion of this mercy is particularly focused on the person and spirit of the Prophet Muḥammad ﷺ and further, that human beings may participate in it through the act of invoking blessings on him, further explained in the well-known *ḥadīth*: "Whoever asks for blessings on me once, God blesses him tenfold" (man ṣallā ʿalayya wāhidatan, ṣalla llāhu ʿalayhi ʿashran).[3]

In its more frequent usage, however, the verb *ṣallā* and its nominative form *ṣalāt* refer to the distinctly Muslim rite of worship which combines postures and movements of the body with recitation and praise. According to one of the earliest written sources in Islam, the *Sīra* of Ibn Hishām,[4] this rite was shown to the Prophet ﷺ directly by the angel Gabriel عَلَيْهِ ٱلسَّلَامُ in the earliest days of the Qur'ānic revelation:

> When the prayer was enjoined, Gabriel عَلَيْهِ ٱلسَّلَامُ came to the Messenger of God ﷺ on the high ground above Mecca and motioned behind him in the direction of the valley. And [in the place] toward which he motioned a spring bubbled forth. [There] Gabriel عَلَيْهِ ٱلسَّلَامُ performed the ablution with the Messenger of God ﷺ looking on, that he might show him how to purify himself for the prayer, and

2 Thus wrote the poet, Maʿan b. Aws al-Muzanī (d. 64/683) as quoted in al-Qālī, *Kitāb al-amālī*, 2:102: "And my tenderness (*layyanī*) and compassion (*taʿaṭṭufī*) toward him remain like a mother inclines (*taḥannū*) toward her child."

3 Muslim, *Ṣaḥīḥ*, 408.

4 Ibn Hishām (d. 213/828), in fact, is credited with editing and preserving the contents of an even earlier, lost biography compiled by Ibn Isḥāq (d. 150/761 or 159/770), making these works among the earliest recorded sources.

> the Messenger ﷺ himself performed this ablution as he saw [the angel] do it. Then Gabriel عَلَيْهِ السَّلَام arose and performed the prayer, and the Messenger of God ﷺ prayed beside him, and then he departed.... [After this], the Messenger of God ﷺ came to [his wife] Khadija and performed the ablution for her, to show her how to purify herself for the prayer, as he had seen Gabriel do, and she performed the ablution as the Messenger of God ﷺ had. Then he led her in the prayer just as Gabriel had led him, and she performed the prayer as he did.[5]

After the Prophet ﷺ taught the prayer to his wife, the next person to learn it was his cousin, ʿAlī b. Abī Ṭalib, who was ten years old at the time, then he taught his friend and supporter, Abū Bakr al-Ṣiddīq, and then others. Following this initial revelation of the prayer, there appears to have been a period of time when it was prayed only twice a day, before sunrise and before sunset, following the Qurʾānic verse which reads, *So be patient—the promise of your Lord is true—and ask forgiveness for your sins and glorify Him in the evening and early morn* [40:55].[6] There was also a period of time when the prayers which are now prayed in four cycles[7]—in the midday, afternoon, and night prayers—were prayed in two.[8]

It was not until the last year before the migration from Mecca to Medina, around 622 (CE), that the complete number and times of the prayer were established definitively. This came by way of the event known as the Night Journey and Ascent (*al-Isrāʾ wa-l-miʿrāj*), during which the Prophet ﷺ was miraculously transported from the courtyard of the Kaʿba in Mecca to the 'furthest mosque' (i.e., al-Aqṣā Mosque) in Jerusalem, from which he was taken up through the seven heavens and entered into the divine presence where his community was commanded to pray fifty times a day. To quote Martin Lings' translation of the passage from Ibn Hishām:

---

5 Ibn Hishām, *al-Sīrat al-nabawiyya*, 2:82.

6 Al-Suhaylī, *al-Rawḍ al-unuf*, 2:284.

7 Throughout the translation, the word *rakaʿ*, which denotes the cycle of movement in the prayer that begins with standing and recitation and is followed by one bowing and two prostrations, is translated to the word "cycle."

8 A *ḥadīth* in al-Bukhārī, *Ṣaḥīḥ* and Muslim, *Ṣaḥīḥ*.

> The Prophet said: "On my return, when I passed Moses—and what a good friend he was unto you!—he asked me: 'How many prayers have been laid upon thee?' I told him fifty prayers every day and he said: 'The congregational prayer is a weighty thing, and thy people are weak. Return unto thy Lord, and ask Him to lighten the load for thee and thy people.' So I returned and asked my Lord to make it lighter, and He took away ten. Then I passed Moses again, and he repeated what he had said before, so I returned again, and ten more prayers were taken from me. But every time I returned unto Moses he sent me back until finally all the prayers had been taken from me except five for each day and night. Then I returned unto Moses, but still he said the same as before; and I said: 'I have returned unto my Lord and asked Him until I am ashamed. I will not go again.' And so it is that he who performeth the five in good faith and in trust of God's bounty, unto him shall be given the meed of fifty prayers."![9]

This rite and the various forms which it can take is the subject of *The Mysteries of the Prayer*. At times al-Ghazālī takes on an authoritative role on Shāfiʿī jurisprudence, explaining the details of the conditions, postures, and movements of the prayer, to the extent that "an aspirant to the hereafter" must know them. In a few limited places, he also speaks as an Ashʿarī theologian, expounding on what it means "to know something" and the interplay between intention and action. Throughout the work, however, he is above all a Sufi teacher, a physican of the heart, who knows well the illnesses of the soul and their remedies; he reminds us that ultimately "presence of heart is the prayer's breath of life." To inform the worshiper how to realize this lifegiving presence and how to ensure that it flows to every member of the body is the goal of this book and, in its broadest sense, the goal of every page of the *Revival of the Religious Sciences*.

---

9 Ibn Hishām, 2:255. The translation is that of Martin Lings in *Muhammad*, 103. This is also described in al-Bukhārī, *Ṣaḥīḥ*, 3887, and Muslim, *Ṣaḥīḥ*, 162.

Acknowledgments

This translation has come about with the help of many people. I would like to thank my colleagues and friends Fouad Aresmouk and Brahim Zoubairi for their help with some of the more enigmatic aspects of al-Ghazālī's Arabic, and Hicham Rajaʿi, teacher at the Qurʾānic school of Sī Zwīn near Marrakesh and Friday *imām* of the Sidī ʿAbd al-ʿAzīz mosque, for patiently helping me understand certain questions in Shāfiʿī *fiqh*. My eternal gratitude goes to my wife Jamila for her feedback on the text, and for her support and love always and in all things.

In the Name of God, the Merciful and Compassionate

The Mysteries of the Prayer and Its Important Elements

[al-Ghazālī's Introduction]

Book 4 of the *Revival of the Religious Sciences*

PRAISE be to God who envelops His servants with His kindnesses and fills their hearts with the lights of *dīn*[1] and its practices; whose descent, by degrees of mercy from the throne of majesty to the heaven of this world, is one portion of His infinite compassion; who is unique in His power and grandeur, yet unlike earthly sovereigns, urges His creatures to ask Him and supplicate Him, saying, "Is there anyone who calls on Me that I might answer? Is there anyone who seeks forgiveness that I might forgive?"[2] Unlike earthly rulers, He opens the door, raises the veil, and allows His servants to speak to Him through prayer, in whatever situation they might be, in congregation or alone. Indeed, while this world's feeble sovereigns allow an audience only in exchange for favors or bribes, God not only allows it, but in His mercy, urges and beckons His creatures to it! So glory be to Him! How immense are His concerns

1 *Dīn*, often translated as "religion," more accurately means a way of life based on belief, devotion, and virtue.

2 This is part of a *ḥadīth* in both Muslim, *Ṣaḥīḥ* (758) and al-Bukhārī, *Ṣaḥīḥ* (1145): "Our Lord, blessed and exalted be He, descends each night to the heaven of this earth when the last third of the night remains and says, 'Who is it that calls upon Me that I might answer him? Who is it that asks of Me that I might give to Him? Who is it that seeks My forgiveness that I might forgive him?'"

and mighty His dominion, and how perfect is His kindness and all-inclusive His goodness!

And may blessings and salutations of peace be upon Muḥammad, His chosen prophet and friend, and upon his family and Companions, the keys to guidance and lamps in the darkness.

To proceed, prayer is the pillar of *dīn*, the handhold of certitude, the principal means of drawing near to God, and the glowing mark of devotional practice. In [works such as] *Basīṭ al-madhhab*, *al-Wasīṭ*, and *al-Wajīz*, we have looked into its principles and particularities according to the science of *fiqh* [jurisprudence], [and] carefully treated its rarer issues and exceptions, that these works might form a library on which a *muftī* might rely, in [which he might] seek safety, and [to which he might] refer with confidence.

In this present book, however, we confine ourselves to what an aspirant must know about the external actions and internal mysteries of the prayer, [and] uncover [as we do] the finer points of its most hidden dimensions by examining the meaning of humility, sincerity, and intention, all of which are not usually discussed in conjunction with the science of *fiqh*.

This book is arranged in seven chapters:

Chapter 1: On the Merits of Prayer
Chapter 2: On the Details of the Outward Elements of the Prayer
Chapter 3: On the Details of Its Inward Elements
Chapter 4: On the *Imām* and [His] Example
Chapter 5: On the Friday Prayer and the Manners [Relating] to It
Chapter 6: Various Questions Which Are Generally Troubling to People and About Which an Aspirant Should Know
Chapter 7: On Supererogatory [Prayers] and Others

1

On the Merits of Prayer, the Prostration, the Congregational [Prayer], the Call to Prayer, and Others

The Merits of the Call to Prayer

The Messenger of God ﷺ said,

> On the day of resurrection there will be three men untroubled by the reckoning and untouched by fear, standing on a dune of black musk until what concerns the people is done: a man who reads the Qurʾān seeking the countenance of God and, in that way, leads people in the prayer who are pleased with him; a man who gives the call to prayer in a mosque and beckons people to God عَزَّوَجَلَّ, seeking only the countenance of God عَزَّوَجَلَّ; and a man who is tested by slavery (*riqq*) but does not let that bar him from accomplishing the work of the hereafter.[1]

And he said ﷺ, "Anyone [and anything]—a human, a jinn, or anything else—that hears the muezzin [caller to prayer] will bear witness for him on the day of resurrection."[2]

---

1 Al-Tirmidhī, *Sunan*, 1986, with similar wording. The wording above is found in al-Khaṭīb al-Baghdādī, *Tārīkh Baghdād*, 4:124. According to some texts of the *Iḥyāʾ*, the third person described is "a man tested in sustenance (*rizq*)."

2 Al-Bukhārī, *Ṣaḥīḥ*, 609.

And also, "The hand of the most merciful is upon the head of the caller to prayer until he finishes the call."[3]

Concerning God's words, *And who is better in speech than one who invites to God and does righteousness and says, "Indeed, I am of the Muslims"* [41:33], it has been said that [these verses] were revealed concerning those who make the call to prayer.[4]

The Prophet صَلَّى ٱللَّهُ عَلَيْهِ وَسَلَّمَ also said, "When you hear the call, say what the caller says."[5] This is recommended for all but the two phrases that begin, "Hasten to…" (*ḥayy ʿalā*), in which case one should say, "There is no strength nor power except by God" (*lā ḥawla wa-lā quwwata illā bi-llāh*).[6]

After the words, "The prayer has been established," [just before the prayer begins], it is recommended to say, "God has established it and has made it endure as long as the heavens and the earth remain."[7]

After the phrase, "The prayer is better than sleep," [in the call for the *fajr* prayer], it is recommended to say "You have spoken the truth, said what is good, and given true counsel!"

Then, after the caller has finished, the worshipers should say, "O God, Lord of this perfect call and of the prayer about to be performed, give Muḥammad nearness, excellence, and an exalted degree, and grant him the station of the praised which You have promised him. Verily, You are the One who never breaks a promise."[8]

According to Saʿīd b. al-Musayyib, "Whoever performs the prayer in the wilderness will have an angel on his right and an angel on his left praying with him, but if he makes the call and then performs the prayer, a multitude of angels as vast as the mountains will pray behind him."[9]

---

3 Al-Ṭabarānī, *al-Muʿjam al-awsaṭ*, 2008; Ibn ʿAdī, *al-Kāmil*, 5:49.

4 Ibn Abī Shayba, *al-Muṣannaf*, 2361, based on a saying from ʿĀʾisha رَضِيَ ٱللَّهُ عَنْهَا. Also see al-Suyūṭī, *al-Durr al-manthūr*, 7:325.

5 Al-Bukhārī, *Ṣaḥīḥ*, 611; Muslim, *Ṣaḥīḥ*, 383.

6 Muslim, *Ṣaḥīḥ*, 385.

7 Abū Dāwūd, *Sunan*, 528. The phrase is 'aqāmaha l-lāhu wa-adāmahā mā dāmati al-samawātu wa-l-arḍu.'

8 Al-Bukhārī, *Ṣaḥīḥ*, 613; al-Nasāʾī, *Sunan*, 2:27.

9 Mālik, *al-Muwaṭṭaʾ*, 1:74.

The Merits of the Obligatory Prayers

God most high says, *Indeed, prayer has been decreed upon the believers a decree of specified times* [4:103], and the Prophet صَلَّى ٱللَّٰهُ عَلَيْهِ وَسَلَّمَ said,

> God has ordained five daily prayers for His servants. Whoever prays them without neglecting anything by falling short in what is their due has a vow with God to enter heaven, while someone who does not has no such vow. If God so wills, He will punish him, and if He so wills, He will cause him to enter heaven.[10]

The Prophet صَلَّى ٱللَّٰهُ عَلَيْهِ وَسَلَّمَ also said [to some of the Companions]:

> "The five prayers are like a stream of fresh water flowing past your door in which you immerse [yourself] five times a day. Would you see on anyone who did this the least remnant of dirt?"
>
> They answered, "No, not the least!"
>
> He said, "Even as that water removes dirt, so too do the five prayers remove sin."[11]
>
> He also said صَلَّى ٱللَّٰهُ عَلَيْهِ وَسَلَّمَ, "The five prayers are expiation for what happens between [the prayers] for anyone who avoids the major sins."[12]
>
> And [the Prophet صَلَّى ٱللَّٰهُ عَلَيْهِ وَسَلَّمَ] said, "What distinguishes us from the hypocrites is that we keep the night [*ʿishāʾ* prayer] and dawn [*fajr* prayer]. This they are not able to do."[13]
>
> And, "Whoever meets God [on the day of judgment], having abandoned the prayer, God will not accept any of his good deeds."[14]
>
> And, "The prayer is the pillar of *dīn*. Whoever abandons it has torn down his *dīn*."[15]

---

10 Abū Dāwūd, *Sunan*, 1420; al-Nasāʾī, *Sunan*, 1:230; Ibn Māja, *Sunan*, 1401.

11 Muslim, *Ṣaḥīḥ*, 668.

12 Muslim, *Ṣaḥīḥ*, 231.

13 Mālik, *al-Muwaṭṭaʾ*, 1:130.

14 "The first thing that will be reckoned of the servant on the day of resurrection will be the prayer. If that is in order, then the rest of his deeds will be in order as well, and if that has been ruined, then the rest of his deeds are ruined as well." Al-Ṭabarānī, *al-Muʿjam al-awsaṭ*, 1880.

15 Al-Bayhaqī, *Shuʿab al-īmān*, 2550, but without the second sentence.

When the Prophet صَلَّى ٱللَّٰهُ عَلَيْهِ وَسَلَّمَ was asked, "What practice is best?" he replied, "The prayer in its times."[16]

And he also said, "Whoever keeps the five prayers, completes their necessary purification and [guards] their times, will [have] a light and a proof on the day of resurrection, while whoever abandons them will be resurrected with Pharaoh and Hāmān."[17]

The Prophet صَلَّى ٱللَّٰهُ عَلَيْهِ وَسَلَّمَ also said, "The prayer is the key to heaven."[18]

He said صَلَّى ٱللَّٰهُ عَلَيْهِ وَسَلَّمَ,

> After the affirmation of His oneness, there is nothing more beloved to God from what He has enjoined upon His creation than the prayer. If there had been, then that would be how the angels would worship Him. But some of them are bowing, some of them are prostrating, some of them are standing, and some of them are sitting.[19]

The Prophet صَلَّى ٱللَّٰهُ عَلَيْهِ وَسَلَّمَ also said, "Whoever intentionally abandons the prayer becomes a disbeliever,"[20] which is to say that he is almost outside the faith because he has let go of its handhold and let its pillar collapse. This is like saying about someone who is near a town, "He has reached it and entered it."

The Prophet صَلَّى ٱللَّٰهُ عَلَيْهِ وَسَلَّمَ also said, "Whoever intentionally abandons the prayer removes himself from those under the protection of Muḥammad صَلَّى ٱللَّٰهُ عَلَيْهِ وَسَلَّمَ."[21]

Abū Hurayra رَضِيَ ٱللَّٰهُ عَنْهُ said,

If someone performs the ablution well, then leaves his home with the intention of praying, he is in the prayer as long as that is what he intends. With one step, a good deed is written for him, and with the next, a bad deed effaced. So if one of you hears the call (*iqāma*) signaling the beginning of the prayer, do not rush [to

---

16 Al-Bukhārī, *Ṣaḥīḥ*, 527; Muslim, *Ṣaḥīḥ*, 75.

17 Ibn Ḥanbal, *Musnad*, 2:169; Abū Dāwūd, *Sunan*, 430; Ibn Māja, *Sunan*, 1403. Hāmān is mentioned twice in the Qurʾān, in 28:38 and 40:36, as being the Pharaoh's minister.

18 Al-Tirmidhī, *Sunan*, 4.

19 Abū Ṭālib al-Makkī, *Qūt al-qulūb*, 2:100. The positions mentioned are those of the prayer.

20 Al-Ṭabarānī, *al-Muʿjam al-awsaṭ*, 3372.

21 Ibn Ḥanbal, *Musnad*, 6:421.

reach it], for the greatest of you in reward will be the one who lives furthest [from the mosque].

And when they asked, "And why is that, O Abū Hurayra?"

He replied, "Because of the many steps [he needs to take]."[22]

It has been related that on the day of resurrection the first of a servant's deeds to be looked on will be the prayer. If it is found to be complete, then it will be accepted from him along with all his other deeds, and if it is found to be deficient, then it will be rejected along with all his other deeds.[23]

And the Prophet ﷺ said, "O Abū Hurayra, enjoin on your family the prayer, and God will provide for you from where you do not reckon."[24]

According to one of the scholars, "The one who prays is like a merchant for whom there is no profit until he has secured his capital: no supererogatory worship will be accepted until he has completed the obligatory."[25]

And when the time of prayer came, Abū Bakr رضي الله عنه used to say, "Rise, and put out the fire you have kindled!"[26]

The Merits of Perfectly Completing the Main Parts of the Prayer

The Prophet ﷺ said, "The obligatory prayer is like a scale. Whoever gives it full measure is given full measure."[27]

---

22 Mālik, *al-Muwaṭṭaʾ*, 1:33.

23 Mālik, *al-Muwaṭṭaʾ*, 1:173, with similar wording.

24 The commentary notes that although this *ḥadīth* has no traceable source, its meaning is substantiated by other *ḥadīths*, as, for example, what is found in al-Ṭabarānī, *al-Muʿjam al-awsaṭ*, 898, narrated by ʿAbdallāh b. Salām: "If a period of hardship came upon the family [of the Prophet ﷺ], he would enjoin upon them the prayer and quote the verse, *And enjoin prayer upon your family* [*and people*] *and be steadfast therein* [20:132]. Al-Zabīdī, *Itḥāf*, 3:11.

25 Al-Bayhaqī, *al-Sunan al-kubrā*, 2:387.

26 Al-Ṭabarānī, *al-Muʿjam al-awsaṭ*, 9448; Abū Nuʿaym, *Ḥilya*, 3:42 with wording similar to this.

27 Ibn al-Mubārak, *Zuhd*, 1190; al-Bayhaqī, *Shuʿab al-īmān*, 2882.

And Yazīd al-Raqāshī said, "The Prophet's prayer ﷺ was as even as if it had been measured in a scale."[28]

The Prophet ﷺ also said, "Two men from my people may stand, and bow, and prostrate in the same prayer and yet between their prayers [is a difference as vast as] what is between heaven and earth,"[29] by which he was referring to reverence. And he ﷺ said, "On the day of resurrection, God عَزَّوَجَلَّ will not look upon a servant who does not rise up from his bowing and prostration until his back is completely straight."[30]

And he ﷺ said, "Does the one who turns his face away in the prayer not fear that God will change it into the face of a donkey?"[31] And also,

> The prayer of one who prays it on time, who extends the places washed in ablution, and completes its necessary bowing, prostration, and reverence, rises in a glowing whiteness saying, "May God protect you as you have protected me!" And the prayer of someone who prays it late, who does not extend the places washed in ablution, and does not complete the necessary bowing, prostration, and reverence, rises in a shadowy blackness saying, "May God neglect you as you have neglected me." Then, when that prayer is where God wills it to be, it is folded up like an old garment and thrown back in the face of the one who prayed it.[32]

And the Prophet ﷺ said, "The worst of people who steal is someone who steals from the prayer."[33]

Ibn Masʿūd and Salmān رَضِيَ اللَّهُ عَنْهُمَا said, "The prayer is a measure. Whoever fills it completely will be given completely in return, while

---

28 Ibn al-Mubārak, *Zuhd*, 103. "Even" (*mustawiyya*) is said to mean that its recitation, bowing, and prostration were in proportion to one another.

29 Ibn al-Mubārak, *Zuhd*, 97.

30 Ibn Ḥanbal, *Musnad*, 2:525.

31 Al-Bukhārī, *Ṣaḥīḥ*, 691; Muslim, *Ṣaḥīḥ*, 427, with the wording, "Does the one who raises up his head in the prayer before the *imām* does..."

32 Al-Ṭabarānī, *al-Muʿjam al-awsaṭ*, 3119; al-Bayhaqī, *Shuʿab al-īmān*, 2871.

33 Ibn Ḥanbal, *Musnad*, 3:56.

you know whoever stints based on what God has said concerning those who deal in fraud (*al-muṭaffifīn*)."[34]

The Merits of the [Prayer in] Congregation

The Prophet ﷺ said, "The prayer in congregation is twenty-seven times better than one prayed alone."[35]

And it was related by Abū Hurayra that the Prophet ﷺ noticed some people missing at one of the prayers and said, "I considered asking someone to lead the prayer with the people [in the mosque] and then going to those men who stayed home and ordering that their houses be set afire." And in another version, "Then going to those men who stayed home and ordering that their houses be set afire with a bundle of firewood. If one of them knew that he would find a meaty bone or sheep's trotters, he would be here for it."

By this he meant the *ʿishāʾ* prayer.[36]

---

34 Abū Ṭālib al-Makkī, *Qūt al-qulūb*, 2:101; Ibn al-Mubārak, *Zuhd*, 1192. Here the allusion is to those who pray in a deficient way, for example, by not completing one of its postures. They are comparable to those mentioned at the beginning of Sūrat al-Muṭaffifūn (83): When they receive something they expect an exact and full measure, even though when they give, they intentionally fall short. The *sūra* begins, *Woe to those who give less [than due], who, when they take a measure from people, take in full but if they give by measure or by weight to them, they cause loss* [83:1–3].

35 Al-Bukhārī, *Ṣaḥīḥ*, 645; Muslim, *Ṣaḥīḥ*, 649.

36 Al-Bukhārī, *Ṣaḥīḥ*, 644; Muslim, *Ṣaḥīḥ*, 651. In the Ḥanbalī school, this *ḥadīth* is cited as evidence that to pray in congregation in the mosque is an individual obligation (*farḍ ʿayn*) for men, whereas other schools consider it a confirmed *sunna* (*al-sunnat al-muʾakkida*). In Ibn Rajab, *Fatḥ al-bārī* (the commentary on the *Ṣaḥīḥ* of al-Bukhārī), another *ḥadīth* is cited which adds context to this one. It is also attributed to Abū Hurayra:

> The Prophet ﷺ delayed the *ʿishāʾ* prayer until well into the night—nearly one-third of it had passed—and then went to the mosque and found only a few people scattered throughout. On seeing this, he became very angry—I do not know if I had ever seen him so angry before—and said, "If a man had invited people to some meat on a bone or sheep's trotters, they would have come and not stayed home as they stay home from this prayer. I even considered having a man lead the prayer while I went to the houses of these people and burned them down around them!"

And ʿUthmān رَضِيَ اللَّهُ عَنْهُ related these words from the Prophet صَلَّى اللَّهُ عَلَيْهِ وَسَلَّمَ: "If someone prays ʿ*ishāʾ* [in congregation], it is as if he has stood half the night in prayer. And if someone prays dawn [*fajr*] [in congregation], it is as if he has stood the entire night in prayer."[37]

He صَلَّى اللَّهُ عَلَيْهِ وَسَلَّمَ also said, "Whoever prays with the congregation fills his breast with worship."[38]

Saʿīd b. al-Musayyib said, "For twenty years the muezzin has not made the call without my being in the mosque."[39] And Muḥammad b. Wāsiʿ said, "There are only three things I desire from this world: A brother who will correct me if I stray, nourishment from lawful provision which has no claim upon it, and a prayer in congregation in which forgetfulness is lifted from me and merit is recorded."[40]

It is related that Abū ʿUbayda b. al-Jarāḥ led some people in the prayer and when he finished, he said, "Satan kept at me [in that prayer] until I saw in myself something superior to others. I will never act as *imām* again!"[41]

Ḥasan said, "Do not pray behind anyone who does not follow the learned." And al-Nakhaʿī said, "Anyone who leads people in the prayer without knowledge is like a man who does not know an addition from an omission!"

Ḥātim al-Aṣam said, "I missed one of the prayers in congregation and Abū Isḥāq al-Bukhārī alone offered me his condolences, whereas had I lost a child, ten thousand would have done so because people think a tribulation in *dīn* matters less than a tribulation in the world."

And Ibn ʿAbbās رَضِيَ اللَّهُ عَنْهُمَا said, "He who hears the one who calls to prayer and does not answer him does not want the good, nor is the good wanted for him."[42]

Another version adds "Were there not women and children in those houses...," and another mentions specifically "the men who live around the mosque and are not present for the night prayer."

37 Muslim, *Ṣaḥīḥ*, 656.

38 Al-ʿIrāqī considers this a saying of Saʿīd b. al-Musayyib, al-Zabīdī, *Itḥāf*, 3:15.

39 Ibn Abī Shayba, *al-Muṣannaf*, 3542; Abū Nuʿaym, *Ḥilya*, 2:162.

40 Ibn ʿAsākir, *Tārīkh madīnat Dimashq*, 56:161.

41 Ibn al-Mubārak, *Zuhd*, 834; Ibn Abī Shayba, *al-Muṣannaf*, 4141.

42 Ibn Abī Shayba quotes a saying similar to this in *al-Muṣannaf*, 3485, and attributes it to ʿĀʾisha رَضِيَ اللَّهُ عَنْهَا.

And Abū Hurayra رَضِيَ ٱللَّهُ عَنْهُ said, "It is better for the son of Adam's ear be full of molten lead than for him to hear the call to prayer and not answer it."[43]

It is related that Maymūn b. Mahrān came to the mosque and was told, "The people have already left," to which he responded, "*Verily we belong to God and to Him we are returning!*[44] The excellence of this prayer is more beloved to me than being governor of Iraq!"

And the Prophet صَلَّى ٱللَّهُ عَلَيْهِ وَسَلَّمَ said, "Whoever prays with the congregation for forty days without missing a single opening *takbīr* [saying *Allāhu akbar*], God will write for him two protections: protection from hypocrisy and protection from the fire."[45]

It is said that on the day of resurrection, there will be a people brought to the gathering, [with] their faces like glistening stars, and the angels will ask them,

> "What was your practice [in the world]?"
>
> They will respond, "Whenever we heard the call, we would rise to perform the ablution and be unoccupied by anything else."
>
> Then a people whose faces are like moons will be brought to the gathering, and after being asked [the same question], they will say, "We used to perform the ablution before the time of prayer." Then yet another folk whose faces are like the sun will be brought to the gathering, and they will say, "We used to hear the call from inside the mosque."[46]

And it has been narrated that the early believers (*salaf*) would console each other for three days if they missed the first *takbīr* [of the obligatory prayer in congregation] and for seven [days] if they missed the [obligatory prayer in] congregation.[47]

---

43 Ibn Abī Shayba, *al-Muṣannaf*, 3484.

44 Following the words of the Qurʾān, about those who say, when struck by affliction, *Indeed, we belong to God and to Him we will return* (Innā li-llāhi, wa-innā ʿilayhi rājiʿūn) [2:156]. For Muslims, this is usually the first thing said on hearing of someone's death.

45 Al-Tirmidhī, *Sunan*, 241.

46 A saying similar to this is found in Abū Ṭālib al-Makkī, *Qūt al-qulūb*, 2:101.

47 Al-Zabīdī adds, "as a proof of the merit of the prayer in congregation." *Itḥāf*, 3:17.

The Merits of the Prostration

The Messenger of God صَلَّىٱللَّٰهُعَلَيۡهِوَسَلَّمَ said, "The servant does not draw nearer to God by anything more excellent than a prostration done in secret."[48]

And the Messenger of God صَلَّىٱللَّٰهُعَلَيۡهِوَسَلَّمَ also said: "When a Muslim prostrates to God, God raises him up a degree and removes a bad deed from his [account]."[49]

And it is related that a man said to the Messenger of God صَلَّىٱللَّٰهُعَلَيۡهِوَسَلَّمَ, "Ask God to make me among those who benefit from your intercession and grant me companionship with you in heaven," to which God's Messenger صَلَّىٱللَّٰهُعَلَيۡهِوَسَلَّمَ responded, "Help me do this by [making] many prostrations."[50]

It is said: "The closest a servant may be to God most high is in prostration," and that this is the meaning of the words of God most high, *prostrate and draw near* [*to God*] [96:19].[51]

And concerning God's words, *Their mark is on their faces from the trace of prostration* [48:29], it is said that this [may be understood to mean] the earth that remains on their faces from [their] prostrations or the light of reverence that shines forth from within [them], the latter being the more correct. It is also said that this is the glow from the ablution that will be on their faces on the day of resurrection.[52]

The Prophet صَلَّىٱللَّٰهُعَلَيۡهِوَسَلَّمَ said,

> When the son of Adam recites a verse of prostration[53] and then prostrates, Satan departs from him crying and saying, "Oh woe to me! This one was commanded to prostrate and he

48 Ibn al-Mubārak, *Zuhd*, 154.

49 Ibn Māja, *Sunan*, 1323.

50 Muslim, *Ṣaḥīḥ*, 489.

51 Quoted in the commentary on this verse in al-Suyūṭī, *al-Durr al-manthūr*, 8:566.

52 Al-Suyūṭī, *al-Durr al-manthūr*, 7:541.

53 A verse of prostration is one of the fourteen or fifteen places in the Qur'ān where the sacred text calls on the faithful to prostrate. On reciting one of these verses or hearing it recited by another, it is considered either mandatory or highly recommended to make a single prostration.

did, so for him there is heaven, while I was commanded to prostrate and I refused, so for me there is the fire."[54]

And it is related that ʿAlī b. ʿAbdallāh b. ʿAbbās would make one thousand prostrations [each] day, such that they used to call him the 'prostrator.'[55]

It has also been recorded that ʿUmar b. ʿAbd al-ʿAzīz رضي الله عنه would only prostrate on earth.[56] And Yūsuf b. Asbāṭ used to say, "O youths! Make efforts while you are healthy, before you are infirm! There is no one I envy except a man who can perform his bowing and prostration completely, since [old age] has come between me and that!"

Saʿīd b. Jubayr said, "I do not regret the loss of anything in this world except the prostration."[57] And ʿUqba b. Muslim said, "There is no quality a servant can have more beloved to God than that of a man who loves to meet Him, and there is no moment a servant can have that is closer to God than when he is in prostration [on the ground]."[58]

And Abū Hurayra رضي الله عنه said, "The closest a servant may come to God is in prostration, so be abundant in calling on Him in that state."[59]

---

54 Muslim, *Ṣaḥīḥ*, 81.

55 Al-Ṭabarānī, *al-Muʿjam al-kabīr*, 10:275; and Abū Nuʿaym, *Ḥilya*, 3:307.

56 Recorded in *al-Risālat al-Qushayriyya*, in the chapter on "Reverence and Humility." This is also mentioned by Ibn Rajab (*Fatḥ al-bārī*), who comments on the *ḥadīth* that states that the Prophet صلى الله عليه وسلم once spread out a headscarf (of his wife Maymūna) and prayed on it. Ibn Rajab notes that ʿUmar b. ʿAbd al-ʿAzīz also prayed on a woman's headscarf but would ask for some earth to be sprinkled on it first. He adds, "And perhaps he did this as an extreme expression of reverence and humility." That is, not because he found anything wrong with prostrating on a scarf.

57 Ibn al-Mubārak, *Zuhd*, 974.

58 Ibn al-Mubārak, *Zuhd*, 279.

59 Muslim, *Ṣaḥīḥ*, 482, as a *ḥadīth* related by Abū Hurayra directly from the Prophet صلى الله عليه وسلم.

The Merits of Reverence

God most high says, *And establish prayer for My remembrance* [20:14].

And God most high says, *And do not be among the heedless* [7:205].

And God most high says, *Do not approach prayer while you are intoxicated until you know what you are saying* [4:43], about which it has been said that [*when you are intoxicated* means] "intoxicated from too many worldly cares" or "intoxicated with the love of this world."[60]

Wahb said, "This verse is meant in a literal sense, but the words, *until you know what you are saying*, include a warning against becoming intoxicated by the world. For how many worshipers have never drunk intoxicants and yet know not what they are saying in their prayer?

The Prophet صلى الله عليه وسلم said, "Whoever prays two cycles free of worldly distractions will be forgiven all his past sins."[61]

And the Prophet صلى الله عليه وسلم also said, "The prayer is submissiveness, humility, urgent need, distress, and remorse; it is to raise your hands and say, 'O God! O God!' Otherwise, it is incomplete."[62]

It is recorded that God most high said in one of the earlier scriptures, "I do not accept the prayer of everyone who prays, but I accept the prayer of the one who is humble before My majesty, who does not come before me in haughtiness and pride, and who feeds the poor and hungry for My sake."[63]

And the Messenger of God صلى الله عليه وسلم said, "The prayer was made obligatory, the pilgrimage and circumambulation were decreed, and [the pilgrimage's] other rites instituted to establish the remembrance of God most high."[64] So if there is no veneration or awe in your heart for the One remembered, the One who is the goal and purpose, what is the value of your remembrance?[65]

---

60 Abū Ṭālib al-Makkī, *Qūt al-qulūb*, 2:97.

61 Al-Bukhārī, *Ṣaḥīḥ*, 164; and Muslim, *Ṣaḥīḥ*, 226.

62 Al-Ṭaḥāwī, *Sharḥ muskhil al-āthār*, 3:124; al-Tirmidhī, *Sunan*, 385.

63 In the biography of Ṭāwūs b. Kaysān, Abū Nuʿaym (*Ḥilya*), relates a similar saying as a *ḥadīth* narrated from the Prophet صلى الله عليه وسلم by Ibn ʿAbbās.

64 Abū Dāwūd, *Sunan*, 1888; and al-Tirmidhī, *Sunan*, 902, but without mention of the prayer.

65 Abū Ṭālib al-Makkī, *Qūt al-qulūb*, 2:98.

To someone who asked him for counsel, [the Prophet] صَلَّى ٱللَّٰهُ عَلَيْهِ وَسَلَّمَ said, "When you pray, pray the prayer of farewell,"[66] by which he meant the prayer of someone saying farewell to his ego, his desires, and his life, and journeying to his guardian Lord, even as the words of God most high affirm: *O mankind, indeed you are laboring toward your Lord with [great] exertion and will meet Him* [84:6], and *fear God. And God teaches you* [2:282], and *fear God and know that you will meet Him* [2:223].[67]

The Prophet صَلَّى ٱللَّٰهُ عَلَيْهِ وَسَلَّمَ also said, "If someone's prayer does not prohibit him from immorality and wrongdoing, he gains nothing from it except distance from God,"[68] for the prayer is intimate discourse with the Lord and how can that exist along with heedlessness?

Bakr b. ʿAbdallāh said, "O child of Adam! If you wish to enter into the presence of your Lord without an invitation, enter!" They asked, "How?" He said, "Complete the ablution perfectly, enter your prayer niche, and there you are—in the presence of your guardian Lord without permission, speaking to Him without intermediary!"[69]

And according to ʿĀʾisha رَضِيَ ٱللَّٰهُ عَنْهَا: "The Messenger of God would speak with us and we would speak with him, but when the prayer time came, it was as if he did not know us and we did not know him,"[70] for he was completely taken up by the majesty of God عَزَّ وَجَلَّ.

And the Prophet صَلَّى ٱللَّٰهُ عَلَيْهِ وَسَلَّمَ said, "God does not look on the prayer of a man whose heart is not present along with his body."[71]

It has been said that when Abraham عَلَيْهِ ٱلسَّلَامُ, God's intimate friend, rose to pray, the beating of his heart could be heard for two miles.[72] And when Saʿīd al-Tanūkhī prayed, tears would not cease to

66 Ibn Māja, *Sunan*, 4171.

67 Abū Ṭālib al-Makkī, *Qūt al-qulūb*, 2:98.

68 Al-Ṭabarānī, *al-Muʿjam al-kabīr*, 11:54. This is a reference to the verse: *Indeed, prayer prohibits immorality and wrongdoing, and the remembrance of God is greater* [29:45].

69 Abū Nuʿaym, *Ḥilya*, 2:229, with similar wording.

70 In commenting on al-Bukhārī, *Ṣaḥīḥ*, 676, Ibn Rajab cites a similar saying, also in the words of ʿĀʾisha رَضِيَ ٱللَّٰهُ عَنْهَا: "When the Messenger of God صَلَّى ٱللَّٰهُ عَلَيْهِ وَسَلَّمَ was with me, he occupied himself with serving his family, but when the call to prayer was made, he did not know us." Ibn Rajab, *Fatḥ al-bārī*, 4:114.

71 Al-Marūzī, in *Taʿẓīm qadri al-ṣalāt*, H. 157, quotes a long *ḥadīth* with similar wording.

72 Ibn ʿAsākir, *Tārīkh madīnat Dimashq*, 6:218.

flow down his cheeks and onto his beard.[73] Once the Messenger of God صَلَّى ٱللَّٰهُ عَلَيْهِ وَسَلَّمَ saw a man absentmindedly playing with his beard during the prayer and said, "If his heart were reverent, his limbs would be as well."[74]

And it is related that Ḥasan saw a man who was playing with some pebbles on the ground while saying, "O God, wed me with the maidens of heaven!" To which Ḥasan said, "What a foul suitor you are—proposing to the maidens of heaven while playing with pebbles on the ground!"[75]

When Khalaf b. Ayyūb was asked, "Do the flies not bother you in your prayer so that you want you to shoo them away?"

> He answered, "I do not want to accustom myself to anything that would ruin my prayer."
>
> They asked, "But how can you stand it?"
>
> He answered, "I have heard that there are criminals who endure a sultan's lashes so that it may be said of them, 'What endurance so-and-so has!' and they are proud of that. And here I am standing before my Lord and a fly is going to make me move around?"

And it is related that when Muslim b. Yassār intended to pray, he would say to his family, "Go ahead and talk. I will not hear you."

It is also related that one day [Muslim b. Yassār] was praying in a mosque in Basra when a part of the building collapsed and people gathered around because of it, but he was unaware of what had happened until he had completed the prayer.[76]

When the time of prayer came, ʿAlī b. Abī Ṭālib, may God be pleased with him and ennoble his face, would tremble and his face would change color. When they asked him, "What ails you, O Commander of the Faithful?" he said, "The time of the trust has arrived—the trust that God offered to the heavens, the earth, and

---

73 Ibn ʿAsākir, *Tārīkh madīnat Dimashq*, 21:202–203.

74 Al-Ḥakīm al-Tirmidhī, *Nawādir al-uṣūl*, 317, and al-Marūzī, in *Taʿẓīm qadri al-ṣalāt*, 151, with similar wording.

75 Abū Nuʿaym, *Ḥilya*, 5:287, attributes a saying with wording similar to that of ʿUmar b. ʿAbd al-ʿAzīz.

76 Abū Nuʿaym, *Ḥilya*, 2:290.

the mountains, and they refused to bear it and shrank from it [in fear] and I have taken it on!"[77]

And it has been reported that when ʿAlī b. al-Ḥusayn made the ablution, he would turn pale, and when his family asked him, "What happens to you during the ablution?" he answered, "Do you understand before whom I intend to stand?"[78]

It is related that Ibn ʿAbbās رَضِيَ ٱللَّهُ عَنْهُمَا said,

> David عَلَيْهِ ٱلسَّلَامُ, speaking intimately to his Lord, asked, "Dear God, who shall dwell in Your house and from whom do You accept the prayer?"
>
> And God answered him through revelation, "O David, the one who shall dwell in My house and whose prayer I accept is the one who humbles himself before My majesty, who spends his days invoking Me, who restrains his soul from its lusts for My sake, feeds the hungry, gives shelter to the stranger, and has compassion for the afflicted. That is the one whose light shines in the heavens like the sun. If he calls to Me, I answer him; if he asks of Me, I give to him, and I grant him understanding in the midst of ignorance, remembrance in the midst of heedlessness, and light in the midst of darkness. His likeness, as compared to ordinary people, is that of Firdaws[79] as compared to earthly gardens: its rivers never dry up, [and] its fruits never spoil."[80]

It is also related that Ḥātim al-Aṣam رَحِمَهُ ٱللَّهُ was once asked about his prayer and said,

> When the time of the prayer is at hand, I complete the ablution and then go to the place where I wish to pray and sit there until I am inwardly and outwardly collected. Then I stand for the prayer, putting the Kaʿba between my eyebrows, the traverse (*ṣirāṭ*) beneath my feet, heaven to my right, the fire to

---

77 This is a reference to the verse, *Indeed, we offered the trust* (*al-amāna*) *to the heavens and the earth and the mountains, and they declined to bear it and feared it; but man* [*undertook to*] *bear it. Indeed, he was unjust and ignorant* [33:72].

78 Ibn Ḥanbal, *al-Zuhd*, 2138; and Ibn Abī l-Dunyā, *al-Riqqa wa-l-bukāʾ*, 148.

79 One of the gardens of paradise.

80 Abū Nuʿaym, *Ḥilya*, 4:18, with similar wording.

> my left, and the angel of death behind me.... and I pray as if it were my last prayer. Then, standing between hope and fear, I pronounce the opening *takbīr* with care, recite the recitation in a measured way, bow for the bowing with humility, prostrate for the prostration with reverence, and sit on my left haunch with my left foot folded flat beneath me and my right foot upright on its big toe—and all this I undertake with sincerity, but then I do not know: is it accepted of me or not?[81]

And Ibn ʿAbbās رضي الله عنه said, "A prayer of two cycles with reflection is better than standing all night [in prayer] with a heedless heart."[82]

The Merits of the Mosque and Places of Prayer

God most high says, *The mosques of God are only to be maintained by those who believe in God and the last day* [9:18].

And the Prophet صلى الله عليه وسلم said, "Whoever builds a mosque for God—be it as humble as partridge's nest—for him God builds a palace in heaven."[83]

And he also said صلى الله عليه وسلم, "Whoever is familiar with a mosque, God most high is familiar with him."[84]

And he said صلى الله عليه وسلم, "Whoever enters a mosque should pray two cycles before he sits down."[85] And he said صلى الله عليه وسلم, "There is no prayer for someone who lives next to the mosque except in the mosque."[86]

And he said صلى الله عليه وسلم, "The angels bless you as long as you are [sitting] in the place where you pray and they say 'O God bless him! O God have mercy on him! O God forgive him!' And this continues until your [ablution] is broken or you leave the mosque."[87]

---

81 Abū Nuʿaym, *Ḥilya*, 8:75, with similar wording.

82 Ibn al-Mubārak, *Zuhd*, 288.

83 Ibn Māja, *Sunan*, 738. A version of this *ḥadīth* also appears in the collections of al-Bukhārī and Muslim.

84 Al-Ṭabarānī, *al-Muʿjam al-awsaṭ*, 6379.

85 Al-Bukhārī, *Ṣaḥīḥ*, 444; Muslim, *Ṣaḥīḥ*, 714.

86 Al-Dāraquṭnī, *Sunan*, 1:419; al-Ḥākim al-Nīsābūrī, *al-Mustadrak*, 1:246.

87 Al-Bukhārī, *Ṣaḥīḥ*, 445; Muslim, *Ṣaḥīḥ*, 649.

And he said صَلَّى ٱللَّٰهُ عَلَيْهِ وَسَلَّمَ, "In the last days, there will be people from this community who go to the mosque, sit in circles, and talk about this world and the love of this world. Do not sit with such people, for God has no need of them."[88]

And he صَلَّى ٱللَّٰهُ عَلَيْهِ وَسَلَّمَ said, "God عَزَّ وَجَلَّ says in one of the scriptures, 'Verily, My houses on earth are the mosques, and My visitors are those who go to them. Blessed be the servant who first purifies himself at home then visits Me in My house, for it is a duty of a host to be generous to his visitors.'"[89]

And he صَلَّى ٱللَّٰهُ عَلَيْهِ وَسَلَّمَ also said, "When you see a man who frequents the mosque, attest to his faith."[90]

Saʿīd b. al-Musayyib said, "Whoever sits in a mosque is sitting with his Lord and so it is most fitting that he speak only the good."[91]

And a saying, either a tradition or a report, [states] "Conversation in the mosque eats good deeds like cattle eat grass."

Al-Nakhaʿī said, "They used to consider walking to the mosque on a dark night something that vouchsafed heaven."[92]

And Anas b. Mālik said, "If someone lights a lamp in the mosque, the angels and the bearers of the throne continue to ask forgiveness for him for as long as the mosque is lit by that lamp."[93]

According to ʿAlī, may God ennoble his face: "When a servant dies, the places where he prayed and his deeds ascended to heaven weep for him." Then he recited, *And the heaven and earth wept not for them, nor were they reprieved* [44:29].[94]

---

88 Al-Ḥākim al-Nīsābūrī, *al-Mustadrak*, 4:323; al-Ṭabarānī, *al-Muʿjam al-kabīr*, 10:198; Abū Nuʿaym, *Ḥilya*, 4:109.

89 Abū Nuʿaym, *Ḥilya*, 10:213; and al-Ṭabarānī, *al-Muʿjam al-kabīr*, recount sayings close to this in wording.

90 Al-Tirmidhī, *Sunan*, 2617; Ibn Māja, *Sunan*, 802.

91 Ibn al-Mubārak, *Zuhd*, 416.

92 Ibn al-Mubārak, *Zuhd*, 424, Ibn Abī Shayba, *al-Muṣannaf*, 6500; Abū Nuʿaym, *Ḥilya*, 4:225.

93 Al-Haythamī, *Bughiyat al-bāḥith*, 127.

94 Ibn al-Mubārak, *Zuhd*, 336. Al-Zabīdī, *Itḥāf*, mentions that this was said in response to a man who asked ʿAlī, "Does the earth or sky weep for anyone?" There is also a *ḥadīth* with similar wording in Abū Yaʿlā, *Musnad*, 4022; it states, "Every servant of God has two doorways in the heavens—a door through which his deeds enter and a door through which his deeds and words leave—and on his death, both these doors miss him and weep for him." Then he recited [the verse above] and

Ibn ʿAbbās said, "The earth weeps for him for forty mornings."[95]

And ʿAṭāʾ al-Khurasānī said, "There is no servant who prostrates to God in any place on earth, except that that place will bear witness for him on the day of resurrection and weep for him on the day of his death."[96]

Anas b. Mālik said, "There is no place on earth in which God most high is invoked except that it boasts to the land around it and rejoices for the remembrance of God to the limits of the seven earths. And there is no servant who prays except that the earth where he does so is made beautiful because of it."[97]

It is also said that any place where a people camp the night will either bless them or curse them in the morning.[98]

---

said, "Those were people who did no good on the earth for which the earth would weep, and no good words or deeds ascended to the heavens for which they would be missed and for which the heavens would weep."

95 Ibn al-Mubārak, *Zuhd*, 338.

96 Ibn al-Mubārak, *Zuhd*, 340.

97 Ibn al-Mubārak, *Zuhd*, 339.

98 Ibn al-Mubārak, *Zuhd*, 334.

2

On How to Perform the Outward Elements of the Prayer, Beginning with the *Takbīr* and What Comes Before It

When the person [intending to] pray has completed the ablution and is pure of any impurities on his body, the place of prayer, and his clothes, and his nakedness is covered from his navel to his knees, he should stand straight, face the *qibla*, and balance his weight between one foot and the other, without his feet or legs touching one another.[1] This is what used to be considered a sign of a man's understanding of his *dīn*. The Prophet صَلَّى ٱللَّٰهُ عَلَيْهِ وَسَلَّمَ forbade both *ṣafn* and *ṣafd* in the prayer. *Ṣafd* ("fettering") means to stand with one's feet together, as in the words of the most high, *Bound together in fetters* [14:49]. *Ṣafn* means to raise one foot, as in the words of the most high *Running with feet raised high* [38:31]. This is what [the worshiper] should observe regarding his feet when standing.

He should also take care that his knees and waist are straight. In regard to his head, he may either keep it straight or bow it slightly. The latter expresses more humility and also lowers the gaze.

His gaze should be directed toward the prayer rug on which he is praying. Lacking that, he should stand near the wall in front of

1 Note that al-Ghazālī is describing the method of the Shāfiʿī school of law. For a complete exposition of how this may differ with regard to the other three schools of law in Sunnī Islam, see al-Jazīrī, *Islamic Jurisprudence*.

him, or else draw a line.[2] This limits the extent of his gaze and helps prevent his thoughts from becoming scattered. He should limit his gaze so that it does not exceed the edges of his prayer rug or the line, and he should maintain this until the bowing, without turning to the right or the left. Such is the correct comportment for the standing position [in the prayer].

Then, with his body in balance, facing the *qibla*, and with [his] limbs still, he should [first] recite [the entire *sūra* beginning] *Say, "I seek refuge in the Lord of mankind"* [114:1–6] as a defense against Satan, and then proceed to pronounce the call establishing the prayer (*iqāma*). If there is hope that someone else might join him, he should first make the [complete] call to prayer. After that, he should form [his] intention. So, for example, if he is about to pray the midday prayer (*ẓuhr*), he should say in his heart, "I am praying the obligatory midday prayer for God." This formulation of intention should specify whether [the prayer] is being prayed in its time or being made up, whether it is obligatory or supererogatory, and whether it is for the *ẓuhr*, *ʿaṣr*, or some other [prayer] time. The meanings of these utterances should be present in his heart, for that is the true intention, while the utterances are only reminders and ways of being aware. The worshiper should try to retain this awareness until the end of the opening *takbīr*, lest it be forgotten.

Then, with [his] intention in mind, he should raise his hands from the position of being straight at his sides to the level of his shoulders such that his thumbs are even with his earlobes and his fingertips with the tops of his ears. The palms of his hands should be open, facing the *qibla*, and his thumbs should be likewise, with fingers open, not closed, neither splayed nor tightly closed, but rather in their normal state. Since the transmitted narrations describe both spreading the fingers and closing them, the most inclusive, and thus preferred [position], is to keep them between these two.

When the hands have come to rest in their place, he should begin to pronounce the *takbīr* as he lowers them, all the while keeping [his] intention in mind. Then he should place his hands above his navel

---

2 The commentary adds "if praying in the desert or in the open courtyard of a mosque"; that is, where the ground is sand or soil. Al-Zabīdī, *Itḥāf*, 3:31.

but below his chest, the right on left, out of respect for the right hand, [as] it is borne [by the left]. He should extend the index and middle fingers of the right hand upon the forearm [of the left] while grasping his left wrist with his thumb, small finger, and ring finger.

According to some narrations, the *takbīr* [saying *Allāhu akbar*] should be pronounced as the hands are being raised; according to others, once the hands are [completely] raised; and according to yet others, as they are being lowered. There is nothing wrong with any of these, but I consider it most fitting to [pronounce the *takbīr*] as the hands are lowered. This is because the *takbīr* expresses a bond and placing one hand on the other does as well. So lowering the hands from a raised position to their place as the *takbīr* [is pronounced], beginning with the *alif* [of the divine name] and ending with the *rāʾ* [of the word *akbar*] extends this correspondence between the bond and that action. The [initial] raising of the hands, then, is an introduction to this beginning.

When making the *takbīr*, the worshiper should not move his hands forward as if pushing away nor should he move them back behind [the line of] his shoulders, nor shake them toward the right and left on finishing the *takbīr*. Rather, he should lower them easily and smoothly, placing the right hand on the left when they are lowered.

There is a narration that says that when the Prophet ﷺ uttered the *takbīr*, he lowered his hands and then, when he intended to recite [the prayer], he placed the right hand on the left; if this *ḥadīth* is authentic (*ṣaḥīḥ*), then it is preferred over whatever else we have mentioned.

In respect to the [utterance] of the *takbīr* itself, he should vocalize the *hāʾ* of *Allāhu* with a *ḍamma*[3] and make it short and unstressed, ensuring that between it and the *alif* of *akbar* there is no sound that resembles a *waw* [sound], which might happen if that syllable were stressed, and that between the *bāʾ* and *rāʾ* of *akbar* there is no added *alif* [which would lengthen the *a* sound] into "*akbār*." Lastly, the *rāʾ* of *akbar* should not be pronounced with a *ḍamma*.

This is the form of the *takbīr* and what accompanies it.

---

3 A *ḍamma* is a short 'u' sound.

The Recitation

Then he begins with the opening supplication. It is good for him to say, immediately following the *takbīr*: "God is much greater! (*Allāhu akbar kabīra*)! Praise be to God in abundance! Glory be to God early and late!"[4] Then, "I have turned my face..." to the words, "...and I am among the Muslims."[5]

He then says, "Glory to You O God, and [God be] praised! Blessed be Your name, and exalted Your majesty, and sublime Your praise, and there is no deity other than You,"[6] thus combining various [invocations] that have been transmitted.

If he is praying behind an *imām* who does not leave a silence long enough [after the *takbīr*] in which to recite this invocation, he should shorten it.

He then says, "I seek refuge in God from Satan the accursed,"[7] and proceeds to the recitation of the Fātiḥa [1:1–7], starting with "In the name of God, the Merciful and Compassionate," making sure to pronounce it with all its stresses and doubled letters, all its sounds, and making sure that the letter *ḍād* [in the word *al-ḍāllīn*] is not pronounced as *ẓal.*

At the end of the Fātiḥa [1:1–7], he says *āmīn*, lengthening the sound of the *mīm*, and making sure not to join it to the word *al-ḍāllīn* [*those who go astray*] at the end.

In *fajr*, *maghrib*, and *ʿishāʾ*, the recitation is made aloud, unless the worshiper is praying behind the *imām*, in which case he pronounces only the word *āmīn* aloud.

---

4 Muslim, *Ṣaḥīḥ*, 601. The formula following the *takbīr* is 'Allāhu akbaru kabīran, wa-l-ḥamdu li-llāhi kathīran, wa-subḥān Allāhi bukratan wa-aṣīla(n).'

5 Muslim, *Ṣaḥīḥ*, 771. The entire supplication is: "I have turned my face in pure monotheism to the One who fashioned the heavens and the earth and I am not among the polytheists. My prayer and my sacrifice, my life and my death belong to God, Lord of the worlds, without partner, thus have I been commanded and I am among the Muslims."

6 In Abū Dāwūd, *Sunan*, 775; al-Tirmidhī, *Sunan*, 242; and al-Nasāʾī, *Sunan*, 2:132; this supplication is conveyed as the practice of the Prophet صَلَّى ٱللَّهُ عَلَيْهِ وَسَلَّمَ, while in Muslim, *Ṣaḥīḥ*, 399, it is related as something people heard ʿUmar رَضِيَ ٱللَّهُ عَنْهُ say.

7 'Aʿūdhu bi-l-llāhi mina al-shayṭāni al-rajīm.'

Then he recites a *sūra* or portion equal in length to three or more verses of the Qurʾān, taking care not to connect the end of the *sūra* to the *takbīr* uttered for the bowing. Rather, he should leave a silence between them equal to the length of time it takes to say *Subḥān Allāh* once.

In *fajr*, he should recite from the longer of the *mufaṣṣal*,[8] in *maghrib* from the shorter ones,[9] and for *ẓuhr*, *ʿaṣr*, and *ʿishāʾ*, from the medium-length [*sūra*s],[10] such as *By the sky containing great stars* [85:1–22] or something close to it in length. If traveling, for *fajr*, he should recite, *Say, "O disbelievers...* [109:1–6] and *Say, "He is God,* [*who is*] *One"* [112:1–4]. These two *sūra*s should also be recited for the [supererogatory] prayer of two cycles before *fajr*, or at the beginning of the circumambulation of the Kaʿba, or [in the prayer of] greeting a mosque. In all these cases, [the recitation is done] while the worshiper stands with his hands placed as we have described at the beginning of the prayer.

The Cycle (*rukūʿ*) and What Accompanies It

Then he bows, taking care to observe certain matters as he does. He should pronounce the *takbīr* of the bowing, raising his hands as he does so, and extend the utterance so that it ends when the motion of bowing ceases. Also, when bowing, he should place the palms of his hands on his knees, his fingers outspread, with [the backs of the hands] facing the *qibla* and in line with his lower legs. He should keep his knees straight, not bent, his back straight, with his neck and head forming a straight line. If the worshiper is a man, he should keep his elbows out from his sides, and if a woman, she should keep them close by her sides.

---

8 The *mufaṣṣal* are those *sūra*s toward the end the Qurʾān, beginning around *sūra* 49.

9 From approximately *sūra* 98 to the end of the Qurʾān.

10 From approximately *sūra* 78 to *sūra* 90.

He should then say: "Glory be to my Lord the almighty"[11] three times, and it is good to increase this to seven or ten times unless he is the *imām* [leading others].

[The worshiper] then rises up from the bowing to the standing position, raising his hands and saying "God hears the one who praises Him!"[12] Then, with his body still, he says, "Our Lord, Yours is the praise,[13] praise that fills the heavens, fills the earth, and fills whatever You will beyond them!"[14] This standing should not be prolonged except in the case of the prayer of glorification (*ṣalāt al-tasbīḥ*), [the prayer] during an eclipse (*kusūf*),[15] or in the [obligatory] dawn prayer (*ṣubḥ*).

In this latter case, after [standing up from] the second bowing and before the prostration, the worshiper should utter the *qunūt* supplication, using the words transmitted [from the Prophet صَلَّى ٱللَّٰهُ عَلَيْهِ وَسَلَّمَ].[16]

---

11 'Subḥāna rabbīya al-ʿaẓīm.'

12 'Samiʿa llāhu li-man ḥamida.'

13 'Rabbanā laka al-ḥamd.' In some narrations, this has been recorded as 'Rabbanā, wa-laka al-ḥamd,' meaning, "Our Lord, and Yours is the praise." Both versions were recorded in sound *ḥadīth*s.

14 'Rabbanā laka al-ḥamd milʾa al-samawāti wa-milʾa al-arḍi wa-milʾa mā shiʾta min shayʾin baʿd.' Muslim, *Ṣaḥīḥ*, 471.

15 These and other supererogatory prayers are described in chapter 7.

16 One of the best-known versions of this supplication is,

> O God, guide me among those whom You have guided, pardon me among those whom You have pardoned, take charge of me among those of whom You have taken charge, bless me in what You have given me, and deliver me from evil You have decreed. You are the One who decrees and none shall decree [anything] over You, and none who takes You as their friend is abased. Blessed be You, our Lord, and exalted! And may God send blessing to the Prophet and his people and salutations of peace.
>
> 'Allāhumma, ihdinī fī man hadayt, wa-ʿāfinī fī man ʿāfayt, wa-tawallanī fī man tawallayt, wa-bārik lī fīmā ʿaṭayt, wa-qinī sharra mā qaḍayt, innaka taqḍī wa-lā yuqḍā ʿalayk, wa-innahu lā yadhillu man wālayt, tabārakta rabbanā wa-taʿālayt! Wa-ṣalla allāhu ʿalā l-nabīyi wa-ālihi wa-sallam.'

Al-Bayhaqī reported that this supplication was made with the *fajr* prayer (*al-Sunan al-kubrā*, 2:209), whereas many other sources associate it with the *witr* prayer at night.

The Prostration

Pronouncing the *takbīr*, the worshiper then proceeds into the prostration, placing his knees, forehead, nose, and outstretched hands on the ground, and pronouncing the *takbīr* for prostration as he does [so], but not raising his hands as he did for the bowing.

The first part of his body placed on the ground should be his knees, then both hands, then his face so that the forehead and nose touch the ground. For men, the elbows should be kept out from the sides of the body, but not for women; for men, the feet should be apart from one another, but not for women. Once in prostration, there should be an empty space [formed by] raising the abdomen up from the thighs with the knees apart. This, too, applies to men, not women. He should also take care that his hands are in line with his shoulders and that his fingers are not spread open, but are rather closed with the thumbs closed against them. If they are not, however, no harm is done. He should avoid placing his forearms flat on the ground, the way a dog does, for that is prohibited. Then, [while in prostration], he should say, "Glory be to my Lord most high!"[17] three times, and if [he does so] more, that is good unless he is the *imām* [leading others].

Then he rises up from the prostration and comes to rest in a balanced sitting position, uttering the *takbīr* as he raises his head and sits on his left foot with his right foot perpendicular to the earth. He places his hands on his thighs, fingers open, although there is no narration concerning whether they must be closed or open, and [while in that seated position] he says, "Lord forgive me, have mercy upon me, provide for me, guide me, restore me, pardon me, and grant me well-being."[18] At this point, the worshiper should not sit for a long [time], unless he is praying the prayer of glorification. Then he should make the second prostration in a similar fashion, and [when he] rises up from it, he [should] sit for a brief rest and do this in every cycle [that is] not followed by the

17 'Subḥāna rabbīya al-aʿlā.'

18 'Rabbi ighfirlī, wa-irḥamnī, wa-irzuqnī, wa-ihdinī, wa-jburnī, wa-ʿāfinī, wa-ʿafu ʿannī.'

testimony. Then he [should] stand, placing his hands on the ground but without bringing either of his feet forward. For this standing, he prolongs his utterance of the *takbīr*, to fill the time midway from rising up from the seated position until midway to standing completely straight, so that the *hāʾ* of *Allāh* comes when he sits back up from prostration, the *kāf* of *akbar* while he leans on his hands to stand up, and the *rāʾ* of *abkar* midway toward standing completely straight. [In other words], the utterance of the *takbīr* will be done from the mid-point of rising up [from prostration] to the mid-point of rising to the [complete] standing position, leaving only the very beginning and end [of this movement] without its utterance. This [description] corresponds to the most general view [of how to make this movement].

He prays the second cycle as he did the first, beginning with the words "I seek refuge in God from Satan the accursed," [said before reciting the Fātiḥa (1:1–7)].

Reciting the Testimony

[At the end of the] the second cycle, he recites the first testimony, after which he invokes blessings upon the Messenger of God ﷺ and on his family, placing his right hand upon his right thigh with all the fingers of the right hand closed except the index finger, but it is also correct if the thumb is not folded. He points upward with his right index finger only at the words "except God" (*illa llāh*) but not when saying, "There is no deity" (*lā ilāha*). For this testimony he sits on his left foot as he did between the two prostrations.

In the final testimony, he completes the supplication that was transmitted following the invocation of blessings on the Prophet ﷺ.[19] Its elements are like those of the first testimony,

---

19 There are many narrations concerning the words of this supplication. In Muslim, *Ṣaḥīḥ*, 588, the Prophet ﷺ is reported to have said,

> When one of you pronounces the testimony, let him ask [for] protection from four things, saying: "O God, I seek refuge in You from the punishment of the fire, from the punishment of the grave, from the tribulations of life and death, and from the evil of the tribulation of the Antichrist (*al-masīḥ al-dajjāl*)."

except, in this final one, he sits on his left hip, since it is not followed by standing again. Rather, he settles in place, causing his left foot to lie flat and out [from his left hip], and keeping the right foot upright [and perpendicular to the ground], with the tip of the big toe pointed toward the *qibla* unless this is too difficult for him. [When he ends the prayer], he says, "Peace be upon you and the mercy of God," and turns far enough to the right so that his right cheek could be seen by someone behind and to [the right] of him. He then turns to the left in the same way, repeating a second salutation of peace. [The first is done] with the intention of ending the prayer with salutations of peace to whoever is on his right, both the angels and the Muslims, and the second to whoever is on his left, both the angels and the Muslims. In both cases, he utters these final salutations in a short manner, without stretching out the words, for the short utterance is *sunna*.

This is the form of the prayer of the solitary worshiper.

He raises his voice in uttering the *takbīr* just loudly enough so that he can hear [it] himself.

The *imām* should form the intention to lead the prayer in order to gain the merit of prayer in congregation. If he does not, the prayer of the people who expressed [their] intention to follow him is still sound, and thereby they gain the merit of the congregation.

He should recite the opening supplication and [the formula of] seeking refuge silently, as a solitary worshiper would, and then the Fātiḥa [1:1–7] and a *sūra* aloud in both cycles of *fajr*, and the first two cycles of *ʿishāʾ* and *maghrib*, as a solitary worshiper would.

[The *imām*] says the word "*āmīn*" aloud in the prayers that are recited aloud, as do those who are following him; they should say this at the same time he does, not afterward. Following the recitation of the Fātiḥa [1:1–7], the *imām* should pause to catch his breath and during this pause, those following him should recite the Fātiḥa, so that in the prayers recited aloud, they might listen [attentively] to the *imām*'s recitation [of the *sūra*]. One following the *imām* does not, however, recite the *sūra* in the prayers he says aloud unless he cannot hear the *imām*'s voice.

Raising his head from the bowing position, the *imām* says, "God hears the one who praises Him,"[20] and the follower [says the same]. The *imām* should not exceed three repetitions of the glorification while bowing and prostrating, nor add anything to the testimony after the words, "O God bless Muḥammad and the people of Muḥammad." In the last two cycles [of the prayer], the *imām* should make his recitation of the Fātiḥa [1:1–7] brief so as not to make the prayer too long for people, nor should he add to his supplication in the final testimony such that it becomes longer than the time it takes for the testimony and invocation of blessings on God's messenger ﷺ.

When the *imām* pronounces the closing salutations of peace, he should intend thereby both people and angels, and when the people say it, their intention should be to return his greeting.

The *imām* should then remain still for a time until people have finished saying the closing salutations, and then turn to face them. If there are women praying behind the men, however, he should remain in his place facing the *qibla* until they have left. None [of the men] should get up to leave until the *imām* does so; he may leave either to the right or left, although I prefer the right.

In the *qunūt* supplication[21] of *fajr*, the *imām* should refer not only to himself [using the singular], but to the entire assembly by saying: "O God, guide us..." (*Allāhumma ihdinā*). This he says aloud while the people raise their hands [in supplication] to the level of the breast, and wipe them over their faces at the end, in keeping with a *ḥadīth* that was transmitted concerning this.[22] Otherwise, the general rule is that the hands are not raised, as in the supplication that comes at the end of the testimony.

---

20 'Samiaʿ llāhu li-man ḥamida.'

21 Here *qunūt* means "standing in devotion." This supplication is made while standing and, according to the Shāfiʿī school, is said with hands raised.

22 "Whenever the Messenger of God ﷺ raised his hands in supplication... he did not lower them until he had wiped them over his face," al-Tirmidhī, *Sunan*, 3386.

Matters That Are Prohibited in the Prayer

The Messenger of God ﷺ prohibited *ṣafn* and *ṣafd*,[23] both of which we have already mentioned. [Prayer in] *iqʿāʾ*, *sadl*, *kaff*, *ikhtiṣār*, *ṣalb*, *muwāṣila*, and that of the *ḥāqin*, *ḥāqib*, and *ḥāziq*, or by someone who is hungry, angry, or wearing a face veil are also prohibited.

The word, *iqʿāʾ*[24] literally means "to sit like a dog," that is, on the haunches with the paws on the ground. But for scholars of *ḥadīth*, it means sitting [during the prayer] on bended knees with nothing touching the earth except the tips of one's toes and knees.

The term *sadl*,[25] according to the view of scholars of *ḥadīth*, means to enwrap oneself in one's robes, with hands inside, while bowing and prostrating in the prayer. Such was the habit of the Jews in their worship and [Muslims] were prohibited from imitating them.[26] Included here would be the long shirt (*qamīṣ*): one should not bow or prostrate with one's hands inside the shirt. It is also said that this term refers to the act of draping the bottom half of a loincloth (*izār*) over one's head so that its two ends hang down to the left and the right without its being placed on the shoulders. The first of these two [definitions, i.e., enwrapping oneself in one's robe] is, however, more accurate.

The term *kaff* means to bunch up one's garment in the front and back when one intends to make the prostration. It is also used to signify gathering one's hair [into a braid or plait]. One should not pray with braided or plaited hair, as this is prohibited for men [but not women], in accordance with the *ḥadīth*: "I was told to prostrate on seven bones and not to bunch up either my hair or my garment."[27]

---

23 Defined at the beginning of chapter 2 as standing with one's feet together or with one foot raised. The rest of these terms are defined below.

24 Al-Tirmidhī, *Sunan*, 282; Ibn Māja, *Sunan*, 894.

25 Abū Dāwūd, *Sunan*, 643; al-Tirmidhī, *Sunan*, 378.

26 The *ḥadīth* cited here is, "The Messenger of God prohibited *sadl* in the prayer and also [prohibited] a man's covering his mouth."

27 Al-Bukhārī, *Ṣaḥīḥ*, 809; Muslim, *Ṣaḥīḥ*, 490.

Thus, Aḥmad b. Ḥanbal رَحِمَهُ ٱللَّهُ disapproved of wearing a loincloth over a shirt in the prayer because he viewed it as [a form of] "bunching up."

The term *ikhtiṣār* means placing one's hands on one's waist.[28]

[The term] *ṣalb* means standing [in the prayer] with outstretched arms.[29]

[The term] *muwāṣila* ("joining") may apply to five things. Two refer to the *imām*: he must not connect the recitation to the opening *takbīr*,[30] nor connect the recitation to the bowing. Two refer to those who pray behind the *imām*: they should not connect their utterance of the opening *takbīr* to that of the *imām*, nor [should they connect] their final salutation to that of the *imām*. The meaning [of *muwāṣila*] that applies to both the *imām* and the follower is that they should not connect the [first closing] salutation, which is obligatory, to the second. Rather, the two should be separated [by a brief silence].

The *ḥāqin* is someone who needs to urinate, the *ḥāqib* is someone who needs to defecate, and the *ḥāziq*[31] is someone wearing foot coverings that are too tight for his feet. All these [situations] are obstacles to reverence in the prayer.

For the same reason, [the prayer is prohibited] for someone who is hungry or burdened by concerns. Prohibiting someone [who] is hungry is understood from his words صَلَّى ٱللَّهُ عَلَيْهِ وَسَلَّمَ, "If the evening meal is ready and the time for prayer has come, begin with the evening meal,"[32] that is, unless the time is short or one's heart is at ease [in praying first].

There is also a narration that says, "Do not enter into the prayer with a scowl on your face and do not pray while you are angry."

And Ḥasan said, "Every prayer in which the heart is not present is more likely to bring punishment [than reward]."[33]

---

28 In al-Bukhārī, *Ṣaḥīḥ*, 1220; Muslim, *Ṣaḥīḥ*, 545, the *ḥadīth* states, "The Prophet صَلَّى ٱللَّهُ عَلَيْهِ وَسَلَّمَ prohibited a man from praying with his hands on his waist."

29 Abū Dāwūd, *Sunan*, 903; al-Nasā'ī, *Sunan*, 2:127. *Ṣalb* means, literally, a cross; the prohibition is against forming this shape with one's arms and body.

30 That is, the *imām* cannot say, "Allāhu akbar al-ḥamdu li-llāh rabbī l-ʿālamīn...."

31 Muslim, *Ṣaḥīḥ*, 560.

32 Al-Bukhārī, *Ṣaḥīḥ*, 5465; Muslim, *Ṣaḥīḥ*, 557.

33 Recorded by al-Ṭawsī, *al-Arbaʿīn*, 11, as a saying of Ḥasan al-Baṣrī.

The [following] *ḥadīth* [states that]: "Seven things [which occur] in the prayer are from Satan: a nosebleed, drowsiness, whisperings of doubt, yawning, scratching, turning away, and absentmindedly playing with something."[34] One version of this also includes, "Forgetfulness and doubt."[35]

One of the early Muslims said, "Four things in the prayer [denote that someone] is ill-mannered: turning [to the right or left], wiping [the dust from prostration off] one's face, clearing away pebbles on the ground [where one is going to prostrate], and praying in a path where people need to pass."[36]

[The Prophet صلى الله عليه وسلم] also prohibited interlacing the fingers,[37] cracking the knuckles,[38] covering the face,[39] and putting the palms of both hands together and placing them in between the thighs when bowing. One of the Companions رضي الله عنه said, "We used to do that, then he prohibited it."[40]

Also, blowing on the earth when prostrating in order to clean something from it,[41] or smoothing out the pebbles on the ground,[42] is also disapproved, for all these actions are superfluous [to the prayer]; nor should a worshiper raise his foot and place it upon his thigh, or lean against a wall when standing, such that if the

---

34 With one's beard or garment, for example.

35 Al-Tirmidhī, *Sunan*, 2748, with similar wording. Al-Bukhārī, *Ṣaḥīḥ*, 751, states, "The Prophet صلى الله عليه وسلم was asked about turning away in the prayer and he replied, 'It is a robbery by which Satan steals from the servant's prayer." And Muslim, *Ṣaḥīḥ*, 2203, states that ʿUthmān b. Abī l-ʿĀṣ asked about whisperings in the prayer, and the Messenger of God صلى الله عليه وسلم said to him, "That is a devil named Khanzab. If you sense him, seek refuge in God." The words "forgetfulness" (*sahw*) and "doubt" (*shakk*) here may apply to forgetting or having doubt about the text one is reciting, or forgetting how much of the prayer has been completed. "Doubt" may also concern the ablution, as al-Ghazālī discusses in the *Mysteries of Purification*, book 3 of the *Revival of the Religious Sciences*.

36 This is a quote from Abū Ṭālib al-Makkī, *Qūt al-qulūb*, 2:97.

37 Ibn Ḥanbal, *Musnad*, 4:241.

38 Ibn Māja, *Sunan*, 965.

39 Abū Dāwūd, *Sunan*, 643; Ibn Māja, *Sunan*, 966. This refers to men.

40 Al-Bukhārī, *Ṣaḥīḥ*, 790; Muslim, *Ṣaḥīḥ*, 535.

41 Al-Ṭabarānī, *al-Muʿjam al-kabīr*, 5:137.

42 Abū Dāwūd, *Sunan*, 945; al-Tirmidhī, *Sunan*, 379; al-Nasāʾī, *Sunan*, 6:3.

wall were not there, he would fall. The most prevalent view is that [leaning against anything] invalidates the prayer.[43]

Distinguishing the Obligatory from the *Sunna* Elements of the Prayer

What we have mentioned thus far includes [elements that are considered] obligatory, *sunna*, [good] manners, and correct form (*hayʾa*), and the aspirant on the path to the hereafter should observe them all.

Of these, [there are] twelve obligatory elements: (1) intention; (2) the opening *takbīr*; (3) standing; (4) the recitation of the Fātiḥa [1:1–7]; (5) bowing low enough for the palms to reach the knees and the body to come to a rest; (6) rising up from [the bowing] into a standing position; (7) prostrating such that the body comes to a rest, although placing the hands [on the ground] is not obligatory; (8) rising up from the prostration to a seated position; (9) sitting for the last testimony; (10) [pronouncing] the last testimony; (11) invoking blessings on the Prophet ﷺ; and (12) the first salutation, though having the intention to end the prayer [when this salutation is pronounced] is not obligatory.

Anything other than these [twelve] is not considered obligatory. Rather, it may be either *sunna* or a form that pertains to a *sunna* or an obligatory element.

There are four actions that are considered *sunna*: (1) raising the hands when pronouncing the opening *tabkīr*; (2) raising them for [the *takbīr* just before] bowing; (3) raising them when rising up [from the bowing] to a standing position; and (4) sitting for the first testimony.[44]

What we have mentioned about spreading the fingers or the limits to which they are raised [when pronouncing the *takbīr*] [relates to one's physical] form [during the prayer]. Keeping the right foot

---

43 This would not apply, however, to someone whose health necessitated praying while seated in a chair.

44 That is, in the prayers that have three or four cycles.

perpendicular to the ground and the left foot flat are forms that pertain to sitting. Inclining the head and not turning to the right or to the left are forms that pertain to the standing position and beautiful posture, and staying seated for a brief rest before standing up from the prostration is also not numbered among the principle actions of the *sunna*, but are, rather, ways of beautifying the form of rising from prostration to standing. These things in themselves are not the purposes [of the actions], and thus are not singled out for mention.

Invocations in the prayer [that are] considered *sunna* are the opening supplication, then the [formula of] seeking refuge, then saying "*āmīn*," which is a confirmed *sunna*, then the recitation of a *sūra*, then pronouncing the *takbīr* of transition from one position to another, then the glorification in the bowing and prostration, then what is said on rising up from each of them, then the first testimony and the invocation of blessings on the Prophet ﷺ that follow it, then the supplication at the end of the final testimony, and finally, [pronouncing] the closing salutation.

Although we have combined all these under the name *sunna*, there are different degrees of importance; if omitted, four among them necessitate the prostration to correct [for] forgetfulness.

[1] Of the actions [mentioned above], one of them, sitting for the first testimony, is at this level of importance. [It is important] because it affects the order of the prayer in the eyes of an onlooker, who can understand [by seeing it] whether the prayer is of four cycles or not. This differs from an action such as raising the hands, which does not alter the order [of actions] in the prayer. For this reason, the former [actions] are termed the "portion" (*baʿḍ*) and it is said that [omitting] "any of the portions" necessitates the prostration of forgetfulness.

[2] In respect to invocations, there are three that necessitate prostration if omitted: the *qunūt* supplication, the first testimony, and the invocation of blessings on the Prophet ﷺ. These differ [in importance] from the utterances of the *takbīr* of transition from one position to another, or the glorification in the bowing, prostration, and rising up from them. Bowing and prostrating are special postures in themselves by which [the prayer] takes on the

quality of worship, and this is [true] even without invocation or *takbīr* [when it accompanies them]. So omitting them does not alter the form of worship.

Sitting for the first testimony is an ordinary [human posture];[45] it exists [in the prayer] only for the purpose of [pronouncing] the testimony. Thus, if it is [mistakenly] omitted, it affects the visible form of the prayer. Such is not the case, however, for the supplication recited [just after the opening *takbīr*] or the *sūra*, for if they were [mistakenly] omitted, the standing posture would still be filled with the recitation of the Fātiḥa [1:1–7] and would be distinguished from an ordinary [human posture]. If the supplication at the end of the final testimony [is mistakenly omitted], it is a similar case.

[Omission of] the *qunūt* supplication would seem the least likely to need to be corrected by the prostration [of forgetfulness], but it was for [its recitation] that standing [after the second cycle] in the *fajr* prayer is enjoined. In this respect, it is similar to sitting for the rest. If the latter is prolonged and [one recites therein the testimony], it becomes sitting for the first testimony.

So standing would remain simply a prolonged, ordinary act if it did not contain the obligatory invocation. Its prolongation makes the *fajr* prayer unique; and in its being devoid of an obligatory invocation is a caution concerning the principle of the standing position in the prayer.[46]

If you said: "The difference between the *sunna* and obligatory elements of the prayer is well-known: if you omit an obligatory element, the prayer is invalid and could entail punishment, but this is not the case [for the *sunna*]. And as for distinguishing one *sunna* element from another—all of them are described as "recommended" (*istaḥbāb*), and there is no punishment in omitting them all, while reward may be hoped for [when] all of them are observed, so what is the point [of differentiating between them]?"

---

45 That is, standing and sitting are ordinary, habitual human postures, while bowing and prostrating are postures that are specific to worship.

46 Al-Ghazālī seems to be saying that a prayer is only invalidated by the omission of some element that visibly alters the outward appearance of it. This is not entirely clear, however, from the text, and even al-Zabīdī says about this passage, "The distinction that the author is making here is something strange and not mentioned by anyone else before him." Al-Zabīdī, *Itḥāf*, 3:107.

[If you were to ask this], then know that both [the major and minor *sunna* elements] share in reward and punishment, and the fact that they are recommended does not remove the differences between them. We illustrate this to you by way of an analogy. A human being only becomes a complete, existent human through his intelligible dimension, which is internal, and [through] the organs of the body, which are tangible. The internal dimension is life and spirit. The tangible dimension is the physical form of the limbs.

Without certain of those organs, like the heart, the liver, the brain—every one of which is essential for life—there is no human being. Then there are other organs, such as the eyes, the hands, the feet, and the tongue, that are not essential for life but which, if lacking, remove some of the meaning of life (*maqāsid al-ḥayyat*).[47] There are still others, such as the eyebrows, the beard, the eyelashes, and the complexion, that are not essential for life, nor [do they] accomplish its purposes, but, if lacking, decrease the beauty [of the human form]. And finally, there are some physical features that are not essential for beauty, but they add to its perfection, such as the curve of the eyebrows, the blackness of the beard and eyelashes, the symmetry of the limbs, and the mixture of ruddiness and whiteness in the complexion. All these are of differing degrees.

Similarly, worship is a form shaped by the law; when we take on [this form], it makes us worshipers. Its spirit and inner life is reverence, intention, the heart's presence, and sincerity, as we explain later. Now we are only considering its internal aspects.

Thus, the bowing, prostration, standing, and all the other essential elements play a role in the prayer similar to that of the heart, head, and liver in the body: without them there is no prayer. The *sunna* elements we have mentioned, such as raising the hands, making the opening supplication, and [pronouncing] the first testimony, are like the hands, eyes, and feet. The prayer is not lost without them, just as life may continue without those physical organs, but a person who loses them becomes disfigured, flawed, and undesirable because of their loss. Indeed, someone who would reduce the prayer to its

47 Many verses of the Qurʾān mention hearing, sight, and speech as gifts by which we can know God and express gratitude to Him.

bare minimum is like a person who presents a king with a servant who is alive but has no limbs.[48]

As for the formal details connected to the *sunna*, they are ways to add beauty, just as the eyebrows, beard, eyelashes, and good complexion add to human beauty.

And as for the subtle manners within those *sunna* [actions], they are what complete its beauty, just as the curve of the eyebrows, shape of the beard, and others [complete human beauty].

So the prayer that you have is a means of drawing near and a gift that you bring into the presence of the King of kings, like a beautiful servant girl that someone who wishes to approach a sultan might present as a gift. And this precious gift that you present to God سُبْحَانَهُ وَتَعَالَىٰ is what will be returned to you on the day of the greatest showing. The choice is yours whether it is beautiful or ugly. If you make it beautiful, it is for your own soul, and if you do it badly, it is against your own soul.

So it should not be your goal [to study] the science of *fiqh* in order to distinguish between what is *sunna* and what is obligatory, and for this to have no connection to your understanding other than the fact that because you know that it is permitted to omit a *sunna*, you omit it! That is like a doctor saying, "If a man loses an eye, it does not take away his existence!" [True], but it does take away his chance to become someone more acceptable to the sultan.

This is the way in which you should understand the place of the *sunna*, [its] formal details, and manners [of the prayer]. Any prayer in which someone does not complete the bowing and prostration [well] will be the first to argue against him and will say, "May God neglect you just as you neglected me!" So read the narrations we have conveyed about how to perfectly complete the main elements of the prayer, so their affect [on the prayer] is clear to you.

---

48 Al-Marūzī, *Taʿẓīm qadri al-ṣalāt*, 84.

3

The Inward Requisites [of the Prayer]: Practices of the Heart

In this chapter, we speak about the connection [between] the prayer [and] humility and the concentrated presence of heart. Then we speak of the internal, intelligible aspects of the prayer, their definitions, means, and treatment. Then we speak of the details concerning what [internal dispositions] should accompany each of the main elements of the prayer, so that it may truly serve as provision for the hereafter.

Humility and Presence as Requisites in the Prayer

Know that the scriptural evidence for [both of these] is abundant. Of it, there are the words of God most high, *And establish prayer for My remembrance* [20:14]. In its literal sense, this commandment makes [remembrance] obligatory in the prayer; the opposite of remembrance is heedlessness (*ghifla*). How can we say that someone who is heedless throughout the prayer has prayed it for the remembrance [of God]?

The words of God most high, *And do not be among the heedless* [7:205], on the other hand, are a prohibition, and their literal sense is [that heedlessness is] forbidden.

[There are also] the words of God most high, *And do not approach prayer while you are intoxicated until you know what you are saying* [4:43]. This prohibition concerns drunkenness, but it also includes the state of heedlessness of someone drowning in cares, whisperings of doubt, and worldly thoughts.

In addition, there are the words of the Prophet ﷺ: "The prayer is nothing other than submission and humility."[1] The syntax of this sentence, which uses the emphatic particle (*innamā*) as well as the definite article (*alif lam*), conveys a sense of limiting the meaning as well as affirmation and negation,[2] and linguists understand this to be analogous to the words of the Prophet ﷺ, "The right of pre-emption [in inheritance] applies to nothing except what is not divided."[3]

There is also the saying of the Prophet ﷺ: "If someone's prayer does not prohibit him from immorality and wrongdoing, he gains nothing from it except distance from God,"[4] and praying heedlessly will not forbid immorality and wrongdoing.

Who else but the heedless are meant by the words of the Prophet ﷺ: "There are those who stand in prayer and gain nothing from it except weariness and distress."[5]

He also said ﷺ, "The servant gains nothing from the prayer except that of which he is mindful,"[6] and this is confirmed by the saying, "A worshiper praying is in intimate discourse with

1 Al-Ṭaḥāwī, *Sharḥ muskhil al-āthār*, 3:124, and with similar wording in al-Tirmidhī, *Sunan*, 385.

2 These two constructs indicate that the phrase could be rendered: "Truly the prayer is submission" or "The prayer is nothing but submission."

3 Al-Bukhārī, *Ṣaḥīḥ*, 2213; Muslim, *Ṣaḥīḥ*, 1608. That is, it only applies to what is divided. In this case, for example, pre-emption means that if someone wants to sell his house or land and he has an heir, that heir has the first right to buy it. His or her right pre-empts that of anyone else.

4 Al-Ṭabarānī, *al-Mujʿam al-kabīr*, 11:54. The reference is to the verse, *Indeed, prayer prohibits immorality and wrongdoing, and the remembrance of God is greater* [29:45].

5 Ibn Māja, *Sunan*, 1690; and Ibn Ḥanbal, *Musnad*, 2:373, with wording close to this.

6 Abū Nuʿaym, *Ḥilya*, 7:61; Abū Dāwūd, *Sunan*, 796.

his Lord most high,"[7] for mindless speech is certainly not intimate discourse.

That is, if a person were heedless while paying *zakāt*, [the mere act of giving] would still be a powerful means of opposing selfishness. Fasting, too, can overcome the power of the ego and break the control exerted by the passions, which are the tools of God's foe, Satan, and so it is possible to achieve its end even while [one is] heedless. The same holds true for the pilgrimage (*ḥājj*): to accomplish its rites is extremely hard and in some cases painful, whether or not the heart is always present while [one] does so.

The prayer, however, is only invocation, recitation, bowing, prostration, standing, and sitting.

Invocation, for its part, is intimate discourse with God most high. Its purpose is either discourse and conversation or [articulating] words and sounds as a way of testing the tongue by action; just as the stomach and genitals are tested by abstinence in fasting, the whole body is tested by the hardships of the pilgrimage, and the heart is tested by the difficulty of giving alms and parting with precious wealth.

There is no doubt, however, that this latter view [of invocation] is false. Nothing is easier than heedlessly wagging the tongue. As an action alone, it is no test at all. Rather, the purpose of forming a word is to express something, and expression means there is something in the mind to express, which cannot be [true] if the heart is not present. What do the words *Guide us to the straight path* [1:6] mean if the heart is distracted when they are said and if the purpose in saying them is not need and supplication? What is hard about moving the tongue heedlessly, especially if this has become merely a habit?

Such is the judgment concerning invocations.

In fact, I would say that if you were to take a solemn oath, saying, "Truly I am going to thank a particular person, and praise him, and ask for his help," and then you uttered words to that effect, but [you] were asleep when you did so, you would not have fulfilled your oath. And if the person [you wished to address] were there with you

---

7 The *ḥadīth* in al-Bukhārī, *Ṣaḥīḥ*, 405; and Muslim, *Ṣaḥīḥ*, 551, states, "Whenever one of you rises for the prayer, truly he is in intimate discourse with his Lord."

when you said those words, but it was dark and you were unaware of his presence and did not see him, you would not have fulfilled your oath, because you were still not addressing your words to him. And if these words passed over your tongue, and the person was there with you, but even in broad daylight you were so distracted, so drowned in other thoughts that you had no intention of directing what you said to him, you would still not have fulfilled your oath.

The goal, without a doubt, in the recitation and invocation [of the prayer] is praise and exaltation, humbleness and supplication, and the One being addressed is God, but a worshiper's heart covered by heedlessness is veiled from God and does not see or [experience] consciousness of Him. He is heedless of the One to whom he is speaking, and his tongue simply moves out of habit. How far is this from the purpose of the prayer, which was ordained in order to polish the heart, renew the remembrance of God, and deepen the bond of faith!

Such is the judgment about recitation and invocation.

In short, there is really no way to deny these specific characteristics of the verbal aspect of the prayer, nor to make any distinction between it and the physical aspect.

The bowing and prostration, for example, are for the purpose of veneration, and were it permissible to venerate God by these actions alone, while being in a state of heedless distraction, then it would be equally permissible for the worshiper to venerate an idol placed before him, of which he is heedless, or [venerate] the wall in front him, of which he is [also] heedless.

In that case, [these actions] are no longer veneration. They are no more than movements of the back and head, devoid of any difficulty that would make it a test—or, indeed, make it the "pillar of the *dīn*," [which is] the [act] that separates Islam from disbelief, that takes precedence over the pilgrimage and all other acts of worship, and that alone may [even] entail the slaying of someone who purposefully abandons it.

I do not see that all this importance was given to the prayer for its external actions alone, unless they are combined with the purpose of intimate discourse with God. That is what gives it precedence over fasting, giving alms, making the pilgrimage, and other forms of sacrifice and worship that try the ego by parting with its possessions. God most high says [speaking of the sacrificed cattle on the pilgrimage]: *Their meat will not reach God, nor will their blood, but what reaches Him is piety from you* [22:37]. This means that what is sought is the quality foremost in your heart that leads you to follow God's commandments. Then how could there be a commandment to pray if it had no bearing on actions?

Therefore, this is proof, from the spiritual perspective, that presence of heart is a requisite condition of prayer.

And if you were to say, "If you judge a prayer [which lacks this] to be invalid, and you make it a condition for the prayer's validity, then you disagree with the consensus of jurists (*fuqahāʾ*) who consider it a requirement only at the moment when the opening *takbīr* is pronounced."

Know then, as we said in the *Book of Knowledge*, that the jurists do not deal with the inner dimension. They are not concerned with [the state of hearts], or with the path to the hereafter. They base their judgments on the outward actions of the limbs of the body, and those are sufficient to deliver [people] from capital punishment or the reprimand of the ruler. The question of whether such actions alone will benefit [someone] in the hereafter, however, is beyond the limits of *fiqh*, and it is impossible to claim any consensus concerning it. There are, however, sayings like what was conveyed from Bishr b. al-Ḥārith, as quoted by Abū Ṭalib al-Makkī, that Sufyān al-Thawrī said, "If someone has no reverence, his prayer is ruined."[8]

And Ḥasan [al-Baṣrī] is quoted as having said, "Any prayer without the heart's presence is more likely to bring chastisement."[9]

And to quote Muʿādh b. Jabal, "Whoever intentionally knows, while he is praying, who is praying to his right and left has no prayer."[10] This saying was [also] narrated with a chain of transmission [as a *ḥadīth*].

And the Prophet ﷺ said, "A servant may pray, yet there will not be written for him even one-sixth, [or] even one-tenth of it.

8 Abū Ṭālib al-Makkī, *Qūt al-qulūb*, 2:97.

9 Al-Ṭawsī, *al-Arbaʿīn*, 11, and it is mentioned in Abū Ṭālib al-Makkī, *Qūt al-qulūb*, 2:97.

10 Abū Ṭālib al-Makkī, *Qūt al-qulūb*, 2:97.

All that is written for the servant of his prayer is that of which he is mindful."[11] Even if this had this been conveyed from [someone] other than the Prophet ﷺ, it would have become canon, so how can it not be followed?

ʿAbd al-Wāḥid b. Zayd said, "The consensus of scholars is that a servant gains nothing from his prayer except that of which he is mindful." So [ʿAbd al-Wāḥid b. Zayd] considers this a matter of consensus (*ijmāʿ*).

There are, in fact, countless sayings along these same lines, conveyed by scholars with the highest scruples and by the learned who use their knowledge for the hereafter. The right thing to do is to study the legal proofs, the narrations and sayings concerning this prerequisite, and at the same time recognize that a ruling (*fatwā*) concerning human responsibility must always take into account human shortcomings. It is simply impossible to require that all people [bring] their hearts into a state of concentrated presence throughout the whole of the prayer. In this, everyone, with few exceptions, would fall short. Given the fact that when faced with necessity, a blanket ruling is not possible, the most that can be required is [for the worshiper] to try and realize what the words ["presence" or "reverence"] mean, even if only for a moment, and the best moment for this is when pronouncing the opening *takbīr*. So, it is to this moment that we have limited [what we deem to be] responsibility.

In doing this, we hope that the state of someone who is heedless throughout his prayer, except for the opening *takbīr*, is not the same as the state of someone who omits [even that instant of concentration]. At least in a general way, the former is making an effort to undertake actions outwardly, and concentrates for a moment. How could it be otherwise, when we consider the fact that if someone forgets that he does not have the ablution and prays, even though his prayer is invalid in the eyes of God most high, he nonetheless receives some reward for what he thought he was doing, and [this

11 Abū Dāwūd, *Sunan*, 796, with the wording: "A man will finish his prayer and no more than one-tenth of it will be written for him, or one-ninth, one-eighth, one-seventh, one-sixth, one-fifth, one-fourth, and one-third, or half." The last sentence in the above narration is reported in Abū Nuʿaym, *Ḥilya*, 7:61.

reward] is based on his shortcomings and justifications. Yet along with this hope, he should be fearful that his state may be worse than that of someone who prays the whole prayer without [presence of heart]. And this is because someone who first comes to serve but then [immediately] forgets all respect for the Presence [he is in] and speaks with heedless disdain [may be] in a much worse state than someone who refuses to serve in the first place.

Whenever the means to [experience] fear and hope present themselves in opposition, and [whether or not] an issue is risky in itself, you have a choice between caution or ease. And [I have] no desire to disagree with the jurists in what they have ruled concerning the validity [of the prayer of someone] in a state of heedless distraction, for [their ruling] takes into account situations of necessity, as has been already explained.

Anyone who knows the mystery of the prayer knows that a state of heedless distraction is its opposite, but as we mentioned in the chapter dealing with the difference between outward and inward knowledge[12] in the book of *The Principles of the Creed*, people's shortcomings are one of the reasons for not trying to explain to anyone and everyone the mysteries of the law that have been disclosed to certain people.

Let us then limit our discussion to this issue, for this should suffice the aspirant on the path of the hereafter and we have no intention to confront quarrelsome dissenters at this time.

Our main point is that presence of heart is the prayer's breath of life. The smallest breath needed to keep it alive is at the moment of the opening *takbīr*. To lose even this means the death [of the prayer], while to the extent that we can increase it, the breath of life will spread to all the parts of the prayer. And how many a living person without movement is closer to the dead? Such is the case with the prayer of someone who is heedless for all of it except the opening *takbīr*. We ask for God's goodly aid!

---

12 Al-Ghazālī, book 2, *The Principles of the Creed*, section entitled "Inquiry [on the Difference Between the Outward and the Inward]," 44.

The Inner Dispositions by Which the Life of the Prayer Is Completed

Know that many expressions are used to refer to these inner dispositions, but they can be summarized by six: presence of heart, understanding, veneration, awe, hope, and modesty.

Let us mention each in detail, then speak of their causes, and finally the remedy by which one can acquire these [six]. Their details [follow]:

The first is presence of the heart (*ḥuḍūr al-qalb*). By this, we mean [that one must] empty the heart of anything other than what concerns it and the One to whom it speaks, so that knowledge is joined to word and deed, and thoughts are not directed to anything other than those two elements. When the mind is distracted from what it is doing, and the heart knows what it is doing, and does not neglect anything, then there is presence of the heart.

Understanding (*tafahhum*) the meaning of the words [uttered in the prayer] is something beyond presence of heart. The heart may be present to [the act of] pronouncing the words, but not present to the meaning of those words. So when we speak of "understanding," we mean that there is also knowledge of the meaning of what is being said.

Certainly, in respect to this station, people differ greatly since they do not share a [single] understanding of the meanings of the Qurʾān and the expressions of praise and glorification. Indeed, how many [times might] a worshiper pray, then understand a subtle meaning that his heart had never before conceived of. Thus, the prayer will prohibit lewdness and profligacy. Once the worshiper understands [the Qurʾān and glorification more deeply], the prayer [will] prohibit lewdness without a doubt.

Veneration (*taʿẓīm*), for its part, is something beyond presence of heart and understanding, for a man may speak to a servant with his heart present and [with an] understanding [of] the meanings [of what is said] and yet have no veneration for [the servant] at all. Thus, veneration is something in addition to those two other qualities [presence of heart and understanding].

Awe (*hayba*) is something in addition to veneration; it refers to the state of fear that arises from veneration. Someone who does not experience fear cannot experience awe; someone who fears a scorpion, or the evils of human nature, or other lowly things, is not said to be "in awe," whereas someone who fears a mighty ruler is [in awe]. Awe is thus fear that arises from the majestic.

Hope (*rajāʾ*) is something clearly additional to all this. How many may hold a king in veneration, be in awe of him, and fear his power, but have no hope of any reward from him. A servant of God, however, should always be hopeful that his prayer will bring recompense from the almighty, just as he should always be fearful that his shortcomings will bring chastisement.

Shame (*ḥayāʾ*) is also in addition to these other [dispositions]. It is founded on the consciousness of our shortcomings and sins. It is only possible to conceive of veneration, fear, and hope without shame if one has no consciousness of his shortcomings and sins.

The Means Through Which These Six Dispositions Arise

Know that presence of heart comes by way of aspiration. If there is something that really matters to you, your heart will follow [it], and if not, [your heart will] not [follow it]. In fact, whenever something matters to you, your heart will be present willingly or unwillingly, for such is its nature and how it is governed. If your heart is not present in the prayer, it does not simply rest, but rather wanders to whatever worldly concerns present themselves. So there is no method or remedy to make it present except to find what is important to you in the prayer, and that will not happen as long as it is not clear that what we truly desire—which is faith and certainty that *the hereafter is better and more lasting* [87:17]—depends on prayer, and prayer is the means to it. When this conviction is combined with a deep knowledge of the paltriness of this world and its concerns, [then] out of that union arises the heart's presence in the prayer.

In a similar manner, if you stand before certain great and powerful people, people who cannot [truly] harm or benefit you, your heart becomes present. If it is not present when you are speaking to the King of kings, in whose hand is both this physical world and the dominion of the heavens (*ʿālam al-malakūt*), both benefit and harm, then the reason is no more than the weakness of your faith.

So make every effort now to strengthen your faith; the method of doing this will be examined elsewhere.

As for understanding, it is achieved, besides presence of heart, by sustained reflection and focus on the meaning [of what is being recited]. The remedy is the same as that for the presence of heart: reflect, and [make] a concerted effort to repel distracting thoughts. Repelling distracting thoughts means cutting off the material from which they are formed, by which I mean removing the means of the distractions. As long as that material is not cut out, there will be no [way] to turn those thoughts away, for "whoever loves something remembers it often."[13] The remembrance of what is loved cannot but assail the heart, and so you will see that the prayer of someone who loves what is other than God is never free from distracting thoughts.

And as for veneration, this is a state of the heart that is born of two forms of [experiential] knowledge.

One of is them is knowledge of God's majesty and grandeur, which is one of the principles of faith. If someone does not acknowledge God's greatness, his soul will never venerate Him.

The second is knowledge of the paltriness of the ego, its lowly nature, and its state as a subjugated servant.

Out of these two forms of knowledge is born a sense of submission, contrition, and humility toward God سُبْحَانَهُ وَتَعَالَىٰ and that is what is called veneration. If knowledge of the paltriness of the ego is not intermingled with knowledge of God's grandeur, then a disposition toward veneration and humility will never be reached. Someone who thinks he needs no one else and who feels completely self-sufficient may know what the attribute of grandeur means from another human being, but humility and veneration will never be

13 Al-Daylamī, *Musnad al-firdaws*, 1830, and in Abū Nuʿaym, *Ḥilya*, 2:165, as a saying of Ḥasan al-Baṣrī, with the words, "Tomorrow, each person will be with what concerned him most. Whoever is concerned with something remembers it often. There is no here and now for the one who has no hereafter, and whoever chooses his worldly life over his next life has neither this world nor the next."

his state because the other element of the pair—knowledge of the lowliness and the neediness of the self—is lacking.

As for awe and fear, these are states of the soul born out of a servant's knowledge of God's power and control, the inexorable nature of His will, the servant's own insignificance, and the knowledge that if God were to bring about the destruction of the first and the last [in creation], it would not diminish His dominion in the least. For behold the tribulations and afflictions that have befallen the prophets and saints even though God, unlike earthly rulers, has the power to repel them.[14]

In short, the greater one's knowledge of God, the greater one's humility and awe. The causes for this will be dealt with [more deeply] in the book *On Fear and Hope*, in the Quarter of Deliverance.[15]

Hope, for its part, comes about through knowledge of God's kindness, generosity, all-inclusive grace, and the subtleties of His creation, and by knowing that His promise is true, that heaven is reached by way of prayer. When [the servant] is certain of God's promise, and knows His kindness, hope cannot but arise from this union.

As for shame, this arises from a servant's sense that his devotional practice falls short, and from the knowledge that he cannot fulfill what is [truly] due before the grandeur of God, [who is] mighty and majestic. It is strengthened by the knowledge of his own flaws and deficiencies, lack of sincerity, inner impurity, and inclination to choose this fleeting world in all that he does, along with the knowledge of the great things that the majesty of God requires of him, and [the knowledge] that God sees into his secrets and deepest thoughts, however sensitive or hidden they may be. If this knowledge is truly attained, there cannot but arise from it the state called "shame."

These, then, are the means [by which] these dispositions [arise]. Any time you seek to attain [one of them], the prescription for doing so is to bring to mind the means, for in knowledge of the means is knowledge of the remedy. What links all these means is faith and

---

14 Al-Zabīdī, *Itḥāf* (3:123) adds, "Whose treasuries are depleted when they give and who are powerless to ward off any disaster that might befall them."

15 Book 33 of the *Revival of the Religious Sciences*.

certitude. By the former, I mean the kinds of knowledge I have mentioned, and by the latter, I mean that they be free from doubt and completely govern the heart, as we explained previously in the *Book of Knowledge*. The heart reveres [God] to the extent of its certitude, as the saying of ʿĀʾisha رَضِيَ ٱللَّهُ عَنْهَا [confirms]: "The Messenger of God صَلَّى ٱللَّهُ عَلَيْهِ وَسَلَّمَ used to converse with us and we with him, but when the time of prayer arrived, it was as if he did not know us and we did not know him."[16]

It has been related that God عَزَّ وَجَلَّ spoke to Moses عَلَيْهِ ٱلسَّلَامُ through revelation, saying,

> O Moses! When you invoke Me, invoke Me with trembling limbs and be reverent and focused on My invocation. When you invoke Me, let your tongue translate what is in your heart, stand before Me as a lowly servant, and converse with Me with a fearful heart and a truthful tongue.[17]

And it is related that God [also] spoke to him through revelation and said, "Tell the recalcitrant sinners of your people not to invoke Me, for I have sworn to Myself that whoever mentions Me, I shall mention, and when the recalcitrant sinners mention Me, I mention them with a curse."[18] This concerns the recalcitrant sinner, not someone who is negligent and distracted while invoking Him. But what about someone who is both?

It is to the degree that these dispositions are in their hearts that people may be divided into those who complete their prayer neglectfully, without their hearts being present for even an instant, and those who complete their prayer without their hearts being absent for even an instant. The latter, in fact, may be so absorbed by the import of what they are doing that they cease to be conscious of anything around them, as in the case of Muslim b. Yassār who was unaware that a pillar had collapsed in the mosque and the people had crowded around it.[19] Indeed, there are those who

---

16 Ibn Rajab, *Fatḥ al-bārī*, 4:114.

17 Al-Dīnawarī, *al-Majālisa*, 379; and Abū Nuʿaym, *Ḥilya*, 6:55.

18 Abū Ṭālib al-Makkī, *Qūt al-qulūb*, 1:57.

19 Ibn ʿAsākir, *Tārīkh madīnat Dimashq*, 58:135, and also quoted in Abū Ṭālib al-Makkī, *Qūt al-qulūb*, 2:102.

pray in congregation for a long time without ever knowing who is praying on their right or left.[20] [Abraham عَلَيْهِ ٱلسَّلَامُ was so overwhelmed by awe in prayer] that his heartbeat could be heard for two miles,[21] and there have been others whose faces would turn pale and whose sides would quake with fear. None of this should sound implausible, since it can be witnessed many times over in the affairs of worldly people, who fear earthly sovereigns, despite their weakness and impotence, and the paltriness of whatever can be gained from them. Someone may go to solicit a favor from a king or minister and if, after he left their presence, you were to ask him about who else was there or what the king was wearing, he would not be able to tell you, for his concern with the king had completely distracted him from seeing his clothes or anyone else around him.

So for each [person] there are levels according to his practice, and the portion of each person in the prayer is to the measure of his fear, humility, and veneration. What God سُبْحَانَهُ وَتَعَالَىٰ looks upon is not outward movements but rather hearts, as one of the Companions رَضِيَ ٱللَّٰهُ عَنْهُ said, "People will be gathered on the day of judgment according to the form their prayer took: its tranquility and serenity and the bliss and delight they found in it."[22]

And he spoke the truth, for "Everyone will be gathered according to the condition in which they died,"[23] and everyone dies according to the condition in which they lived, by which is meant the condition of the heart, not of the individual form. Their forms in the hereafter will be fashioned from the qualities of their hearts, and none shall be delivered, *But only one who comes to God with a sound heart* [26:89]. We ask God, in His kindness and generosity, for His goodly accord!

---

20 He is referring to Saʿīd b. Jubayr, as mentioned in Abū Ṭālib al-Makkī, *Qūt al-qulūb*, 2:97.

21 Ibn ʿAsākir, *Tārīkh madīnat Dimashq*, 6:218.

22 Abū Ṭālib al-Makkī, *Qūt al-qulūb*, 2:98.

23 Muslim, *Ṣaḥīḥ*, 2878, with the wording: "Every servant will be resurrected according to the state in which he died."

The Effective Remedy for a Heart Which Is Not Present in Prayer

Know that the believer must be full of veneration for God عَزَّوَجَلَّ, fear [of His chastisement], hope [for His mercy], [be] ashamed of his shortcomings, and never [be] without these dispositions once faith [has entered his heart]. If they are as strong [within him] as the strength of his certitude, then the lapses [he might experience] when praying can only be because his thoughts become scattered, his attention [becomes] divided, his heart is not present in its intimate discourse with God, or he is praying in a state of heedlessness. Nothing, in fact, distracts in the prayer except unprovoked passing thoughts, so the remedy for presence of heart is to repel those thoughts. Since this is only possible by repelling their causes, you should know what those causes are.

What causes passing thoughts to enter the mind may be either external or essentially internal.

External causes are things that [first] strike the ear or appear to the eye, then seize [our] interest until [that interest] follows them and turns in the direction [of those causes]. [Our] thoughts are then pulled toward something completely different, one [thing] after another. Sight becomes the reason for thoughts, and then these thoughts lead to others. While someone with a powerful intention and lofty aspiration may not be distracted by what comes to him through the senses, someone who is weak cannot help but become [distracted].

So the remedy here is to eliminate those external causes by lowering our gaze, or praying in a darkened room, or ensuring that there is nothing in front of us that may distract our senses, and praying near a wall so as to limit the range of our vision. Similarly, one should avoid praying on roads outside, or in places adorned with decorative carvings, or on colorful rugs. There are servants, in fact, who worship in small darkened rooms with only enough space for the prostration so that their attention can be more focused, and the strongest of them go to mosques with their gazes lowered, and do not look any further than the place where they prostrate, and [they] would consider it part of the prayer's perfection to be unaware of who is to their right or their left. Ibn ʿUmar رَضِيَ اللَّهُ عَنْهُ would make sure he removed from his place of prayer [even] a copy of the Qurʾān or a sword, and [he would] erase something written [on the wall].

The internal causes of distraction [on the other hand] are more difficult. For someone whose concerns lead him down each and every pathway of this world, [his] thoughts are not just confined to a single thing but rather fly from side to side. Lowering the gaze does him no good because what has already occurred in his heart is distraction enough.

For someone like this, the solution is to force himself back to an understanding of what is being recited in the prayer and to occupy himself exclusively with that. In this, it will help if he prepares himself before [even pronouncing] the opening *takbīr* by renewing within himself the remembrance of the hereafter, [the importance] of discourse [with God], of the dreadful station of standing before Him, and the terror of the vantage point (*muṭṭalaʿ*).[24] Also, before he pronounces the opening *takbīr*, he should empty his heart of whatever occupies it, so as not to leave himself any distraction, following what the Messenger of God صَلَّى اللَّهُ عَلَيْهِ وَسَلَّمَ said to ʿUthmān b. Abī Shayba, "I forgot to tell you to put a cloth over the cooking pots in the room, for there should be nothing in the room that distracts people from their prayer."[25]

---

24 A *ḥadīth* reported in Ibn Ḥanbal, *Musnad*, 11:484; al-Bayhaqī, *Shuʿab al-īmān*, 10105, and elsewhere reads: "The Messenger of God صَلَّى اللَّهُ عَلَيْهِ وَسَلَّمَ said, 'No one should wish for death, for the terror of the vantage point (*muṭṭalaʿ*) is mighty, and part of happiness is for God to prolong the servant's life and grant him complete repentance (*ināba*).'" The "vantage point" is said to be a place from which one will look down, as it were, on the tumultuous events of the day of resurrection.

25 Abū Dāwūd, *Sunan*, 2030. In the version al-Ghazālī quotes, the *qidra* ("cooking pot") is to be covered, but in Abū Dāwūd, the noun is *qarnayn* ("two horns"), in which case the *ḥadīth* would read, "I forgot to tell you to put a cloth over the two horns that are in house [of God, that is, the Kaʿba], for there should be nothing in the house [of God] that distracts people during their prayer." This latter version is cited in al-Zabīdī, *Itḥāf*, as the correct one; he states that the "two horns" refer to the horns of the ram provided to Abraham عَلَيْهِ السَّلَامُ for the ransom of his son and which had been left in the Kaʿba for millenia.

This method, then, consists in calming the mind, but if someone cannot quiet his agitation, then nothing will save him except a purgative that will expel the diseased matter from the deepest recesses of his soul. This means that he [needs to] look at the things that distract his mind and keep his heart from being present; without a doubt, they can all be traced back to worldly matters that concern him because of his appetites and desires. Therefore, he should discipline his [lower] soul by uprooting those desires and severing those connections. Anything, in fact, that distracts him from his prayer is against his *dīn* and part of the forces of his foe, Satan, and so holding onto it is more harmful than being rid of it. Only in its removal will he be free of it. It was narrated that the Prophet ﷺ donned a robe given to him by Abū Jahm; [the robe] had a patterned border and he prayed wearing it. But afterward, he took it off and said, "Take this back to Abū Jahm, for it distracted me in my prayer. Bring me instead his coarse woolen cloak."[26]

Once the Messenger of God ﷺ asked for the strap on his sandal to be replaced, but then, because it was new, he looked at it during his prayer, and so [afterward] he asked that it be taken off and the old strap put back.[27]

And once he had some sandals made and their beauty so enthralled him that he fell prostrate on the ground and said, "I humble myself to my Lord عَزَّوَجَلَّ that He might not hate me." He then went out and gave them to the first beggar he met, and told ʿAlī رَضِيَٱللَّهُعَنْهُ to buy him a pair of simple rawhide sandals, and [he] put them on instead.[28]

Yet another time, he was at the pulpit and was wearing a gold ring—this was before gold was forbidden [for men]—and he cast it away from him and said, "It was distracting me: [I had] one eye on it, and one eye on you."[29]

It is related that Abū Ṭalḥa once prayed in an enclosed garden [he owned], in which there were trees. [During his prayer], he began to marvel at a small, colorful pigeon (*dubsī*) that was flying from

26 Al-Bukhārī, *Ṣaḥīḥ*, 373; Muslim, *Ṣaḥīḥ*, 556.

27 Ibn al-Mubārak, *Zuhd*, 402.

28 Abū Ṭālib al-Makkī, *Qūt al-qulūb*, 2:105.

29 Al-Nasāʾī, 8:194.

tree to tree looking for a way out of the garden, and this caught his eye for so long that he lost track of how much of the prayer he had completed. He [later] mentioned this to the Prophet صَلَّى ٱللَّهُ عَلَيْهِ وَسَلَّمَ and then said, "O Messenger of God, [I give] this garden in charity. Dispose of it however you will."[30]

[A similar incident] was related about another man who was praying in his garden and began looking at the date palms in it and marveling at how much fruit they had, until he [too] lost track of how much of the prayer he had completed. So he went to ʿUthmān رَضِيَ ٱللَّهُ عَنْهُ and said, "This [I give in] charity. Use it in the way of God." So ʿUthmān sold the garden for fifty thousand.[31]

Such are the things people did in order to rid themselves of distractions and atone for their deficiencies in the prayer. This is the decisive way to treat the origin of the affliction when other methods fail. The [other] gentler methods we mentioned—calming [an agitated mind] and bringing oneself back to understanding what is being said—may work for someone whose desires are weak and whose cares only marginally preoccupy his heart, but for someone whose desires are strong and difficult to control, they do not [work]. You will go on attracting these desires to yourself and they will go on attracting you to them until they overwhelm you and the whole of the prayer is spent simply dealing with them.

This is like a man who sits under a tree wanting to clear his mind but the sounds of the sparrows disturb him. He drives them away with the stick in his hand and goes back to his thoughts, but the sparrows keep coming back, and he keeps driving them away until someone says to him "This is a turning waterwheel that does not stop! If you really wish to be rid of [those birds], cut down the tree!" So it is with the tree of desires. The more it grows and branches out, the more distracting thoughts are drawn to it like the sparrows to the tree, or like flies are drawn to garbage, and how much trouble it is to drive them away! In fact, a fly is called *dhubāb* because every time it is driven away (*dhubb*), it returns (*āb*). And so it is with distracting thoughts.

30 Mālik, *al-Muwaṭṭaʾ*, 1:98.

31 Mālik, *al-Muwaṭṭaʾ*, 1:99.

Desires are many and it is rare for a servant to be without them, but all of them arise from one thing: love of this world. It is the origin of every sin, the foundation of every shortcoming, the source of all corruption. Anyone whose soul harbors this love so that he inclines toward it—not simply as provision needed for the journey and as what will aid him in the hereafter—should not expect to find the delight of pure discourse with God in the prayer. In short, if you find your source of happiness in the world, you will not find it in God, nor in intimate discourse with Him سُبْحَانَهُ وَتَعَالَىٰ.

In truth, a man will aspire to whatever gladdens his heart. If it is the world, then that is where his aspiration will inevitably turn. Even so, he should not give up all effort to return his heart to the prayer and keep the sources of distraction [in his life] to a minimum.

This is a bitter medicine, and its bitterness may be so repulsive to certain constitutions that the disease will become chronic and its cure even harder. The greatest [servants] hoped only to pray two cycles that were free of inner discourse about worldly matters and [they] were unable to do so. What hope, then, is there for the likes of us? If only we might be granted one-half or even one-third of the prayer free from whisperings of doubt, it would at least mix a good deed with a bad one.

Trying to combine aspiration for this world and aspiration for the hereafter is like trying to pour water into a vessel full of oil: the more water is poured in, the more oil is displaced. They simply do not mix.

Details of What Should be Present in the Heart for Each of the Essential Elements and Preconditions of the Prayer

We would say that if you are truly among the aspirants of the hereafter, first, do not be mindless of the messages contained in the preconditions and essential elements of the prayer.

The preconditions for the prayer are the call, purification, covering one's nakedness, facing the *qibla*, standing straight, and forming the intention.

As for the call, when you hear it, bring to mind the dreadful summons on the day of resurrection, prepare yourself inwardly and outwardly to answer it, and hasten to do so.[32] Those who hasten to answer this call will be those who are summoned with kindness on the 'day of the greater showing' (*al-ʿarḍ al-akbar*).

So look into your heart when this call [is heard], and if you find it full of happiness and joy, charged with a desire to answer, then know that the summons on the day of judgment will also bring you joy and deliverance. Thus did [the Prophet ﷺ] say, "Give us rest by it, O Bilāl!" That is, give us rest by the prayer and its call, for the coolness of his eye ﷺ was placed therein.[33]

As for the purification, purify your place [of prayer], which is the ground furthest from you; then your garments, [which are] closest to you; then your body, the outer shell nearest you; [and] do not neglect your core, your most essential element, namely your heart.[34] On its account, strive through repentance and remorse for past transgressions and resolve to be rid of [them] in the future. Thus, purify your inner dimension, for that is the place beheld by the Lord you worship.

As for shielding your nakedness, know that this means to cover from the view of others the parts of your body considered shameful. This means the outward form of your body that others may see; but what of the shameful things within you, the vices of your soul, which none looks upon except your Lord عَزَّوَجَلَّ?

Bring to mind, then, those vices, seek for your own soul to conceal them, and be assured that though there is no veil that can conceal them from the eye of God سُبْحَانَهُ وَتَعَالَىٰ, yet they can be atoned for through remorse, shame, and fear. Making them present in your heart will serve to call forth the forces of fear and shame from where they wait hidden, that thereby your soul might be humbled and your heart made lowly. Then you will stand before God in His

---

32 See al-Ghazālī, *The Remembrance of Death and the Afterlife*, 73.

33 Referring to the *ḥadīth* in al-Nasāʾī, *Sunan*, 7:61, and elsewhere: "Of this world, women and sweet scents were made lovable to me, and God placed the coolness of my eye in the prayer."

34 Here al-Ghazālī begins with the ground, the area farthest from the person's heart; then he moves on, to what is nearer to the person, his garments; then to his body itself; and finally, to his core, the heart.

majesty as a servant who has sinned and wronged his own soul, a humbled person full of remorse, returning to his Lord with head bowed in shame and fear.

Turning in the direction of the *qibla* [means] outwardly turning your face away from every other direction and toward the house of God عَزَّوَجَلَّ. Do you think, then, that you are not also required to turn your heart away from every other matter and [turn it] toward God? How can that be? In fact, nothing else [should be] sought! These external [forms] are only a means to activate what is within, to control and calm the limbs of the body by keeping them turned in one direction so that they do not wrong the heart, for if they do so, by movements or by turning in other directions, this would affect the heart and it would turn with them, away from the countenance of God most high.

Let the face of your heart be with the face of your body, and know that just as it is impossible for you to turn in the direction of the sacred house without turning away from everything else, so too, is it impossible for your heart to turn toward God without first being empty of all else. Thus did the Prophet صَلَّىٱللَّهُعَلَيْهِوَسَلَّمَ say, "If the servant rises to pray with his desires, his face, and his heart turned to God, he will leave that prayer as pure as on the day his mother bore him."[35]

As for the standing posture, this means to be upright in your [physical] person and your heart before God عَزَّوَجَلَّ. Let your head, which is the highest part of your body, be inclined and lowered, as a sign that even as this, the highest part of your body, is lowered from its height, so too, your heart must be humble, lowly, free from pride and the desire for high rank. Let your remembrance in this station be of the danger of standing before God and the dreaded vantage place[36] when all creatures are brought forth to be questioned.

Know too that while you are in that position, you are standing before God most high and He is looking upon you. If you are unable to conceive of His majesty, then let your standing in that place be as if you were before one of the great sovereigns of the age. Even

---

35 Muslim, *Ṣaḥīḥ*, 234, 832, with similar wording.

36 The "vantage point" is said to be a place from which one will look down, as it were, on the tumultuous events of the day of resurrection. See also page 53, n. 24.

reckon that as you stand in prayer you are being scrutinized by the constant gaze of a righteous member of your family or someone who you hope will know you to be righteous [as well]. In that situation, your limbs will be still, your senses humbled, and every part of you [will be] quiet out of fear that that feeble and poor human being might otherwise find you lacking humility.

And if you do experience some restraint [by picturing yourself] under the scrutiny of a poor servant [of God], then reprimand yourself and say, "You who claim to know God and to love Him! Are you not ashamed of your insolence toward Him and your deference toward one of His servants? Do you fear people and not fear God, when He is more deserving to be feared?"[37]

Thus did Abū Hurayra رَضِيَ اللَّهُ عَنْهُ ask the Prophet صَلَّى اللَّهُ عَلَيْهِ وَسَلَّمَ, "What is it to be ashamed before God?" and he answered, "You should be ashamed before Him as you would be ashamed before a righteous man of your people," or in another version, "of your family."[38]

As for intention, it means the resolve to answer God عَزَّ وَجَلَّ by fulfilling His commandment through the prayer, praying as perfectly as possible, avoiding all that invalidates or ruins it, and doing all this purely for the sake of God most high, hoping for His recompense, fearing His chastisement, seeking His nearness, and being cognizant that it is by His grace that He allows you to speak intimately with Him, even with your poor comportment and many sins.

Realize in your soul the greatness of speaking intimately with God, and behold who it is you are speaking with, how you are speaking, and of what. At that moment, your brow should sweat with shame, your sides tremble in awe, and your face turn pale with fear.

With respect to the opening *takbīr*, when your tongue utters "God is greater" (*Allāhu akbar*), your heart should not belie it, for if there is anything occupying your heart at that moment that is greater to you than God most high, God bears witness that you are in fact a liar, even though the words are true, just as He bore witness that

---

37 This paraphrases the verse, *while you concealed within yourself that which God is to disclose. And you feared the people, while God has more right that you fear Him* [33:37].

38 Al-Ṭabarānī, *al-Muʿjam al-kabīr*, 6:69; al-Bayhaqī, *Shuʿab al-īmān*, 7343.

the hypocrites were liars when they said that Muḥammad ﷺ was the Messenger of God.[39]

If your desires have more power over you than the commandment of God عَزَّوَجَلَّ, then you are more obedient to them than [you are] to God most high and you have taken them as a god and pronounced the *takbīr* for them. Your saying "God is greater!" is purely with your tongue, while your heart remained behind and did not aid it. How extremely dangerous this would be, were it not for repentance, seeking forgiveness, and [having] a goodly view of God's generosity and pardon.

With regard to the opening supplication, your first words are, "I have turned my face to the One who originated the heavens and the earth." Here, the meaning of "face" is not your physical face, for you have turned that in the direction of the *qibla*, and God سُبْحَانَهُ وَتَعَالَىٰ is beyond any limitation in space to which you might turn your physical face. Rather, it is the face of the heart that must turn to the Creator (al-Fāṭir) of the heavens and the earth. So look to see if the direction to which it has turned is its [own] expectations and concerns in the home and the marketplace as it pursues its desires, or [is it turned toward] the Creator of the heavens and the earth.

Beware that the supplication with which you begin your conversation [with God] is not a lie or fabrication. There is no way to turn toward God most high except by turning away from all else. So strive to turn totally in His direction at that moment, and if you are unable to do this throughout [the prayer], then at least do it for that moment, that your words might be true.

When you say, "As a pure monotheist and Muslim" (*ḥanīfan musliman*), call to mind the fact that "a Muslim is someone from whose tongue and hand Muslims are safe."[40] If this has not been true in your case, then you are a liar and you must make every effort not to be one in the future and feel remorse for those situations that have passed.

---

39 This refers to the verse *When the hypocrites come to you,* [*O Muḥammad*], *they say, "We testify that you are the Messenger of God." And God knows that you are His Messenger, and God testifies that the hypocrites are liars* [63:1].

40 Al-Bukhārī, *Ṣaḥīḥ*, 10; Muslim, *Ṣaḥīḥ*, 40.

When you say, "And I am not one of the polytheists," call to mind what is meant by "hidden polytheism" (*al-shirk al-khafī*), for the words of God most high, *So whoever would hope for the meeting with his Lord—let him do righteous work and not associate in the worship of his Lord anyone* [18:110], were revealed concerning someone who worships for the sake of God as well as for people's praise.[41] Be careful, then, to guard yourself from this kind of polytheism and feel humility in your heart if you have described yourself as not being among the polytheists, but are not free from this kind of polytheism. For the name "polytheism" applies, whether it be little or much.

And when you say, "My life and my death belong to God," know that this is the state of a servant who is effaced from his ego, present to his Lord. So if this phrase comes from someone whose pleasure and anger, standing, sitting, thirst for life, and fear of death all stem from the things of this world, then it in no way fits the situation.

And when you say, "I take refuge in God from Satan, the accursed," know that Satan is the foe who lies in wait to turn your heart from God عَزَّوَجَلَّ, and he envies the fact that you can speak and prostrate to the Lord, while he was cursed for the single prostration he did not make, and he was not accorded a second chance to [make it]. Your seeking refuge in God most high from Satan is not simply with words but by giving up what Satan loves, and replacing it with what God عَزَّوَجَلَّ loves. If a wild beast or a foe wants to tear someone to pieces or kill him, and the person says, "I seek the shelter of that safe fortress," and yet remains where he is, those words are useless. No, nothing will shelter him except actually changing the place where he is. And if a person is pursuing appetites loved by Satan but hated by God the most merciful, simply uttering a phrase will do him no good.

Rather, let his words be joined with a resolve to actually seek refuge in the secure citadel of God عَزَّوَجَلَّ from the evil of Satan, and that citadel is *lā ilāha illā llāh*, even as God عَزَّوَجَلَّ says, in what was related by our Prophet صَلَّىٱللَّهُعَلَيْهِوَسَلَّمَ, "*Lā ilāha illā llāh* is My citadel

41 *Shirk*, translated above as "polytheism," literally means "associating" [someone] or "making [someone] a partner" with God.

and whoever enters My citadel is safe from My chastisement."[42] To be one who dwells in God's citadel means to have no other deity than God سُبۡحَانَهُۥ وَتَعَالَىٰ, but someone who takes his own desires as a god is in the field of Satan, not in the citadel of God عَزَّوَجَلَّ.

Know that one of Satan's ploys is to distract you in the prayer with thoughts of the hereafter or with plans of how to carry out good deeds, [both of] which prevent you from understanding the meaning of what you are reciting. Know that everything that distracts you from understanding the meaning of your recitation is a whispering of doubt from Satan: the goal is not to move the tongue; the goal is the meaning [of your words].

In respect to the recitation, there are three types of people. The first is a man who moves his tongue, while his heart is heedless. The second is a man who moves his tongue and then his heart follows, so that he understands and hears the recitation as if he were hearing it from someone else. Such is the degree of the companions of the right hand. The third is a man whose heart goes first to the meanings which he then expresses with his tongue. The difference is whether the tongue is the heart's interpreter or its teacher. For those nearest to God (*muqarrabūn*), their hearts do not follow their tongues, but rather their tongues interpret and follow their hearts.

The [following] meanings are interpreted in detail [below].

When you say *In the name of God the All-Merciful, All-Compassionate*, intending to bless the beginning of your recitation of God's words, سُبۡحَانَهُۥ, understand that absolutely everything is from God تَعَالَىٰ and what is meant by *the name* is the named.[43]

If all things are from God, سُبۡحَانَهُۥ, then all praise must belong to God, which means that all gratitude belongs to God since all gifts [both internal and external] are from Him. If you consider that a particular gift comes from another or direct your gratitude toward that one as anything other than a being under the complete control of God تَعَالَىٰ, then in pronouncing His name and

42 Abū Nuʿaym, *Ḥilya*, 3:192.

43 The particle in Arabic which begins the *basmala*, that is, *bi-*, may be translated as "in" or "by" in English.

praising Him, you are falling short to the degree that you turned to that other [being].

And when you say, *the All-Merciful, All-Compassionate*, try to bring to mind God's numerous kindnesses [toward you, so] that His mercy might be made clear for you and your hope might be uplifted.

Then, as you say *the Master of the day of recompense*, let your heart be moved by veneration and fear; [your] veneration [is] for His greatness inasmuch as there is no dominion (*mulk*) except God's, and [your] fear is for the dreadfulness of the day of recompense and reckoning of which God is the possessor.[44]

Then, as you say *It is You we worship*, renew your sincerity toward God; and as you say *You we ask for help*, renew the awareness of your weakness and need, and relinquish your [own illusory] claims to power and strength. Affirm that your obedience to Him would not be possible were it not for God's assistance, which led to your success in obeying Him, and summoned you to worship Him, and made you among those who speak to Him in intimate discourse. [And affirm] that if God's help and accord [were] denied you, you would be among those who are cast away with Satan, the accursed.

Then, when you have finished the [formula of] seeking refuge, the *basmala*, the praise, and the expression of your need for [God's] help, make your supplication specific; this is nothing other than the most important need you have, as you say *Guide us to the straight path*, the path that brings us near You and leads us to what is pleasing to You. Add to this the explanation, affirmation, and witnessing [that this is the path] of those upon whom God showered the gift of guidance from among the prophets, the veracious, the martyrs, and the righteous, not [the path] of those with whom God is angry, those who have no faith, the Jews, Christians, and Sabeans who have gone astray. Then, with hopes that your prayer will be answered, say *āmīn*.

44 Al-Ghazālī is referring to the connection between the word *mālik* (possessor or owner), and *mulk* (possession or domain). The other accepted pronounciation of this divine name is *Malik* (with the first vowel short), meaning 'Sovereign.'

If you recite the Fātiḥa [1:1–7] in this manner, you do so in a way similar to those of whom God most high says, in what was transmitted by the Prophet صَلَّى ٱللَّٰهُ عَلَيْهِ وَسَلَّمَ,

> I have divided the prayer between Me and My servant, half is for Me and half is for My servant…and My servant shall have what he seeks. The servant says, "*Praise be to God, Lord of the worlds*," and God عَزَّوَجَلَّ says, "My servant has praised Me and exalted Me."

This is the meaning of the [worshiper's] words: "God hears the one who praises Him" (*samiʿa lāhu li-man ḥamida*), and so on, to the end of the *ḥadīth*.[45]

If you gained nothing else from your prayer except that God, in His majesty and grandeur, mentions you, that would be gift enough. So what if He were to grant you the recompense and grace that you hope for from Him?

In the same way, you should understand what you recite in the *sūra*, as we shall explain in the book on the *Etiquette of the Recitation of the Qurʾān*.[46] You should not be heedless of God's commandments, prohibitions, promises, threats, admonitions, narrations of His prophets, mention of His favors and graces, and for each of these there is a required disposition: for the promise [of paradise], hope; for the threat [of hell], fear; [for] a commandment or prohibition, resolve; [for an] admonition, the sense of being admonished; [for a] favor or grace, gratitude; and [for] the narrations concerning the prophets, rapt attention.

It has been recorded that Zurāra b. Awfā came to the verse *And when the trumpet is blown* [74:8] in his recitation and fell lifeless to the ground.[47]

And whenever Ibrāhīm al-Nakhaʿī heard God's words, *When the sky is split* [*open*] [84:1], he was seized by such a trembling that his limbs shook.[48]

---

45 Muslim, *Ṣaḥīḥ*, 395.

46 Book 8 of the *Revival of the Religious Sciences*.

47 Al-Tirmidhī mentions this incident following *ḥadīth* 445, noting that Zurāra b. Awfā was the chief judge (*qāḍī*) of Basra; he adds, "I was among those who carried [his body] back to his home."

48 In some editions, the man mentioned is Ibrāhīm b. Adham.

ʿAbdallāh b. Wāqid said, "I saw Ibn ʿUmar praying [and he was] completely overwhelmed. It is fitting that his heart be burnt by the promise and threat of His Lord, for he is but a sinful and lowly servant before an All-Powerful and Compelling Ruler."

These meanings [differ] according to [the various] degrees of [peoples'] understanding, and these [degrees] are, in turn, related to one's portion of knowledge and purity of heart, which have no limit. Prayer is the key to hearts wherein the mysteries of words are unveiled.

Such are the dispositions required in the recitation, just as they are [required] in pronouncing the invocation and glorification.

[The worshiper] should keep the sense of awe throughout the recitation. He should recite slowly in measured phrases, not rapidly without pause, for the former aids in reflection. And the tone of his voice should differ when reciting verses of mercy or punishment, promise or threat, praise, veneration, and glorification.

When al-Nakhaʿī would come to a verse such as *God has not taken any son, nor has there ever been with Him any deity* [23:91], his voice would lower as if he were ashamed to mention such a thing.

And it has been related that [at the resurrection] it will be said to the reciter of the Qurʾān, "Recite distinctly, in a slow, measured voice, as you were wont to do in the world."[49]

In respect to standing for the duration [of the recitation], this signifies [that] the heart remains with God عَزَّوَجَلَّ in a single attitude of presence. The Prophet صَلَّىٱللَّهُعَلَيْهِوَسَلَّمَ said, "God عَزَّوَجَلَّ faces the one praying as long as he does not turn away."[50]

And just as is it necessary to keep your head and eye from turning in other directions, it is necessary to keep your innermost being from turning toward anything other than the prayer. If this happens [i.e., you become distracted], remind yourself that God is looking upon you, and how ugly it is to disrespect the One with whom you are speaking by ignoring Him, [and how important it is] that you might return to Him.

Keep reverence in your heart, for to be free inwardly and to turn away outwardly is a result of reverence. Whenever there is reverence

49 Abū Dāwūd, *Sunan*, 1464; al-Tirmidhī, *Sunan*, 2914.

50 Abū Dāwūd, *Sunan*, 900; al-Tirmidhī, *Sunan*, 2863; al-Nasāʾī, *Sunan*, 3:8.

within, there will be reverence without, even as the Prophet ﷺ said when he saw a man praying while absentmindedly toying with his beard, "For this one, if his heart were reverent, his limbs would be as well."[51] It is the shepherd who controls the flock, and thus the supplication: "O God, make good the shepherd and make good the flock as well,"[52] is a reference to both the heart and the body's limbs.

When [Abū Bakr] al-Ṣiddīq رضي الله عنه prayed, it was as if he were a post, and Ibn al-Zubayr رضي الله عنه was [still], as if made of wood.[53] One of [the saintly] was so still in his bowing that sparrows would land on him as if he were an inanimate object.[54]

All this comes naturally when someone is standing before someone worldly,[55] [who is] deemed powerful, so how is it not the same for someone who knows the King of kings when standing before Him?

He who stands in humble stillness before someone other than God, but whose limbs are restless when he stands before God lacks knowledge of God's majesty and [awareness of] the fact that He looks upon his soul and mind.

Concerning the words of God عز وجل *Who sees you when you arise, And your movement among those who prostrate* [26:218–219], ʿIkrima said, "[God sees him in] his standing, his bowing, his prostration, and his sitting."[56]

As for the bowing and prostration, when you do these, you should renew your remembrance of the greatness of God most high, and when you raise your hands,[57] do so seeking protection in God's

---

51 This is related as a *ḥadīth* by al-Ḥakīm al-Tirmidhī in *Nawādir al-uṣūl* and by al-Marūzī, in *Taʿẓīm qadri al-ṣalāt* as a saying of the Companion Ḥudhayfa al-Yamanī.

52 Mentioned by Abū Nuʿaym in *Ḥilya* (10:286) as a phrase from one of Junayd's supplications.

53 Ibn Abī Shayba, *al-Muṣannaf*, 7322; al-Marūzī, *Taʿẓīm qadri al-ṣalāt*, 87.

54 This was recorded concerning al-ʿAnbas b. ʿUqba in Ibn Ḥanbal's *al-Zuhd*, 2086, and something similar is mentioned in Abū Nuʿaym, *Ḥilya* (2:114) concerning al-Rabīʿ b. Khuthaym.

55 Lit., 'sons of this world,' that is, someone important by worldly standards.

56 In this verse, the "you" is singular, addressed to the Prophet ﷺ. Ibn Abī Ḥatim, *Tafsīr*, 16032.

57 It is considered *sunna* in the Shāfiʿī school to raise the hands on rising up from bowing and prostrating.

clemency from His chastisement and following the *sunna* of His Prophet ﷺ. Then return to Him in lowliness and humility through your bowing, and try to soften your heart and renew your reverence, conscious of your own lowliness and the might of your guardian Lord, your own indigence and the sublimity of your Lord, and seek help, through what your tongue utters, to keep that consciousness in your heart. In this way, pronounce the glorification of your Lord and bear witness to His greatness—that He is greater than all who are great—repeat it from your heart, and in doing so, affirm it. Then rise up from your bowing with hope that He will have compassion for your lowliness, and affirm that hope in yourself by saying, "God hears the one who praises Him," meaning "He answers the one who thanks Him."

Then immediately follow that with the thanks which bring increase,[58] saying "My Lord, all praise is Yours," and multiply it by adding, "[Praise] that fills [all that is in] the heavens and [all that is on] the earth!"

Then bow down in the prostration. This is the highest degree of submission, for you place the noblest part of your body, your face, on the lowliest of things, the ground (*turāb*). If it is possible for you not to have anything between you and it, so that you prostrate directly on the earth, then do so, for it will bring greater humility and is more conducive to lowliness.

When you put your ego in this lowly place, know that you have put it in its [true] place and returned the branch to its root, for you were created from earth and to earth you will return. As you prostrate, once again renew in your heart [your affirmation of] the greatness of God and say, "glorified be my Lord, the most high," and affirm it by repetition, since one utterance alone is of weak effect. Then, when your heart has been touched by this and you have manifested your lowliness, be hopeful of the mercy of God, for His mercy hastens not toward pride and vanity but toward weakness and humility.

Raise your head from the prostration, magnifying God as you do so [with the words *Allāhu akbar*], then ask for your needs to be

58 Here he is referring to the verse, *And [remember] when your Lord proclaimed, "If you are grateful, I will surely increase you [in favor]; but if you are ungrateful, indeed, My punishment is severe"* [14:7].

fulfilled as you say, "Lord forgive me, have mercy on me, and pardon me for You know [of my sins],"[59] or whatever other supplication you wish, then affirm your humility through repetition, and make [the prostration] yet again.

And as for the testimony, when you sit for this, sit with propriety and proclaim that all the prayers and all the good and wholesome things you may do—which are part of your outward character—belong to God, as does the dominion (*mulk*); [all of this is] the meaning of the *taḥiyyāt*.[60] [Visualize] the noble person of the Prophet ﷺ in your heart and say, "Peace be upon you, O Prophet, and the mercy of God and His blessings," and be assured that your salutations will reach him and he will return even greater [salutations] to you.

Then send greetings of peace to yourself, and to all of God's righteous servants, and do so in the hope that God will return your greetings in an abundance as great as all those righteous servants.

Bear witness to God's oneness and to the message of Muḥammad ﷺ, renew at that moment God's covenant by repeating the twofold testimony, and seek safety and protection therein.

At the end of your prayer, supplicate God with [one of the] supplications transmitted from the Prophet ﷺ, and do so with humility, reverence, urgency, and the conviction that it will be answered, and include as well a prayer for your parents and for all the faithful.

And when you pronounce the closing greeting of peace, direct it to the angels and to all those present, with the intention of ending the prayer. Do so full of gratitude to God سُبْحَانَهُ وَتَعَالَىٰ for giving you the chance to complete this act of worship, and imagine that you are bidding farewell to this, your prayer, and that you might not be alive to pray another, even as the Prophet ﷺ said to the someone who asked him for counsel: "Pray the prayer of farewell."[61]

---

59 Abū Ṭālib al-Makkī, *Qūt al-qulūb*, 2:95.

60 Al-Zabīdī notes in his commentary, "This word can mean salutation, remaining (*baqā*), dominion, or greatness. Every aspect of these [qualities] belongs to God...." Al-Zabīdī, *Itḥāf*, 3:158.

61 Ibn Māja, *Sunan*, 4171.

Let your heart feel dread and shame for your shortcomings in the prayer and fear that it may not be accepted, that you will be found despicable because of some outward or inward sin, and your prayer [will be] thrown back in your face, yet at the same time hope that God, in His generosity and grace, will accept it.

When Yaḥyā b. Waththāb completed his prayer, he would remain in his place for some time afterward, as if troubled,[62] and Ibrāhīm [al-Nakhaʿī] would also remain in his place for some time after the prayer, as if he were ill.[63]

Such is the detailed description of the prayer of the reverent, *They who are, during their prayer, humbly submissive* [23:2], *And they who carefully maintain their prayers* [23:9], *Those who are constant in their prayer* [70:23], and those who commune with God as worshipful servants as much as they are able.

Let a person apply himself to praying, and to the extent that it is made easy for him, let him rejoice, while to the extent that it escapes him, let him feel loss, and make greater efforts in that domain.

As for the prayer of those who pray mindlessly, it is full of peril unless God envelops them in His mercy—and His mercy is all-encompassing and His generosity overflowing.

We ask God to envelop us in His mercy, and shelter us in His forgiveness, for there is no other means for us except to acknowledge our powerlessness to fulfill the obedience [He is due].

❁ ❁ ❁

Know that the prayer made without defect, sincerely for the sake of God عَزَّوَجَلَّ, [that] fulfills the inner conditions of humility, veneration, and shame as we have mentioned, is a means by which light reaches the heart, and this light is key to esoteric knowledge. God's saints, to whom knowledge of the domains of the heavens and earth and divine mysteries are disclosed, are granted these

62 Ibn Abī Shayba, *al-Muṣannaf*, 36519.

63 Ibn Saʿd, *Ṭabaqāt*, 8:396.

disclosures in the prayer, and especially in prostration, which is where the servant comes closest to his Lord عَزَّوَجَلَّ, even as God most high says, *But prostrate and draw near* [*to God*] [96:19].

The mystical disclosures granted to the worshiper in the prayer appear to the extent that his soul is clear of the obscurities of this world, and they differ in strength or weakness, abundance or scarcity, and in whether they are evident or hidden. Thus, to one of them, something is disclosed in its actual form, while to another it is as a likeness: this world, for example, [might be] seen in the form of a corpse, and Satan in the form of a dog crouching over it and beckoning to it.

The substance of what is disclosed to people also differs. For some, [this substance] is the attributes of God most high and His majesty, and to others it is His acts, and to others it is the details pertaining to the knowledge of conduct. There are innumerable hidden means by which such meanings are identified, but the greatest of them is aspiration. If aspiration is directed toward any particular thing, that is the first thing disclosed.

Tongues are quick to deny these things because such matters are only seen when reflected in a polished mirror, and because a mirror that is completely tarnished is veiled from guidance. [This is] not due to any stinginess on the part of the One who bestows guidance, but rather [due] to the accumulated layers of rust on the place to which guidance flows. Human nature is predisposed to deny what is not present. Indeed, if the fetus in the womb had intelligence, it would deny the possibility that a human being could exist in the open air. And if a child had discernment, he would perhaps deny what the savants claim to observe concerning the domains of the heavens and earth.

This is the way people are at every stage: [they are] ready to deny anything beyond the stage [they are in], and someone who denies the stage of sanctity will also deny the stage of prophethood. People were created in different stages and no one should deny what is beyond his own level.

Indeed, since some have sought this [level of perception] only for the sake of disputation and [to present] confusing arguments rather than for the sake of purifying their hearts from what is other than God عَزَّوَجَلَّ, they have failed to reach it altogether and so deny that it even exists.

But if someone has not been granted these disclosures, he must at least be among those who believe in the unseen and affirm it until he has witnessed it by way of experience. According to a narration passed down,

> When the servant stands for the prayer, God lifts the veils between Him and His servant and turns to him with His countenance, angels stand in prayer [in the area] between his shoulders and the sky and say "*Āmīn*" to his supplication, goodness rains down from the clouds to the parting of his hair, a caller calls, "If this one in intimate discourse knew with whom he was speaking, he would not turn away," the doors of heaven open to him, and God عَزَّوَجَلَّ boasts to the angels of the sincerity of the one who prays to Him.[64]

'Opening the doors of heaven' and 'God's turning to him' are ways of speaking about the disclosures that we have mentioned.

And it is written in the Torah: "O child of Adam, do not be too weak to stand before Me praying and weeping, for I am God, the One who drew near to your heart, and in the unseen world you saw My light."[65] He said,[66] "And we have seen that this tenderness, weeping, and opening which the worshiper finds in his heart is from the nearness of his Lord most high." Since this nearness cannot be a physical proximity,[67] it has no meaning except as guidance, mercy, and disclosure.

It is also said that when the servant prays two cycles, ten rows of angels marvel at him, and in each row there are ten thousand, and God boasts of him to one hundred thousand angels. That is because in the prayer the servant combines the standing, sitting, bowing, and prostration, while God has divided that among forty thousand angels: those who stand do not bow until the day

---

64 Abū Ṭālib al-Makkī, *Qūt al-qulūb*, 2:100.

65 Abū Ṭālib al-Makkī, *Qūt al-qulūb*, 2:100.

66 "He said" refers to Abū Ṭālib al-Makkī.

67 "Physical proximity is an impossibility for God, inasmuch as He transcends all that is particular to physical bodies." Al-Zabīdī, *Itḥāf*, 3:165.

of resurrection; those who prostrate do not rise up until the day of resurrection, and the same holds true for those who bow and sit. This is because whatever God has given them of nearness and degree remains with them continuously as a single state, without increase or decrease, even as He says, [*The angels say*], "*There is not among us any except that he has a known position. And indeed, we are those who line up* [*for prayer*]. *And indeed, we are those who exalt God*" [37:164–166]. The human being differs from the angels, however, by the fact that he may ascend to ever higher degrees and never ceases to draw nearer to God most high. He has the advantage of being able to increase in nearness, while the door of increase is closed to the angels عَلَيْهِمُ السَّلَامُ. Each one of them has only the degree in which he is and the worship he has been given to complete. He may not go to any other, nor does he tire: *And those near Him are not prevented by arrogance from His worship, nor do they tire. They exalt* [*Him*] *night and day* [*and*] *do not slacken* [21:19–20].

The key to this increase is prayer. God most high says, *Certainly will the believers have succeeded: They who are during their prayer humbly submissive* [23:1–2]; He praises them, after their faith, especially for the prayers [they pray] with humility. Then He completes the description of those who succeed through prayer, and says, *And they who carefully maintain their prayers...* [23:9], and then [He] mentions the fruits of these qualities: *Those are the inheritors who will inherit al-Firdaws. They will abide therein eternally* [23:10–11]. He thus begins by describing them as the prosperous ones and ends by describing them as the inheritors of paradise.

I do not believe, however, that mindlessly wagging the tongue is what leads to this station, which is why God mentions the opposite of their state: [*And asking them*], "*What put you into Saqar?*" *They will say*, "*We were not of those who prayed*" [74:42–43]. Those who prayed are the inheritors of paradise.[68] They bear witness to God's light and are graced by His nearness to their hearts.

We ask God to make us among them, and to preserve us from the chastisement of one whose words are beautiful but whose deeds

---

68 This is also an allusion to the following verses: *And they who carefully maintain their prayers, those are the inheritors who will inherit al-Firdaws. They will abide therein eternally* [23:9–11].

are ugly. God is truly the most generous, the giver of grace, and eternally good. May He bless each chosen servant.

Stories of Those Who Were Humble in Their Prayers

Know that humility is the fruit of faith and the result of having attained certitude of God's majesty. Anyone who is granted this will be humble both in the prayer and in [doing things] other than the prayer—in complete solitude, or even when answering the call of nature in the wash room. Humility arises out of the experiential knowledge that God looks upon His servant, and the experiential knowledge of God's majesty and one's own shortcomings. If these three are present, then humility is born and it is not confined to the prayer.

Thus, it has been narrated about one of the pious, that he did not raise his head to the sky for forty years out of shame and humility before God سُبْحَانَهُ وَتَعَالَىٰ.[69]

And al-Rabīʿ b. Haytham was so strict in keeping his gaze lowered that some people thought he was blind. For twenty years he was a regular visitor to the home of Ibn Masʿūd and whenever the maidservant saw him, she said to Ibn Masʿūd, "Your blind friend has come," and he would laugh. When he knocked at the door, the maidservant went out and saw him, head down, gaze lowered and when Ibn Masʿūd saw him, he said, quoting the Qurʾān, "*And, [O Muḥammad], give good tidings to the humble [before their Lord]* [22:34]. If Muḥammad صَلَّى ٱللَّهُ عَلَيْهِ وَسَلَّمَ had seen you, you would have gladdened him," or in another version, "he would have loved you!" or in another, "he would have laughed."[70]

One day he was walking with Ibn Masʿūd in the blacksmith's quarter of the bazaar and when he beheld the bellows blowing into

---

69 This is related about the Prophet Solomon عَلَيْهِ ٱلسَّلَامُ by Ibn al-Mubārak, *Zuhd*, 176; and Ibn al-Jawzī records this concerning several of the saintly, including Abū ʿUbada al-Khawwāṣ; it was said that he did not raise his gaze to the sky for seventy years (Ibn al-Jawzī, *Ṣifat al-ṣafwa*, 4:190).

70 Ibn Ḥanbal, *al-Zuhd*, 1989; al-Ṭabarānī, *al-Muʿjam al-kabīr*, 10:151; Abū Nuʿaym, *Ḥilya*, 2:107; Abū Ṭālib al-Makkī, *Qūt al-qulūb*, 2:102.

the fire, he passed out and fell to the ground. Ibn Masʿūd sat by his head until the time for the prayer arrived, but he still did not come to, so he carried him home on his back, and there he remained unconscious until the same time the next day, thus missing five prayers, with Ibn Masʿūd by his side saying, "This, by God, is fear."[71]

And al-Rabīʿ said, "When I am praying, all that matters to me is what I am saying and what is being said to me."[72]

ʿĀmir b. ʿAbdallāh was [also] among those who were humble in the prayer. He used to [pray] while his daughter would bang on a tambourine or the women of the house would talk about whatever they wished, and he would neither hear nor understand them.

One day he was asked, "Does your soul speak to you about anything in the prayer?" He answered, "Yes. It speaks to me about standing before God عَزَّوَجَلَّ and then being conducted toward one of two abodes." He was also asked, "Do you find worldly matters [distracting] as we do?" To which he replied, "I would rather be used as a target for lances than to find in my prayer what you do!"[73]

And he used to say, "Even if the veils were removed, it would not increase my certitude."[74]

Another of them was Muslim b. Yassār. As we have related concerning him, he was unaware that a column in the mosque had fallen while he was praying.[75]

There was also one whose diseased limb needed to be amputated, but they could not find a way to do it. Then someone said, "In the prayer he will not feel what is happening to him." So it was done while he was praying.[76]

---

71 Ibn Ḥanbal, *al-Zuhd*, 1945; Abū Nuʿaym, *Ḥilya*, 2:110; Abū Ṭālib al-Makkī, *Qūt al-qulūb*, 2:102.

72 Abū Ṭālib al-Makkī, *Qūt al-qulūb*, 2:102. The commentary says, "By his words 'what I say,' he means his recitation and invocation, and by his words 'what is being said to me,' he means [what God is saying to him through His book], intimate discourse [with his heart], and by answering [his prayers]." Al-Zabīdī, *Itḥāf*, 3:167.

73 Abū Ṭālib al-Makkī, *Qūt al-qulūb*, 2:102.

74 Abū Ṭālib al-Makkī, *Qūt al-qulūb*, 2:102.

75 Ibn ʿAsākir, *Tārīkh madīnat Dimashq*, 58:135; Abū Ṭālib al-Makkī, *Qūt al-qulūb*, 2:102.

76 This was recorded concerning ʿUrwa b. al-Zubayr in Ibn Abī l-Dunyā, *al-Maraḍ wa-l-kaffārāt*, 141, and Ibn ʿAsākir, *Tārīkh madīnat Dimashq*, 40:261, but without mentioning that the amputation was done during the prayer.

One of them said, "The prayer is part of the hereafter. When you begin [praying], you leave this world."[77]

And another was asked, "Does your soul speak to you about worldly matters in the prayer?" He answered, "No, not in the prayer and not out of the prayer."[78]

One of them was asked, "Do you start remembering [worldly] things in the prayer?" He answered, "Is there anything I need to remember more beloved to me than the prayer?"[79]

Abū l-Dardāʾ رَضِيَ ٱللَّهُ عَنْهُ said, "It is an indication of a man's understanding that he attends to what he needs to before the prayer so that he may enter the prayer with his heart unburdened."[80]

Some of them would make their prayer brief out of fear of whisperings of doubt. It has been related, for example, that ʿAmmār b. Yāsir prayed once and it was very short.

> [Someone] said to him, "You made that prayer very short, O Abū l-Yaqẓān," to which he replied, "Did you see me omit anything?"
>
> They said no.
>
> He replied, "I was trying to avoid the onset of forgetfulness from Satan, for the Messenger of God صَلَّى ٱللَّهُ عَلَيْهِ وَسَلَّمَ said, "A servant will pray and yet not even one-half, one-third, one-fourth, one-fifth, one-sixth, or one-tenth of it will be written for him."
>
> And also, "What is written for the servant of his prayer is only that of which he is aware."[81]

And it was said that Ṭalḥa, al-Zubayr, and a circle of the Companions رَضِيَ ٱللَّهُ عَنْهُمْ used to pray the shortest prayers of anyone, saying, "We are striving against Satan's whisperings."[82]

---

77 Abū Ṭālib al-Makkī, *Qūt al-qulūb*, 2:102.

78 Al-Suhrawardī, *ʿAwārif al-maʿārif*, 2:547.

79 Abū Ṭālib al-Makkī, *Qūt al-qulūb*, 2:102.

80 Ibn al-Mubārak, *Zuhd*, 1142.

81 Abū Dāwūd, *Sunan*, 796; al-Marūzī, *Taʿẓīm qadri al-ṣalāt*, 90; and Abū Ṭālib al-Makkī, *Qūt al-qulūb*, 2:102.

82 ʿAbd al-Razzāq, *al-Muṣannaf*, 2:367.

It has also been related that ʿUmar b. al-Khaṭṭāb رَضِيَ اللَّهُ عَنْهُ spoke from the pulpit of the mosque, saying, "The sides of a man's beard may turn gray without his ever having completed one prayer for God most high." He was asked, "And how can that be?" He answered, "Because he never prays with total reverence, total humility, and completely turning toward God عَزَّوَجَلَّ."[83]

Abū l-ʿĀliyya was asked about [the meaning of] the words of God most high, [*But*] *who are heedless of their prayer* [107:5]. He said, "This [refers to] someone so forgetful in his prayer that he completes it not knowing how many cycles it contained, whether an even number or odd."

Ḥasan said, "This is someone who forgets the time of prayer until it passes."

And another of them said, "This is someone who, if he prays at its earliest time, does not feel happy because of it and if he prays late, does not feel sad because of it, for he does not see praying early as something good, or praying late as a sin."[84]

Know that some of the prayer is reckoned, some written, and some not, even as the recorded traditions state. When a jurist (*faqih*) says, "The prayer cannot be separated into parts in terms of its validity," it has another sense, which we have mentioned. But the meaning of which we now speak is what is referred to in the *ḥadīth*s that say, if something is deficient in the obligatory prayers, it may be corrected by supererogatory prayers.[85]

And in a tradition, it is reported that Jesus عَلَيْهِ السَّلَام said, "God most high says, 'By obligatory devotions My servant is delivered

---

83 Ibn Abī l-Dunyā, *al-Tahajjud wa-qiyyām al-layl*, 483, Abū Ṭālib al-Makkī, *Qūt al-qulūb*, 2:103.

84 Abū Ṭālib al-Makkī, *Qūt al-qulūb*, 2:103.

85 He is referring to a *ḥadīth* recorded in Abū Dāwūd, *Sunan*, 864; and al-Tirmidhī, *Sunan*, 413: "The first thing to be reckoned of people's deeds on the day of resurrection will be the prayer. And our Lord عَزَّوَجَلَّ will say to the angels—and He knows better—'Look at My servant's prayer. Is it complete or deficient?' If it is complete, it will be written for him completely, and if it is deficient, then [God] will say, 'Look to see if My servant has any supererogatory worship.' If he does, He will say, 'Complete My servant's obligatory worship from his supererogatory,' and thus will deeds be taken."

from My punishment; by supererogatory worship, My servant draws near to Me.'"[86]

And the Prophet ﷺ said, "God most high says, 'My servant is not delivered from My punishment except by completing what I have made obligatory on him.'"[87]

It is related that the Prophet ﷺ once prayed and omitted a verse from his recitation. Then after a supererogatory prayer, he said, "What did I recite?" and the people were silent. So he asked Ubayy b. Kaʿb رَضِيَ ٱللَّٰهُ عَنْهُ, and he said, "You recited [such-and-such] *sūra* and you omitted [such-and-such] verse. I did not know, however, whether it had been abrogated or forgotten," at which the Prophet ﷺ said, "O Ubayy, you have it!" and then turned toward the others and said,

> What is wrong with a folk who come to pray, complete their rows, and with their Prophet before them, do not know what he is reciting to them from the book of their Lord? This is what the children of Israel did and God عَزَّوَجَلَّ revealed to their prophet: "Say to your people, 'You are here for Me in your bodies, you give Me your tongues, but you are absent from Me with your hearts, so what you are doing is in vain!'"[88]

Here, too, is textual proof that to hear what the *imām* recites and understand it replaces an individual's recitation.

One of them said, "A man may make a prostration which he thinks is bringing him closer to God عَزَّوَجَلَّ but if the sins he committed in that prostration were to be parceled out to all the people of his town, all [the people] would be lost!" And it was asked, "How can that be?" He said, "Because while he is prostrating before God, his heart's attention is on some desire and is aware [only] of some vanity that has taken hold of him."[89]

Such are the qualities of the humble.

---

86 Abū Ṭālib al-Makkī, *Qūt al-qulūb*, 2:103.

87 Ibn al-Mubārak, *Zuhd*, 1032.

88 Abū Ṭālib al-Makkī, *Qūt al-qulūb*, 2:104, and with similar wording in Ibn al-Mubārak, *Zuhd*, 92.

89 Abū Ṭālib al-Makkī, *Qūt al-qulūb*, 2:104.

These stories and traditions, along with what was mentioned previously, show that the principle of the prayer is humility and presence of heart, while [its] actions alone, if completed mindlessly, are of little avail in the final destination. And God knows best, and we ask for His most perfect success (*tawfīq*).

4

On the *Imām* and [His] Example

FOR the *imām*, there are duties before the prayer, during the recitation, in the essential elements of the prayer, and after the closing salutation.

There are six duties before the prayer.

First, no one should be put forward to lead the prayer if he is disliked by the people. If there is disagreement concerning the person who leads the prayer, the decision should be based on what the majority wants, but if the minority are people of goodness and faith, then they should have the first word.

A *ḥadīth* states, "There are three whose prayer does not go beyond their heads:[1] a slave who has fled his master, a woman whose husband is angry with her, and an *imām* leading people who do not like him."[2]

Just as it is prohibited to put someone forward if the worshipers do not like him, it is also prohibited to put someone forward if there is someone more learned in *dīn* or better in recitation, unless that one declines. If there are no other reasons that prevent someone

---

1 That is, their prayers do not ascend to heaven.

2 Al-Tirmidhī, *Sunan*, 360. Al-Zabīdī, *Ithāf*, 3:171, notes that dislike for a particular person to be *imām* must be based on reasons related to the law. The same holds true for the woman mentioned in the *ḥadīth*, and concerning the slave he stipulates, "Unless he fled from his master because of abuse against which he had no one to help him."

from leading the prayer, then he should do so whenever he is put forward and if he himself knows the requirements of the *imām*.

It is also disapproved of for someone [who has been asked to lead a prayer] to refuse, and it is said that once, as some people kept trying to put someone forward just as the prayer was to start, they were swallowed up [by the earth].[3]

As for narrations which say that the Companions رَضِيَ اللَّهُ عَنْهُمْ themselves [would sometimes refuse to lead the prayer], this was because they believed someone else was better, or because they feared forgetfulness, or the peril of guaranteeing the [validity of the] prayer, since the *imāms* are guarantors, and the heart of someone who is not accustomed to that role might become preoccupied and then disturbed [out of concern] that his prayer was not sincere, and out of shyness toward those who put him forward, especially when he recites aloud. Their reluctance was for reasons like these.

Second, if someone is offered the choice of serving as the muezzin or the *imām*, he should choose the latter, even though there is merit in both. Furthermore, it is disapproved that they be done by the same person. Rather, the *imām* should be someone other than the muezzin.

It is disliked for the same person to do both these tasks, but serving as the *imām* is preferable, although some say that the role of the muezzin is preferred, based on the saying about its merit that we have already quoted and also on the saying of the Prophet صَلَّى ٱللَّهُ عَلَيْهِ وَسَلَّمَ, "The *imām* is a guarantor and the muezzin is someone given a trust."[4] So they say, "The *imām* bears the peril of guaranteeing the prayer."[5]

He said صَلَّى ٱللَّهُ عَلَيْهِ وَسَلَّمَ: "The *imām* is one to be trusted. When he bows, bow; when he prostrates, prostrate."[6]

And in a *ḥadīth*: "If [the *imām*] prays perfectly, it is to his favor and to [the followers'] favor, but if he falls short, it is against him but not against them."[7]

---

3 Ibn Abī l-Dunyā, *al-ʿUqūbāt*, 90; and Ibn Abī l-Dunyā, *Mujābū l-daʿwat*, 79.

4 Abū Dāwūd, *Sunan*, 517; al-Tirmidhī, *Sunan*, 207; Ibn Māja, *Sunan*, 981.

5 Al-Zabīdī, *Itḥāf*, 3:173, explains that this is because he bears any errors made by the followers and his recitation aloud replaces theirs.

6 Al-Bukhārī, *Ṣaḥīḥ*, 378; Muslim, *Ṣaḥīḥ*, 411, with wording similar to this.

7 Abū Dāwūd, *Sunan*, 580; Ibn Māja, *Sunan*, 983, with wording close to this.

And he صَلَّى ٱللَّهُ عَلَيْهِ وَسَلَّمَ said, in supplication, "O God, guide the *imāms* and forgive the muezzins" and asking for forgiveness is something greater than asking for guidance, since forgiveness includes guidance.

There is [also] a narration that says, "Whoever calls to the prayer in a mosque for seven years is vouchsafed heaven, and he who calls to the prayer for forty years shall enter heaven without a reckoning."[8] Thus, it has been transmitted that the Companions رَضِيَ ٱللَّهُ عَنْهُمْ would put one another forward to lead the prayer.

In truth, however, the position of *imām* is more excellent, for it was the position of the Messenger of God صَلَّى ٱللَّهُ عَلَيْهِ وَسَلَّمَ as well as of Abū Bakr and ʿUmar رَضِيَ ٱللَّهُ عَنْهُمَا and the leaders who came after them.

Yes, it has the risk of being a guarantor [of the prayer], but with great merit is risk, just as the rank of a ruler or caliph is more excellent according to the Prophet's صَلَّى ٱللَّهُ عَلَيْهِ وَسَلَّمَ saying, "One day of a just ruler is more excellent than seventy years of worship."[9]

But there is danger in it and for that reason, it is necessary to put forward as *imām* the best and most learned, even as the Prophet صَلَّى ٱللَّهُ عَلَيْهِ وَسَلَّمَ said, "Your *imāms* are your intercessors or, in another version, 'your emissaries' before God, so if you wish to make your prayer pure, put forward the best among you."[10]

One of the early Muslims said, "There is nothing more excellent after the prophets than the learned, and after them the *imāms* who lead the prayer, for all of them stand before God عَزَّ وَجَلَّ and His creatures: this one with prophecy, this one with knowledge, and this one with the pillar of *dīn*, the prayer."[11]

This was the evidence that the Companions cited for putting forward Abū Bakr al-Ṣiddīq as caliph; they said, "We looked into this and saw that the prayer was the pillar of *dīn*, so we chose for our world the one whom the Messenger of God صَلَّى ٱللَّهُ عَلَيْهِ وَسَلَّمَ preferred for

---

8 The first phrase of this saying is recorded in al-Tirmidhī, *Sunan*, 206, and Ibn Māja, *Sunan*, 727. In al-Zabīdī's commentary, this *ḥadīth* reads, "He who leads the prayer (*man amma*)..."

9 Al-Ṭabarānī, *al-Muʿjam al-kabīr*, 11:337, with "sixty" instead of "seventy."

10 Al-Dāraquṭnī, *Sunan*, 1:346. The first phrase is related by Abū Ṭālib al-Makkī, *Qūt al-qulūb*, 2:87.

11 Abū Ṭālib al-Makkī, *Qūt al-qulūb*, 2:208.

our *dīn*,"[12] and they did not choose Bilāl, for [the Prophet ﷺ] preferred for him to give the call.[13]

It was reported that a man said to him, "O Messenger of God! Direct me to a deed by which I might enter heaven." He said to him, "Be a muezzin." He answered, "I cannot." He said, "[Then] be an *imām*." He said, "I cannot." He said, "[Then] pray directly behind the *imām*."[14] Perhaps the man thought he would not be accepted [by the people] as *imām*, since the muezzin was for the Prophet ﷺ to choose, but *imām* was for them to decide and choose. After that, however, he saw that it would probably be possible for him [to lead the prayer].

The third duty of the *imām* is to keep track of the times of the prayers and to [lead] the prayers at the earliest time in order to gain God's contentment (*riḍwān*). The excellence of the beginning of the prayer time over the end of it is like the excellence of the hereafter to this world. Thus it has been conveyed from the Messenger of God ﷺ.[15]

And in another *ḥadīth*: "The servant may pray at the end of its time and he does not miss it, but what he missed by not praying it at the beginning of its time would have been better for him than the world and all it contains."[16]

He should not delay the prayer waiting for the congregation to increase in size. Rather, it is for them to make every effort to gain the merit [and arrive] at the beginning of the prayer time. This is better than having a larger number of people praying and better than reciting a longer *sūra* in order [to give others time to join]. It has also been said that if there are two people present [to pray behind the *imām*], they should not await a third, and if there are four people present for the funeral prayer, they should not await a fifth.

---

12 Ibn Saʿd, *Ṭabaqāt*, 3:167, and Ibn ʿAbd al-Barr, *al-Tamhīd*, 22:129, record that ʿAlī رضي الله عنه said, "I looked into the issue, and [seeing that] the prayer was the greatest element of Islam and the mainstay of *dīn*, we choose for our world..."

13 The command of the Prophet ﷺ that Bilāl give the call is recorded in Abū Dāwūd, *Sunan*, 499 and 506; and Ibn Māja, *Sunan*, 1234.

14 Al-Bukhārī, *al-Tārīkh al-kabīr*, 1:36; and al-Ṭabarānī, *al-Muʿjam al-awsaṭ*, 3683.

15 Abū Nuʿaym, *Tārīkh Iṣbahān*, 1:444; al-Daylamī, *Musnad al-firdaws*, 3:131.

16 Al-Dāraquṭnī, *Sunan*, 1:247.

Once the Messenger of God ﷺ was late coming to *fajr*. This [took place during] a journey and he had to make the ablution. So ʿAbd al-Raḥmān b. ʿAwf was put forward and led the prayer, and the Messenger of God ﷺ missed the first cycle with the assembly and stood to complete it. When he had finished, [ʿAbd al-Raḥmān] said, "We were worried." And the Messenger of God ﷺ answered, "You did right! That is what you should do."[17]

He was also late once for the midday prayer (*ẓuhr*) and they put forward Abū Bakr رَضِيَ ٱللَّهُ عَنْهُ. When the Messenger of God ﷺ came, Abū Bakr was already in the prayer, so [the Prophet] stood at his side [to pray].[18]

Also, it is not for the *imām* to await the muezzin. Rather, the muezzin should await the *imām* before beginning the call just before the prayer is to begin (*iqāma*) and when he is present, he should not await anyone else.

The fourth [duty of the *imām*] is to lead the prayer with total sincerity toward God عَزَّوَجَلَّ and fulfill his trust to God in respect to his purification and all other conditions requisite for the prayer.

As for his sincerity, he should not take any compensation for this [task]. The Messenger of God ﷺ told ʿUthmān b. Abī l-ʿĀṣ al-Thaqafī, "Take as a muezzin someone who does not take compensation for giving the call to prayer."[19]

The call is a path to the prayer and it is preferable that one not take any compensation for doing it, but if he takes some provision from a mosque, it may be from the one in charge of the *imām*, from the ruler, or one of the people. There is no judgment that forbids this, but it is disapproved of, and this disapproval in respect to obligatory practices is stronger than [it is] in respect to the supererogatory prayers in Ramaḍān (*tarāwīḥ*). So he may be compensated for being regularly at the [mosque], or for overseeing the upkeep of the mosque for communal worship, but not for the prayer itself.

---

17 Muslim, *Ṣaḥīḥ*, 274.

18 Al-Bukhārī, *Ṣaḥīḥ*, 684; Muslim 421.

19 Abū Dāwūd, *Sunan*, 531; al-Tirmidhī, *Sunan*, 209; al-Nasāʾī, *Sunan*, 2:23; Ibn Māja, *Sunan*, 714.

As for the trust, this means he should be inwardly pure of immorality, the greater sins, and persistence in minor sins. A candidate for the duty of *imām* should strive his utmost to guard against all that. As a representative and intercessor for the faithful, he should be from among the best of people.

He should likewise [be scrupulous] in his outward purity from the occurrences that void the ablution and from unclean substances that no one can see except him. If, while praying, he remembers something that voids his ablution or if he experiences bodily gas, for example, he should not be ashamed [to leave the prayer]. Rather, he should take the hand of [a worshiper] near him and put him in his place, just as the Messenger of God ﷺ did when he remembered, in the midst of the prayer, that he needed to make the greater ablution. He put someone else in his place, went and bathed, and then came back and entered the prayer.[20]

Sufyān said, "Pray behind anyone, good or bad, except someone addicted to wine, someone notoriously dissolute, someone who mistreats his parents, a person involved in heretical innovation, or a fugitive slave."[21]

Fifth, he should not pronounce the opening *takbīr* until the rows of worshipers are straight. So let him look behind him [to the] right and left and if he sees a gap, he should order that it be filled. It has been said that they [the early Muslims] would [pray] shoulder to shoulder and ankle to ankle.[22]

He should not pronounce the opening *takbīr* until the muezzin completes the call of readiness (*iqāma*), and this latter call should be delayed until the call to prayer is finished and [he should allow] enough time] for people to get ready for the prayer. A narration states, "The muezzin should leave enough time between the call to prayer and the call to begin the prayer for people to finish eating and for the one who needs to use the toilet to do so."[23] This is because one

20 Abū Dāwūd, *Sunan*, 233, without mention of putting another forward.

21 Al-Lālakā'ī, *Sharḥ uṣūl iʿtiqād ahl al-sunna*, 1:173.

22 This relates to a quotation from ʿUthmān رضي الله عنه, who is reported to have told worshipers to stand like this in the congregational prayer.

23 Al-Tirmidhī, *Sunan*, 195.

who needs to defecate or urinate is prohibited from praying,[24] and also, it was ordered that the evening meal [should] precede the *ʿishāʾ* prayer so that the heart might be empty of distraction.

Sixth, the *imām* should raise his voice when pronouncing the opening *takbīr* and all the other *takbīr*s as well, while the one following the *imām* should not raise his voice any louder than what he himself can hear. The *imām* should form the intention to lead the prayer in order to gain its merit, but if he does not do so, his prayer is still valid, as is the prayer of those following [him] if they have formed the intention to pray behind the *imām*. They gain the merit of following him even if he does not gain the merit of leading them.

Let the one who is following the *imām* delay pronouncing the *takbīr* until after the *imām* has done so; [they should] begin it just after he finishes.

The *imām* has three duties in the recitation.

The first is to pronounce the opening supplication and the [formula of] seeking refuge silently, just as the solitary worshiper does, and then recite the Fātiḥa [1:1–7] and the *sūra* thereafter aloud in *fajr*, and the first two cycles of *ʿishāʾ* and *maghrib*, just as the solitary worshiper does.

In addition, he pronounces the word *āmīn* aloud in the prayers that are recited aloud, as do the followers, who should say this at the same time the *imām* does, not afterward. He should also pronounce the "*bismi llāhi al-Raḥmān al-Raḥīm*" aloud. Although there is disagreement in what has been reported concerning this, the preference of al-Shāfiʿī رَضِيَ ٱللَّهُ عَنْهُ is to say it aloud.

Second, there should be three [brief] silences when the *imām* is standing, following what was conveyed by Samura b. Jundub and ʿImrān b. Ḥaṣīn about the Messenger of God صَلَّى ٱللَّهُ عَلَيْهِ وَسَلَّمَ.[25]

The first and longest of these comes just after the opening *takbīr*; it should be long enough for those following to recite the Fātiḥa [1:1–7]. This is the time when the *imām* pronounces the opening supplication silently. If he were not silent at this time, they would miss hearing the Fātiḥa and whatever deficiency this gives their

24 Muslim, *Ṣaḥīḥ*, 560.

25 Ibn Abī Shayba, *al-Muṣannaf*, 2854.

prayer would be his fault, while if they do not recite the Fātiḥa [silently] during the period when the *imām* is silent [because they are] preoccupied with something else, the fault is theirs, not his.

The second silence is just after the recitation of the Fātiḥa [1:1–7], so that anyone who did not recite it during the first silence may do so. This silent period should be half the length of the first.

The third silence is right after the completion of the recitation of the *sūra* and before bowing. This is the briefest of the three and it should be just long enough to separate the words of the *takbīr* from the recitation, for joining the two is prohibited.

One praying behind the *imām* does not recite anything except the Fātiḥa [1:1–7]. If the *imām* does not pause [after the Fātiḥa], the one praying behind [him] recites the Fātiḥa along with him and it is the *imām* here who is at fault. If a follower cannot hear the recitation of the *imām* in one of the audible prayers because he is too far away, or [because it is one of] the silent prayers, there is no harm in his reciting a *sūra*.

The third [duty of the *imām* in respect to the recitation] is to recite, in *fajr*, two of the longer *sūra*s that do not exceed one hundred verses, for it is *sunna* to lengthen the recitation of the *fajr* prayer and to pray it while the sky is still dark. However, there is no harm if, by the time it is completed, the first glow of dawn has appeared. Nor is there any harm in reciting, in the second cycle, the last twenty or thirty verses [of one of these *sūra*s] until the end, for they [are] infrequently recited and are therefore stronger in their admonitions and more conducive to reflection. Though some scholars have disapproved of reciting the beginning of a *sūra* and then not completing it, it has been narrated that the Prophet ﷺ began reciting Sūra Yūnus [10:1–109], but when he reached the mention of Moses and Pharaoh [10:75], he stopped and bowed.

It is recorded that in *fajr* [prayer] the Prophet ﷺ recited verses from Sūrat al-Baqara [beginning with] *Say,* [*O believers*], *"We believe in God"* [2:136] and in the second cycle, *Our Lord, we believe in what You revealed* [3:53].

And he heard Bilāl recite from here and there and asked him about it. He replied, "I was mixing one perfume with another," to which [the Prophet ﷺ responded], "You have done well."[26]

In *ẓuhr*, the *imām* should recite up to thirty verses from the longer of the *mufaṣṣal sūras*; in *ʿaṣr* from those that are half that long; and in *maghrib*, from the last of the *mufaṣṣal*.[27]

The last prayer the Messenger of God ﷺ prayed was *maghrib*. In it he recited Sūrat al-Mursalāt [77:1–50] and then he did not pray again before his death.[28]

As a general rule, it is preferable [for the *imām*] to make the prayer brief, especially when there is a large congregation. Concerning this permission, the Prophet ﷺ said, "Whoever leads people in the prayer, should make it brief, for there may be weak [people], the aged, and those with some need to fulfill. But when you pray alone, make it as long as you wish."[29]

Muʿādh b. Jabal led some people in the *ʿishāʾ* prayer and recited Sūrat al-Baqara [2:1–286] and one man among them left the prayer and finished by himself. The people said [later], "The man has become a hypocrite!" So they brought their complaint before the Messenger of God ﷺ, who reproached Muʿādh and said, "Are you a troublemaker, Muʿādh? Recite *Exalt the name of your Lord, the most high* [87:1–19], *By the sky and the night comer* [86:1–17], and *By the sun and its brightness* [91:1–15]."[30]

The *imām* has three duties in the essential elements of the prayer.

The first is for him to make both the bowing and prostration brief, not adding to the glorification more than three repetitions. It was reported that Anas said, "I have never seen a prayer as brief

---

26 Abū Dāwūd, *Sunan*, 1330, with wording similar to this.

27 In the *Etiquette of the Recitation of the Qurʾān*, book 8 of the *Revival of the Religious Sciences*, al-Ghazālī defines the *mufaṣṣal* (lit., 'those with many junctions') as the last seventh of the Qurʾān, from Sūra Qāf [50:1–45] to the end of the Qurʾān. The longer of these would be from Sūra Qāf to Sūrat al-Burūj [85:1–22].

28 Al-Bukhārī, *Ṣaḥīḥ*, 763; Muslim, *Ṣaḥīḥ*, 462.

29 Al-Bukhārī, *Ṣaḥīḥ*, 90, 703; Muslim, *Ṣaḥīḥ*, 467.

30 Al-Bukhārī, *Ṣaḥīḥ*, 705; Muslim, *Ṣaḥīḥ*, 465. Qurʾān Sūrat al-Ṭāriq [86:1–17] is not mentioned in either of these, but it is mentioned in the version reported by al-Bayhaqī, *al-Sunan al-kubrā*, 3:112.

and at the same time, [as] complete as that of the Messenger of God ﷺ."[31]

True, it is also narrated that when Anas prayed behind ʿUmar b. ʿAbd al-ʿAzīz, who was governor of Medina, he said, "I have never prayed behind anyone who so reminded me of the prayer of the Messenger of God ﷺ as this young man does, for we used to repeat the glorification behind him ten times each."[32] It is widely reported, in fact, that they used to repeat the glorification behind the Messenger of God ﷺ in the bowing and prostration ten times each, and that is good, but to do so three times when there is a large assembly is better. If there is no one present, however, except those who have left the workaday world for the sake of worship, then there is no harm in ten.

This resolves the differences between the two narrations.

And as he raises his head from the bowing, the *imām* should say, "God hears the one who praises Him" (*samʿa llāhu li-man ḥamida*).

Second, the one praying behind the *imām* should not bow or prostrate before he does. Rather, he should wait until the *imām*'s forehead is touching the ground where he is prostrating and then incline toward the prostration. This was the way of the Companions when following the Messenger of God ﷺ in the prayer. Similarly, the follower should not begin his bowing until the *imām* is at rest in his.

It has been said that people complete the prayer in three groups. One group has [reward for] twenty-five prayers, they are the ones who pronounce the *takbīr* and bow after the *imām*. One group has [reward for] a single prayer, they are the ones whose actions are at the same time as that of the *imām*. And one group has no prayer, they are the ones whose actions precede that of the *imām*.[33]

As to whether an *imām* who is bowing should remain in that position long enough to give a latecomer time to join the prayer and benefit from praying in congregation, there is disagreement.

---

31 Al-Bukhārī, *Ṣaḥīḥ*, 708; Muslim, *Ṣaḥīḥ*, 469.

32 Abū Dāwūd, *Sunan*, 888; al-Nasāʾī, *Sunan*, 2:224. Here, "ten times each" means ten times in the bowing and ten in the prostration.

33 Abū Ṭālib al-Makkī, *Qūt al-qulūb*, 2:209.

It may be that if this [delay] is done in a spirit of sincerity, there is no harm in it as long as it does not seem excessive to those present, for it is their right that the prayer not be excessively long.

Third, while in the seated position for the testimony, the *imām* should not make the supplication at this time excessively long, nor make a supplication exclusively for himself. He should use the first person plural form, saying, "O God, forgive us," not "O God, forgive me," for it is disapproved of for the *imām* to single himself out in supplication.

There is no harm for him to use as his supplication in the testimony the five phrases that were transmitted from the Messenger of God صَلَّى ٱللَّهُ عَلَيْهِ وَسَلَّمَ, who said,

> We seek refuge in You from the punishment of hell and from the punishment of the grave, and we seek refuge in You from the trials of life and death, and from the tribulations of the Antichrist (al-Masīḥ al-Dajjāl). And if it be Your will to send a people tribulation, take us to You untempted by this tribulation.[34]

It is said that the Dajjāl is called "*masīḥ*" because he will touch (*yamsaḥu*) the entirety of the earth. It has also been said that this is because one of his eyes is "rubbed out" (*mamsūḥ*), that is, erased by blindness.

[The *imām* has] three duties in completing the prayer.

First, in pronouncing the two closing salutations,[35] he should intend thereby the people and the angels.

Second, he should remain in his place for a time after the closing salutation. This is what the Messenger of God صَلَّى ٱللَّهُ عَلَيْهِ وَسَلَّمَ, Abū Bakr, and ʿUmar رَضِيَ ٱللَّهُ عَنْهُمَا [did],[36] then they would pray supererogatory prayers in another place.[37] If there are women praying behind him, [the *imām*] does not stand until they have left.[38]

---

34 Muslim, *Ṣaḥīḥ*, 588, but without the last phrase ("And if it be Your will…"), which is part of the version reported in al-Tirmidhī, *Sunan*, 3233.

35 That is, the words 'al-salāmu ʿalaykum wa-raḥmatu llāhi,' said while turning to the right and then the left.

36 Al-Bukhārī, *Ṣaḥīḥ*, 849. Abū Dāwūd mentions Abū Bakr and ʿUmar رَضِيَ ٱللَّهُ عَنْهُمَا doing this, Abū Dāwūd, *Sunan*, 1007.

37 Al-Bukhārī, *Ṣaḥīḥ*, 848.

38 Al-Bukhārī, *Ṣaḥīḥ*, 850.

In a well-known report, the Prophet صَلَّى ٱللَّٰهُ عَلَيْهِ وَسَلَّمَ did not remain seated [after the prayer] any longer than it took to say, "O God! You are peace, and from You comes peace, blessed be You, O You who are full of majesty and generosity."[39]

Third, when he gets up [after the closing salutations], he should turn toward the people.

It is disapproved for the followers to stand before the *imām* turns to face them. It has been related that Ṭalḥa and al-Zubayr رَضِيَ ٱللَّٰهُ عَنْهُمَا prayed behind an *imām*, and when he had pronounced the closing salutation, they said to him, "How beautifully and perfectly you prayed… except for one thing. After you pronounced the closing salutation, you did not turn to face the people." Then they said to the people, "And how beautifully you prayed, except that you began to leave before the *imām* turned around."[40]

Then the *imām* leaves by whatever direction he wishes, either to the right or left, although the right is preferred. These are [his] duties in relation to the prayers.

In the *fajr* prayer, however, he adds to these the recitation of the *qunūt*,[41] in which he should say "O God, guide us..." not "O God, guide me…." [At the end of each petition], the one praying behind the *imām* should say "*āmīn*," but when the *imām* reaches the words at the end, "You [O God] decree [all] but none shall decree above You" (*innaka taqḍī wa-lā yuqḍā ʿalayk*), it is not fitting for them to say *āmīn*, since this is a form of praise. Instead they should say what the *imām* says, or "And I am among those who bear witness to that" (*wa-ana ʿalā dhālika min al-shāhidīn*)! or "You have spoken the truth and done what is good" (*ṣadaqta wa-barirta*)! or words similar to this.

There is a *ḥadīth* which reports that the hands should be raised for the *qunūt*. If this is an authentic *ḥadīth*, then it is preferred to do so. And if it is therefore different from the supplication at the end of the testimony, for which the hands are not raised, then we

39 Muslim, *Ṣaḥīḥ*, 591.

40 Abū Ṭālib al-Makkī, *Qūt al-qulūb*, 2:213.

41 The root of this word (q-n-t) carries the sense of "obedience" as well as "standing in prayer."

depend on whatever has a textual foundation. In addition, there is a difference between the two supplications, since in the testimony there is already a practice for the hands, which is to place them on the thighs in a certain way. But in the *qunūt*, there is no particular place for [the hands], so it is conceivable that raising them is the [correct] practice here, for such is fitting for supplication. And God knows best.

These, then, are the entirety of the manners related to being an example and *imām*, and God is the One who accords success.

5

On the Merits of the Friday Prayer, the Manners [Relating] to It, Its *Sunna*, and Its Requisites

The Merits of the Friday Prayer

KNOW that [Friday] is a mighty day with which God honored Islam and distinguished the Muslims. God most high says, *When* [*the adhan*] *is called for the prayer on Friday, then proceed to the remembrance of God and leave trade* [62:9]. By these words, He forbade being occupied with mundane affairs and with anything that detracts from hastening to the congregational [prayer].

And the Prophet ﷺ said, "God عَزَّوَجَلَّ made the Friday prayer obligatory for you on this, my day, in this, my place."[1]

And he said ﷺ: "God puts a seal on the heart of whoever who does not attend three [consecutive] Friday congregational prayers without excuse."[2] Another version states, "Such a person has cast Islam behind his back."[3]

---

1 Ibn Māja, *Sunan*, 1081.

2 Abū Dāwūd, *Sunan*, 1052; al-Tirmidhī, *Sunan*, 500; al-Nasāʾī, *Sunan*, 3:88; Ibn Māja, *Sunan*, 1125.

3 Reported as a saying by Ibn ʿAbbās رَضِيَٱللَّهُعَنْهُمَا in ʿAbd al-Razzāq, *al-Muṣannaf*, 3:166; and Abū Yaʿlā, *Musnad*, 2712.

A man kept returning to ask Ibn ʿAbbās رَضِيَ ٱللَّهُ عَنْهُمَا about a man who died and had [never] attended the Friday prayer or the prayer in assembly in the mosque. Ibn ʿAbbās said, "He is in the fire"; the man kept returning each month with the same question, and each time he would say, "He is in the fire."[4]

And it is recorded in a narration:

> The "people of the two books"[5] were given Friday but they disagreed concerning it and were turned away from it, and God most high directed us to it, and chose it for this community, and made it a feast day for us. So [this community] has priority and for the people of the two books is what follows.[6]

And in a *ḥadīth* related by Anas, the Prophet صَلَّى ٱللَّهُ عَلَيْهِ وَسَلَّمَ said,

> Gabriel عَلَيْهِ ٱلسَّلَامُ came to me holding a white mirror in his hand and said, "This is Friday, the day of congregation, which your Lord is showing you, that it may be a day of observance (*ʿīd*) for you and for your people after you."
>
> I said, "What do we have in it?"
>
> He said, "Therein are the best of hours. If someone makes a supplication for some good that has been decreed him at that time, God سُبْحَانَهُ وَتَعَالَىٰ will give it to him, and if it is not decreed, God will keep for him something greater than that in the future, or protect him from some harm that had been written for him, or from something worse in the future. For us,[7] it is the lord of days and we call it in the hereafter the 'day of increase.'"
>
> I asked him why and he said, "Verily your Lord عَزَّ وَجَلَّ has chosen a valley in heaven more fragrant than white musk. On the day of the congregation, He descends from the highest of

---

4 Al-Tirmidhī, *Sunan*, 218; Ibn Abī Shayba, *al-Muṣannaf*, 2105.

5 That is, the Jews and Christians.

6 In al-Bukhārī, *Ṣaḥīḥ*, 876; and Muslim, *Ṣaḥīḥ*, 855; this *ḥadīth* ends with the words, "So people follow us in respect [to Friday]: The Jews tomorrow and the Christians the day after tomorrow."

7 That is, the angels.

> the high (*al-ʿillīyīn*), onto His throne and manifests Himself to [the blessed] that they might gaze on His noble countenance."[8]

And the Prophet ﷺ said,

> Friday is the best day on which the sun rises. It is the day on which Adam عَلَيْهِ السَّلَامُ was created, the day on which he was placed in the garden, the day on which he was cast down to earth, the day on which he repented, and the day on which he died. It is the day on which the hour will arise, the day of increase with God, as the angels called it, and the day on which God most high is beheld in heaven.[9]

According to a narration, "Each Friday God عَزَّوَجَلَّ delivers six hundred thousand souls from the fire."[10]

In a *ḥadīth* related by Anas رَضِيَ اللَّهُ عَنْهُ, the Prophet ﷺ said, "If Friday is safe, the week is safe."[11]

And he said ﷺ,

> Hell is kindled every day before noon when the sun reaches its meridian in the middle of the sky, so do not pray at this time except on Friday, for all of Friday is a prayer and hell is not kindled that day.[12]

Kaʿb said, "Among [the] lands, God عَزَّوَجَلَّ preferred Mecca; among [the] months, Ramaḍān; among [the] days, Friday; and among [the] nights, the 'night of power.'"[13]

And it has been said that birds and poisonous reptiles meet one another on Friday saying "Peace, peace! A salutary day!"[14]

---

8 Al-Shāfiʿī, *Musnad*, 1:536; al-Ṭabarānī, *al-Muʿjam al-awsaṭ*, 2105.

9 Muslim, *Ṣaḥīḥ*, 854; al-Nasāʾī, *Sunan*, 3:114.

10 This is recorded as a *ḥadīth* conveyed by Anas رَضِيَ اللَّهُ عَنْهُ in Abū Yaʿlā, *Musnad*, 3434.

11 Abū Nuʿaym, *Ḥilya*, 7:130; al-Bayhaqī, *Shuʿab al-īmān*, 3434. The commentary explains that this means that "if someone is free of sins on Friday, he or she will be safe from being seized [by death in the midst of sinning] for the rest of the week." Al-Zabīdī, *Itḥāf*, 3:214.

12 Abū Nuʿaym, *Ḥilya*, 1:64, and with similar wording in Abū Dāwūd, *Sunan*, 1083.

13 Abū Ṭālib al-Makkī, *Qūt al-qulūb*, 2:64.

14 Ibn Ḥanbal, *al-Zuhd*, 1377; Abū Nuʿaym, *Ḥilya*, 2:205.

The Prophet ﷺ said, "Whoever dies on Friday or the night before will have written to his good the reward of a martyr and will be protected from the trials of the grave."[15]

Concerning the Requisite Conditions for the Friday Prayer

Know that the Friday prayer shares all the requisites of any other prayer [in the mosque], along with six conditions that distinguish it from all the other [prayers].

The first is the time. If the closing salutation of the *imām* [for this prayer] occurs when the time of the *ʿaṣr* prayer has begun, then the Friday prayer has been missed and the *imām* should complete the prayer as *ẓuhr* of four cycles. Concerning someone who joins the prayer late and completes its last cycle after the time [for the Friday prayer], there is a difference of opinion.[16]

The second is the place. It is not permissible to pray the Friday prayer in the desert, in the wilderness, or in an encampment of tents. Rather, it must be prayed in a place with permanent structures and where forty of those on whom the Friday prayer is incumbent may assemble. Whether it is in a village or town makes no difference, nor is it necessary for the ruler to be present or to give his permission, although it is preferable to ask him.

Third is the number. The Friday prayer may not be established if there are fewer than forty males [who are] free, adult, and of sound mind. They should also be residents of the place and not those who migrate in winter or summer. If they are away, so the number is less than forty, either for the sermon or for the [actual] prayer, it is not valid. The minimum number must be there from the beginning to the end.

---

15 Abū Nuʿaym, *Ḥilya*, 3:155; and in al-Tirmidhī, *Sunan*, 1074, without the phrase "reward of a martyr."

16 That is, there is a difference of opinion as to whether he should complete it as *ẓuhr*.

Fourth is the congregation. If there are forty [men] in a village or town who [normally] pray in different mosques, it would be incorrect to gather for the Friday prayer. And if a latecomer is present for the second cycle, it is permissible for him to complete only one cycle, but if he is too late for that cycle, then he should form the intention to pray the midday prayer (*ẓuhr*) and complete what he missed as such.[17]

The fifth is that the prayer in congregation [should] not be preceded by another in that town. If, however, it is not possible for everyone to gather in one mosque, it is permissible to pray at two, three, or four [times], according to the need. And if there is no need [to pray in more than one mosque], then the right one is the one where the opening *takbīr* is pronounced first. If, however, there is need, then the preferred assembly is where the more excellent of the two *imāms* is leading the prayer, and if they are equal, then in the mosque that is older, and if they are equal, then in the one that is closer [to the worshiper]. Another criteria to be considered is where the most people are gathered.

The sixth is [that the *imām* gives] two sermons. These are obligatory, as is standing as he gives them, and sitting down [briefly] between them.

In the first of the two sermons there are four obligatory elements. [First is] praise to God, the very minimum of which are the words, "Praise be to God" (*al-ḥamdu li-llāh*). The second is the invocation of blessings upon the Messenger of God صَلَّى ٱللَّٰهُ عَلَيْهِ وَسَلَّمَ. The third is counseling the people toward reverent fear (*taqwā*) of God عَزَّ وَجَلَّ. The fourth is reciting a verse from the Qurʾān. These same four elements are obligatory in the second sermon, except that instead of reciting a Qurʾānic verse, the *imām* should make a supplication. It is obligatory for the forty people to hear this sermon.

17 It is not clear from the text how the stipulations concerning latecomers relate to the condition that forty men worship in one mosque.

The *Sunna* Elements

When the sun has passed its meridian, the muezzin has made the call, and the *imām* is seated on the pulpit, any prayer except that of greeting the mosque should cease, and when the *imām* begins the sermon, talking must cease as well.

When the *imām* [takes his seat on the pulpit] and turns to face the people, he should greet them and they should return his greeting with the words "and upon you be peace." Then, when the muezzin completes the call, the *imām* should stand facing the people. He should turn neither to the right nor to the left, and his hands should be occupied with holding a sword, a staff, or the pulpit so that he does not absentmindedly move them around or put one on the other. He should then give the two sermons with a brief seated period between them. He should not use language that is strange to the people, nor be long and drawn out,[18] nor chant; the sermon should be brief, articulate, and comprehensible. It is recommended that he recite a Qurʾānic verse in the second sermon as well.

One entering the mosque should not greet the assembly if the *imām* is giving the sermon and if he does pronounce a greeting, it is not his right to have his greeting returned verbally, although it can be returned with a gesture. Finally, the *imām* should not say "God have mercy on you" to someone who sneezes.

These are the requisites of its validity.

The conditions [which make] it obligatory [are as follows].

[Attending] the Friday prayer is only obligatory for adult males [who are] of sound mind and Muslim. One must also reside in a village where forty people live, who fulfill these conditions, or in a village near it, where the call to prayer can be heard from the side of the village nearest to the village where the call is made by the muezzin using a loud voice; [this is in accordance with] the words of God most high, *When* [the *adhan*] *is called for the prayer on Friday, then proceed to the remembrance of God and leave trade* [62:9].

---

18 *Gharīb al-lugha* (lit., strangeness of language) means he should not speak in a style that is incomprehensible to the congregation. *Lā yumaṭiṭu* (he does not stretch [things] out) means either in the way he expresses things, or in his tone of voice.

[Those required to attend] have permission not to attend the Friday congregation if there is rain, mud, fear [for one's person or possessions], infirmity, or the need to take care of someone who has no other caregiver.

In the case of those excused [from attending the Friday congregational prayer], it is preferred that they delay the *ẓuhr* prayer until people have left the Friday prayer. If someone who is ill, or a traveler, or a slave, or a woman does attend the Friday prayer, their prayer is valid but their recompense is [equal to] praying *ẓuhr*, and God knows best.

Exposition of the Manners Related to the Friday Congregation in their Usual Order

Altogether, there are ten [manners].

The first is to begin to prepare for it on Thursday, with a resolution to go and an expectation of being granted its merit. So, after ʿ*aṣr* on Thursday, [the worshiper] should be occupied with supplications asking forgiveness from God and glorification [of Him], for the special merit of that particular time is comparable to that of the hidden hour on Friday.

One of the early Muslims said, "Truly, God عَزَّوَجَلَّ has a special grace other than the sustenance He provides His servants, which He gives to none except those who supplicate Him on Thursday evening and on Friday."[19]

[The servant] should wash and bleach his clothes on [Thursday] and make ready perfume if he does not have any. He should also empty his heart of all other preoccupations that would prevent him from going to the congregation early.

He should form the intention to fast on Friday, for that holds great merit, but it should be combined with fasting on Thursday or on Saturday, for it is disapproved of [to fast only on Friday].

19 Abū Ṭālib al-Makkī, *Qūt al-qulūb*, 1:66.

He should spend [Thursday] night in prayer and complete a recitation of the Qurʾān, for there is immense merit in this, and the merit of Friday will be applied to it.

That night or Friday [is also a good time] to have intercourse with one's spouse and some scholars consider it a recommended practice, citing the words of the Prophet ﷺ, "God has mercy on the one who rises early, sets out for the mosque early, and gives reason to bathe and bathes."[20] This is said to mean, "he gives his spouse reason to bathe,"[21] if the verb is read as *ghassala*, or, "he washes his clothes [*ghasala thiyābahu*] and "bathes" [*ightasilu*] his body.[22]

This completes the practices to be done in anticipation [of Friday]. [In observing them] we are removed from the ranks of the heedless who, when they rise in the morning, say, "What day is this?" One of the early Muslims said, "The person with the fullest portion of the Friday worship is the one who awaits it and begins to observe it from the previous day, and the person with the sparsest portion is the one who, when he awakes that morning, says 'What is today?'"[23]

For this reason, some of them used to spend [Thursday] night in the mosque.[24]

The second [manner for the Friday observance], is to rise that morning, and start by taking a complete bath just after dawn. If he does not set off for the mosque just after dawn, then the closer the bath is to the time he leaves for the mosque before noon, the better, in order for the cleanliness [of bathing] to be as close as possible [to the time of entering the mosque to await the prayer]. The bath is an affirmed supererogatory practice, and some scholars even hold that it is obligatory, based on the saying of the Prophet ﷺ, "A bath on Friday is obligatory for anyone who has reached puberty."[25]

The best-known point of view comes from a *ḥadīth* related by Nāfiʿ from Ibn ʿUmar رضي الله عنه that [states:] "Let whoever comes

---

20 Abū Dāwūd, *Sunan*, 345; al-Tirmidhī, *Sunan*, 496; al-Nasāʾī, *Sunan*, 3:95; Ibn Māja, *Sunan*, 1087.

21 That is, has sexual intercourse with her.

22 Abū Ṭālib al-Makkī, *Qūt al-qulūb*, 1:65.

23 Abū Ṭālib al-Makkī, *Qūt al-qulūb*, 1:70. Both al-Ghazālī and Abū Ṭālib al-Makkī before him relate this saying using the dialectic form, "*aysh*?"

24 Abū Ṭālib al-Makkī, *Qūt al-qulūb*, 1:70.

25 Al-Bukhārī, *Ṣaḥīḥ*, 858; Muslim, *Ṣaḥīḥ*, 846.

to the Friday congregational [prayer] take a bath,"[26] and also, "Let whoever is present at the Friday congregation, men and women, [first] take a bath."[27]

In fact, when one of the people of Medina wished to insult another, he would say, "You are worse than someone who does not bathe on Friday!"[28]

ʿUmar رَضِيَ ٱللَّهُ عَنْهُ was giving the sermon one Friday when ʿUthmān رَضِيَ ٱللَّهُ عَنْهُ entered the mosque. ʿUmar said to him, "Is this the time?" in disapproval of his not having come early. ʿUthmān رَضِيَ ٱللَّهُ عَنْهُ replied, "After I heard the call, I did nothing except make the ablution." To which ʿUmar رَضِيَ ٱللَّهُ عَنْهُ responded, "And only the ablution, too, when you know that the Messenger of God used to tell us to take a complete bath?"[29]

The permissibility of not taking a [full] bath [for the Friday prayer] is known from [this narration] concerning ʿUthmān's ablution رَضِيَ ٱللَّهُ عَنْهُ, as well as from what was conveyed from the Prophet صَلَّى ٱللَّهُ عَلَيْهِ وَسَلَّمَ, who said, "It is all right for someone to make the ablution for the Friday prayer, but to bathe is better."[30]

One who takes a bath because of impurity (*janāba*), should pour water over his or her body another time with the intention of bathing for Friday, because even if a single bath is sufficient, to form the intention for both and combine the bath for Friday with the bath made necessary because of impurity brings reward and merit.

One of the Companions came in to find [that] his son just bathed and said to him, "Did you do that for the sake of the Friday congregation or because of impurity?" He said it was for the latter, to which his [father] replied, "[Then] bathe again," and quoted to him the *ḥadīth* that everyone who has reached puberty must bathe for the Friday [prayer]. He told him to bathe once more only because [bathing for Friday] had not been his intention.[31]

---

26 Al-Bukhārī, *Ṣaḥīḥ*, 877; Muslim, *Ṣaḥīḥ*, 844.

27 Ibn Ḥibbān, *Ṣaḥīḥ*, 1226.

28 Al-Bayhaqī, al-*Sunan al-kubrā*, 1:299; Ibn Abī Shayba, *al-Muṣannaf*, 5039.

29 Al-Bukhārī, *Ṣaḥīḥ*, 878; Muslim, *Ṣaḥīḥ*, 845.

30 Abū Dāwūd, *Sunan*, 354; al-Tirmidhī, 497; al-Nasāʾī, *Sunan*, 3:94; Ibn Māja, *Sunan*, 1091.

31 Ibn Abī Shayba, *al-Muṣannaf*, 5097.

It is possible [for someone to] say that the goal is [simply] physical cleanliness, which can be achieved without forming any intention. But this argument can also be raised about the ablution, which [is] a means of drawing nearer to God. So its special merit is something that must be sought.

Someone who has made the greater ablution and then has an occurrence which voids the lesser ablution,[32] [should] make [only] the lesser ablution, and the [merit that comes from having made the] greater ablution is not lost. It is preferable, however, to guard against [losing] the lesser ablution.

The third [practice in preparation for the Friday prayer] is to beautify oneself in three aspects: clothing, grooming, and fragrance.

Grooming means using the toothstick, and trimming the hair, nails, moustache, and everything else mentioned in [book 2, *The Mysteries of*] *Purification*.

Ibn Masᶜūd said, "For whoever trims his nails on Friday, God عَزَّوَجَلَّ will remove an ailment from him and give him a cure."[33]

If he went to a public bath on Thursday or Wednesday, he will have fulfilled this purpose.

He should also use the most fragrant of scents that he has on this day, in order that it might overcome any objectionable odors and bring refreshment and sweet-smelling air to the noses of those near him [in the congregation].

For men, the best perfume is something that gives forth its fragrance but has no color, while for women, the best gives forth a color but has [little] fragrance. This has been transmitted in traditions.[34]

And al-Shāfiᶜī رَضِيَ ٱللَّهُ عَنْهُ said, "Whoever cleans his own clothes . . . lessens his worries, and whoever perfumes himself. . . adds to his intelligence."[35]

In respect to clothes, white garments are preferred, for the garments most beloved to God most high are white ones.[36] One

32 Generally understood to mean urination, defecation, or passing wind.

33 Ibn Abī Shayba, *al-Muṣannaf*, 5616. In ᶜAbd al-Razzāq, *al-Muṣannaf*, 3:199, this is recorded as having been said by the Prophet صَلَّى ٱللَّهُ عَلَيْهِ وَسَلَّمَ.

34 In Abū Dāwūd, *Sunan*, 2174; al-Tirmidhī, *Sunan*, 2787; and al-Nasāʾī, *Sunan*, 8:151, as something quoted from the Prophet صَلَّى ٱللَّهُ عَلَيْهِ وَسَلَّمَ. Some oil-based perfumes have color.

35 Ibn al-Jawzī, *Ṣifat al-ṣafwa*, 1:2:152; Abū Nuᶜaym, *Ḥilya*, 5:184.

36 In al-Nasāʾī, *Sunan*, 8:205, as a *ḥadīth*.

should not, however, wear something that makes one stand out; wearing black is not in the *sunna* and has no particular merit. In fact, a large number of scholars disapprove of seeing it, since it is an innovation instituted after the Messenger of God صَلَّىٱللَّٰهُعَلَيۡهِوَسَلَّمَ.

It is [also] a preferred practice [to wear] a turban on this day, and it has been conveyed by Wāthla b. al-Asqaʿ that the Messenger of God صَلَّىٱللَّٰهُعَلَيۡهِوَسَلَّمَ said: "Verily God and His angels bless those who wear a turban on the day of the Friday congregation."[37] If the heat bothers him, there is no harm in taking it off before and after the prayer, but not while hastening from his home to the mosque, nor during the prayer itself, nor during the time that the *imām* ascends the pulpit and gives the sermon.

The fourth is to set out for the mosque early. For anyone within six to nine miles from the mosque it is preferable to leave the house early to attend [the Friday prayer].

The earliest time for this starts from dawn and there is great merit in setting out early.

As he hastens to the mosque, he should be humble and modest, and do so with the intention of making a spiritual retreat in the mosque until the time of the prayer, trying his best to answer God's call to attend the congregation, and hastening toward God's forgiveness and contentment.

The Prophet صَلَّىٱللَّٰهُعَلَيۡهِوَسَلَّمَ said,

> Setting out for the Friday prayer in the first hour is like sacrificing a camel; setting out in the second, like sacrificing a cow; setting out in the third, like sacrificing a sheep; in the fourth, like sacrificing a chicken; and setting out in the fifth, like giving an egg. When the *imām* comes out, the pages are folded up, the pens are lifted, and the angels gather at the pulpit to hear the sermon [lit., 'remembrance']. Whoever enters after that fulfills the duty of the prayer but has none of its special merits.[38]

The first hour is from the *fajr* prayer to sunrise, the second from the rising of the sun until it is fully up, and the third when sunlight has spread out over the earth such that walking on the

37 Al-Ṭabarānī, *Musnad al-Shāmiyīn*, 4:336; Abū Nuʿaym, *Ḥilya*, 5:190.

38 Al-Bukhārī, *Ṣaḥīḥ*, 881; Muslim, *Ṣaḥīḥ*, 850.

ground burns the feet. The fourth and fifth, which come after the sun is midway between the horizon and its meridian, hold scant merit, and going at the time when the sun has reached its meridian [fulfills] the duty of the prayer but contains no merit.

The Prophet صَلَّى ٱللَّٰهُ عَلَيْهِ وَسَلَّمَ said, "There are three things that, if people knew their true value, they would race their camels to seek: the call to prayer, the first row of worshipers in the mosque, and arriving early for the Friday congregation."[39] About this, Aḥmad b. Ḥanbal رَضِيَ ٱللَّٰهُ عَنْهُ said, "And the best of them is arriving early for the Friday congregation."

In a tradition [it was stated:] "On Friday, angels sit by the doors of mosques with pages of silver and pens of gold in their hands to record the first as the first in their order [of entering the mosque]."[40]

Another tradition states:

> The angels notice if a man is missing when he is late in coming to the Friday prayer at his usual time and they question one another about him, "What is he doing and what is it that has delayed him from coming at his usual time." Then they say, "O God, if poverty has delayed him, enrich him! If it is illness, cure him! If it is some work, relieve him of it for the sake of Your worship! And if it is some vain distraction, turn his heart back to Your obedience!"[41]

In the first century [of Islam], the roads could be seen full of people walking with lanterns before the *fajr* prayer, crowding to get to the mosque as if it were a feast day. [Then] this practice disappeared. So it has been said that the first heterodox innovation that appeared in Islam was that people abandoned the practice of going early to the mosque.[42]

How can the faithful not feel ashamed before the Jews and Christians who go early to the synagogues and churches on Saturday and Sunday and how is it that those who seek the things of this

---

39 Abū Ṭālib al-Makkī, *Qūt al-qulūb*, 1:64.

40 Al-Bukhārī, *Ṣaḥīḥ*, 929; and Muslim, *Ṣaḥīḥ*, 850, both narrate this as a *ḥadīth*.

41 Ibn Khuzayma, *Ṣaḥīḥ*, 1771; al-Bayhaqī, *al-Sunan al-kubrā*, 3:226.

42 Abū Ṭālib al-Makkī, *Qūt al-qulūb*, 1:70.

world can get to the open-air markets very early to buy, sell, and profit, while those seeking the hereafter cannot outstrip them?

It is said: "The proximity of people to [the paradisical] vision of the countenance of God سُبْحَانَهُ وَتَعَالَىٰ will be to the [same] extent that they came early to the Friday prayer." Ibn Masʿūd رَضِيَ اللَّهُ عَنْهُ once entered the mosque early and saw three other people already there; this so troubled him that he said in self-reproach, "The fourth of four? And how far [from God] is the fourth of four?"[43]

The fifth [practice] concerns how to enter the mosque. [On entering, the worshiper] should not step over people's necks, nor pass in front of them. Arriving early makes both of these [actions] easy to avoid. A strict warning has been passed down concerning a person stepping over the necks of people: It is said that on the day of resurrection such a person will be made into a bridge for people to walk over.[44]

In a *mursala* narration,[45] Ibn Jarīj said that the Messenger of God صَلَّى اللَّهُ عَلَيْهِ وَسَلَّمَ was giving the sermon on Friday when he saw a man stepping over people so he could sit in the front. When the Prophet صَلَّى اللَّهُ عَلَيْهِ وَسَلَّمَ completed the prayer, he turned in the man's direction until he caught his attention and then said, "What kept you from praying with us today?" He answered, "O Prophet of God…but I did." To which the Prophet صَلَّى اللَّهُ عَلَيْهِ وَسَلَّمَ replied, "Did I not see you stepping over people's backs?"[46] By this he meant that [the man's ill manners] had nullified his prayer.

And in a *ḥadīth* with an unbroken chain of transmission to the Prophet صَلَّى اللَّهُ عَلَيْهِ وَسَلَّمَ, he said, "What prevented you from praying with us?" He answered, "Did you not see me, O Messenger of God?" To which the Prophet صَلَّى اللَّهُ عَلَيْهِ وَسَلَّمَ replied, "I saw that you took your time and then caused harm" (*taʾannayta wa-ādhayta*),[47] which is to say, 'You failed to come early and then hurt those who were present.'

---

43 Ibn Māja, *Sunan*, 1094, relates a *ḥadīth* with wording close to this.

44 Al-Tirmidhī, *Sunan*, 513; Ibn Māja, *Sunan*, 1116.

45 A *mursal ḥadīth* is one conveyed by a Follower (someone from the generation after the time of the Prophet صَلَّى اللَّهُ عَلَيْهِ وَسَلَّمَ and Companions) in which the Companion who heard the *ḥadīth* is not mentioned.

46 Abū Ṭālib al-Makkī, *Qūt al-qulūb*, 1:65.

47 Ibn Abī Shayba, *al-Muṣannaf*, 5515; Abū Dāwūd, *Sunan*, 1118; al-Nasāʾī, *Sunan*, 3:103; Ibn Māja, *Sunan*, 1115.

However, if the first row has been left empty, one may step over people's backs to fill it because they have lost their right by not filling the place of special merit, and Ḥasan said, "Step over the backs of people who sit in the doorways of mosques on Friday, for no respect is due to them."[48]

If, when one enters, only those praying in the mosque are present, he should not utter the salutation since that necessitates a response outside its [proper] place.

The sixth [practice concerns] not passing in front of people and sitting close enough to a pillar or wall so that people may not pass in front of him when [he is] praying.[49] Even if that does not cut off the prayer, it is still prohibited [to pass in front of someone praying], according to the saying of the Prophet صَلَّى ٱللَّهُ عَلَيْهِ وَسَلَّمَ, "It is better to wait forty years than to pass in front of someone praying."[50] And also: "It is better for a man to be ashes in the wind than pass in front of someone praying."[51]

In another *ḥadīth*, both the passerby and the one who prays in a path or does not prevent [someone from passing in front of him] are at fault: "If someone passing in front of a person praying knew the gravity of that action for both of them, he would wait forty years for him [to finish praying, rather] than pass in front of him."[52]

The pillar or wall before him or the prayer mat on the ground define the limit of space for someone praying [which a passerby should not breach] and he should prevent anyone who is about to do so, as the Prophet صَلَّى ٱللَّهُ عَلَيْهِ وَسَلَّمَ said, "[the one praying] should block [the passerby], and if [the passerby] refuses [to stop], he should do it again, and if he refuses again, then [the passerby] should be forcefully repelled, for he is a devil."[53]

Abū Saʿīd al-Khudrī رَضِيَ ٱللَّهُ عَنْهُ once prevented someone who was about to pass in front of him so forcefully that he knocked him to

48 Ibn ʿAsākir, *Tārīkh madīnat Dimashq*, 56:298.

49 Early mosques were constructed with many internal pillars. There were structural reasons for this, as well as aesthetic reasons—to remind worshipers of a palm grove.

50 Al-Bukhārī, *Ṣaḥīḥ*, 510; Muslim 507.

51 Abū Nuʿaym, *Tārīkh Iṣbahān*, 1:317 and Ibn ʿAbd al-Barr, *al-Tamhīd*, 21:149.

52 Al-Sirāj, *Musnad*, 391.

53 Al-Bukhārī, *Ṣaḥīḥ*, 509, 3275; Muslim, *Ṣaḥīḥ*, 505.

the ground—and it may have been that the man clung to him—after which the man brought a complaint against him to [the ruler] Marwān, and [Abū Saʿīd] told him that the Prophet ﷺ had ordered him to act thus [in this way].[54]

And if [the worshiper] does not find a pillar, let him place some object before him that is a forearm[55] in length to mark the boundary of his space [for prayer].

The seventh [practice] is to seek the first row, for its special merit is great, as the *ḥadīth* states, "Whoever causes his family to bathe and bathes himself, hastens to the mosque and arrives early, and gets near the *imām* and listens—for him this will be atonement for whatever sins he committed from one Friday to the next and the following three days as well,"[56] or in another version, "God will forgive his sins until the following Friday."[57] In one version it is also stipulated that he not step over people's backs to get [to the first row].[58]

In seeking the first row, [these] three things should be kept in mind.

The first of these is that if, while close to the *imām* during the sermon, one sees something objectionable that he cannot change—such as the *imām* wearing silk or some other disapproved of [clothing], or [the *imām*] prays wearing a heavy and distracting weapon, or a sword made of gold, or anything else like this, which elicits his disapproval—then it is safer and more conducive to his concentration for him to be in a back row. A number of scholars have done so for that reason.

Thus, when it was said to Bishr b. al-Ḥārith, "We see you coming early but sitting in the last rows," he answered, "What we want is the nearness of hearts, not nearness of bodies,"[59] meaning that it was safer for his heart to sit at a distance.

---

54 Al-Bukhārī, *Ṣaḥīḥ*, 509; Muslim, *Ṣaḥīḥ*, 505.

55 *Dhirāʿ*, sometimes translated as "cubit," varies in English measurements from two to two and a half feet.

56 Al-Ḥākim al-Nīsābūrī, *al-Mustadrak*, 1:281.

57 Al-Khaṭīb al-Baghdādī, *Tārīkh Baghdād*, 6:198.

58 Abū Ṭālib al-Makkī, *Qūt al-qulūb*, 1:65, and with similar wording in Abū Dāwūd, *Sunan*, 347; and al-Ḥākim al-Nīsābūrī, *al-Mustadrak*, 1:283.

59 A saying similar to this is related in al-Khaṭīb al-Baghdādī, *Tārīkh Baghdād*, 7:284; and Ibn ʿAsākir, *Tārīkh madīnat Dimashq*, 10:202.

Sufyān al-Thawrī once saw Shuᶜayb b. Ḥarb sitting near the pulpit listening to a sermon being given by Jaᶜfar al-Manṣūr. When he had completed the prayer, Sufyān came to Shuᶜayb and said, "My heart was distracted from the prayer by how close you were to him. Are you safe from hearing [him] say something that you should oppose but do not?" Then Sufyān mentioned what they[60] had innovated by wearing black [on Friday], to which [Shuᶜayb] answered,

> O Abū ᶜAbdallāh! Is there not a tradition that states, "Draw near [the *imām*] and listen?"[61]
>
> [Sufyān] said, "Woe to you! That was referring to [hearing the sermons of] the rightly-guided caliphs who themselves guided people rightly. But as for [people like these], the farther away you are from them and the less you see them, the closer you are to God عَزَّوَجَلَّ!"[62]

Saᶜīd b. ᶜĀmir said,

> "I once prayed at the side of Abū l-Dardāʾ and he started to move back in the rows until we were in the last one. When we had finished the prayer, I said to him, 'Was it not said that the first row is the best?'[63]
>
> He answered, 'Yes, except that this community has been given mercy and is looked on [by God] among all the communities, and when God looks upon a servant praying, He forgives him and forgives those behind him, so I moved to the back in hopes that He might forgive me [by my being] behind those upon whom He looks.'"[64]

And in some versions, he[65] is quoted as saying, "I heard the Messenger of God صَلَّىٱللَّهُعَلَيْهِوَسَلَّمَ say this."

---

60 By which he was referring to the ᶜAbbāsid caliphs, of whom Jaᶜfar al-Manṣūr was the second.

61 Abū Dāwūd, *Sunan*, 1108.

62 Abū Ṭālib al-Makkī, *Qūt al-qulūb*, 1:69.

63 Muslim, *Ṣaḥīḥ*, 440.

64 Abū Ṭālib al-Makkī, *Qūt al-qulūb*, 1:69.

65 That is, Abū l-Dardāʾ رَضِيَٱللَّهُعَنْهُ.

Thus, if someone moves to the back with the intention of giving preference [to others] and showing good character, there is no harm in it, and here it should be said, "Actions are according to intentions."[66]

Second, if there is not an enclosure near [the *imām*] separate from the mosque[67] for the use of the rulers, then the first row is preferable. Otherwise, it is not. Some scholars, in fact, have disapproved of praying inside [such enclosures].[68] Neither Ḥasan nor Bakr al-Muzānī would pray inside such enclosures since they viewed them as specially built for rulers. This is an innovation in mosques that began after the Messenger of God ﷺ. A mosque is for all people and making a separation in it contradicts this principle.[69] But Anas b. Mālik and ʿImrān b. Ḥaṣīn prayed in an enclosure, without disapproving of it, for the sake of being nearer [to the *imām* to hear the sermon].[70] Perhaps the disapproval of the enclosure relates to a particular situation or to the prohibition of [anyone but the ruler using it], but in respect to the enclosure itself, if it is not used exclusively, then it is not disapproved.

Third, if the pulpit (*minbar*) cuts across any rows and the rows [continue] in two halves on either side of it, then the first row is [considered] the one that is not broken by the pulpit. Al-Thawrī used to say, "The first row is the one in front of the pulpit."[71] It is the row that faces the pulpit because it is unbroken and because anyone who sits in it is opposite the *imām* giving the sermon and will hear him. But it is also possible to say that whatever row is closer to the *qibla* is the closest, without regard to the definition [above].

---

66 Ibn Ḥibbān, *Ṣaḥīḥ*, 388.

67 That is, not built as a permanent part of the architecture of the mosque. See the following footnote.

68 According to the commentary, *maqṣūra* ("enclosure") was something started by the Umayyads for the safety of the ruler and high officials while they were praying; these enclosures continued to be found in mosques up to al-Ghazālī's time. Al-Zabīdī, *Itḥāf*, 3:260. In some cases, these enclosures were made of wood and could be removed when not in use. The Umayyad Mosque in Damascus, with which al-Ghazālī was familiar, has a special *maqṣūra* space as a permanent architectural feature.

69 Abū Ṭālib al-Makkī, *Qūt al-qulūb*, 1:68.

70 Mentioned in Ibn Abī Shayba, *al-Muṣannaf*, 4742.

71 Abū Ṭālib al-Makkī, *Qūt al-qulūb*, 1:69.

It is disapproved of to pray the [Friday] prayer in the marketplaces and open spaces just outside the mosque, and some of the Companions would hit people sitting there and make them leave those spaces.[72]

The eighth [practice]: When the *imām* comes out, one should end any [supererogatory] prayers and any talking and instead occupy oneself responding to the call and listening to the sermon.

It has become a habit among some of the common people to make a prostration when the muezzin stands to give the [last] call [before the sermon]. This practice, however, has no basis in what has been transmitted. If the moment happens to coincide with the recitation of a verse in the Qurʾān that requires a prostration, there is no harm in doing [the prostration] and making a supplication while in prostration, since this is a time of special merit. And there is no basis on which to judge it as forbidden.

It has been related that both ʿAlī and ʿUthmān رَضِيَ ٱللَّٰهُ عَنْهُمَا said,

> He who listens and is quiet has a twofold reward. He who does not listen but is quiet, has a single reward. He who hears while speaking [to another] bears a twofold sin, and he who does not hear and is also speaking [to another] incurs a single sin.[73]

The Prophet صَلَّى ٱللَّٰهُ عَلَيْهِ وَسَلَّمَ said, "Whoever says to a person near him, 'Listen!' or 'Be quiet!' while the *imām* is giving the sermon is talking, and whoever talks while the *imām* is giving the sermon has no Friday prayer."[74]

This shows that if someone wishes to remind another to be silent, he should do so through a gesture or by throwing a pebble, not by speaking. In a *ḥadīth* conveyed by Abū Dharr, he once asked Ubayy while the Prophet صَلَّى ٱللَّٰهُ عَلَيْهِ وَسَلَّمَ was giving the sermon, "When was this verse revealed?" and Ubayy motioned for him to be silent. Then, when the Messenger of God صَلَّى ٱللَّٰهُ عَلَيْهِ وَسَلَّمَ descended from the

72 Abū Ṭālib al-Makkī, *Qūt al-qulūb*, 1:69.

73 Abū Ṭālib al-Makkī, *Qūt al-qulūb*, 1:68. Better-known versions of this saying are recorded in Ibn Ḥanbal, *Musnad*, 1:93 and Abū Dāwūd, *Sunan*, 1051.

74 Al-Tirmidhī, *Sunan*, 512, and al-Nasāʾī, *Sunan*, 3:103 without the last phrase, "and whoever talks…"

pulpit [to lead the prayer], Ubayy said to Abū Dharr, "Go, for you have no Friday prayer." Abū Dharr [later] complained of him to the Prophet ﷺ who said, "Ubayy was right."[75]

Even if someone is far from the *imām*, he should not speak, [not] of religious knowledge or anything else, but rather remain silent, for [any such talk] may start [the other worshipers] speaking in low voices that will eventually disturb those listening [to the sermon]. Nor should anyone sit in a circle of those who are speaking. Even if someone is too far to hear [the sermon], it is still preferable to be silent.[76]

Indeed, if it is disapproved of for someone to even pray a [supererogatory] prayer while the *imām* is delivering his sermon, then it is much more disapproved of for someone to talk, and ʿAlī (may God ennoble his face) said, "[Supererogatory] prayer is disapproved of at four times: after *fajr*, after *ʿaṣr*, at midday, and when the *imām* is giving the sermon."[77]

Ninth, when [the worshiper] prays the Friday prayer, he should observe all that we have mentioned concerning other prayers. So if he hears the recitation of the *imām*, he does not recite anything other than the Fātiḥa [1:1–7]. Also, on completing the Friday prayer, he should recite *Praise be to God* [1:1–7] seven times, followed by *Say, "He is God, [who is] One..."* [112:1–4] seven times, and the two *sūras* of seeking refuge [113:1–5 and 114:1–6] seven times each before talking to anyone. According to one of the early Muslims, the one who keeps this practice will have a refuge from that Friday until the next and be protected from Satan.[78]

It is also a preferred practice to say, after the Friday prayer,

> O God (Yā Allāh)! You [are] the infinitely wealthy (Yā Ghanī); You [are] the praised One (Yā Ḥamīd); You begin [all things] (Yā Mubdiʿa); You repeat [all things] anew (Yā Muʿīd); You [are] the Most-Merciful (Yā Raḥīm); You [are] the One who

75 Ibn Māja, *Sunan*, 1111; Ibn Khuzayma, *Ṣaḥīḥ*, 1807.

76 We must bear in mind that in the time of al-Ghazālī, the mosques where the Friday prayers were held were huge structures that could hold thousands of worshipers and the *imāms* spoke without the amplification that is common in mosques today.

77 Abū Ṭālib al-Makkī, *Qūt al-qulūb*, 1:68.

78 Ibn Abī Shayba, *al-Muṣannaf*, 5621, 30218.

loves (Yā Wadūd)! Suffice me by what You have made lawful from what You have forbidden, and suffice me by Your grace from all that is other than You!

It is said that anyone who supplicates Him regularly with this supplication, God سُبْحَانَهُ وَتَعَالَىٰ will make [him] independent of people and provide for him from a direction he does not expect.[79]

After the Friday prayer, he should pray six cycles [as supererogatory worship]. It has been related from Ibn ʿUmar رَضِيَ ٱللَّهُ عَنْهُمْ: "The Prophet صَلَّى ٱللَّهُ عَلَيْهِ وَسَلَّمَ used to pray two cycles [of supererogatory prayers] after the Friday prayer,[80] or according to Abū Hurayra, four,[81] or according to ʿAlī and ʿAbdallāh b. ʿAbbās, six.[82] All these are correct in different situations, but the best is the [prayer] that is most complete.

Tenth: Remain in the mosque until *ʿaṣr*; staying until *maghrib* is even better.

It is said, "Whoever prays *ʿaṣr* in the mosque will have the reward of the greater pilgrimage, while whoever prays *maghrib* in the mosque will have the reward of the greater and lesser pilgrimages (*al-ḥājj wa-l-ʿumra*)."[83] But if someone fears that he is vulnerable to pretensions or wanting people to see him making a spiritual retreat, or if he fears becoming involved in matters that do not concern him, then it is better to return home invoking God عَزَّ وَجَلَّ, reflecting on His signs and verses, thanking Him for his success (*tawfīq*), fearing [because of] his own shortcomings, watching over his heart and tongue, and continuing this until sunset so that the noble hour is not lost.

Nor should he speak to people in the [Friday] mosque or other mosques about worldly matters, even as the *ḥadīth* states, "There will come a time when people will talk, in the mosque, about

---

79 Abū Ṭālib al-Makkī, *Qūt al-qulūb*, 1:69.

80 Al-Bukhārī, *Ṣaḥīḥ*, 1169; Muslim, *Ṣaḥīḥ*, 882.

81 Muslim, *Ṣaḥīḥ*, 881.

82 This is recorded in ʿAbd al-Razzāq, *al-Muṣannaf*, 3:247 and al-Ṭabarānī, *al-Muʿjam al-kabīr*, 9:31, as conveyed by ʿAlī رَضِيَ ٱللَّهُ عَنْهُ, and in Abū Dāwūd, *Sunan*, 1130, and Ibn Abī Shayba in *al-Muṣannaf*, 5412, as conveyed by ʿAbdallāh b. ʿUmar رَضِيَ ٱللَّهُ عَنْهُمَا.

83 Abū Ṭālib al-Makkī, *Qūt al-qulūb*, 1:70.

mundane concerns. God most high has no need of them, so do not sit among them."[84]

Concerning Manners and *Sunna* Practices Other than the Ones in the Previous List and Covering the Entire Day and These Are Seven

The first of these is to attend gatherings for the purpose of religious knowledge in the early morning or after the ʿ*asr* prayer, but [do] not [attend] gatherings around storytellers, for there is no good in their words.[85]

All [day on] Friday the aspirant should continue doing good works and making supplications in the hope that when the noble hour comes, he will be involved in what is good.

He should not join any circles [of discussion] before the prayer, for according to ʿAbdallāh b. ʿUmar رَضِيَ ٱللَّهُ عَنْهُمَا, "The Prophet صَلَّى ٱللَّهُ عَلَيْهِ وَسَلَّمَ forbade forming circles on Friday before the prayer"[86] unless it was around a scholar reminding [those present] of 'the days of God,'[87] educating them about their *dīn*, and speaking in the mosque in the early morning. In this case, sitting in [that circle] combines going early and listening, and listening to knowledge that will [bring] benefit for the hereafter is more excellent than being occupied with supererogatory prayers, even as Abū Dharr related, "Attending a gathering devoted to knowledge is more excellent than praying a thousand cycles."[88]

Commenting on the words of God most high, *And when the prayer has been concluded, disperse in the land and seek from the bounty of God* [62:10], Anas b. Mālik said, [concerning the meaning

84 Ibn Abī Shayba, *al-Muṣannaf*, 36458; al-Bayhaqī, *Shuʿab al-īmān*, 2701.

85 The commentary defines "storytellers" (*quṣṣāṣ*) as "those who, sitting on raised seats, recount to people stories of past communities and distract them from the remembrance of God most high." Al-Zabīdī, *Itḥāf*, 3:274.

86 Abū Dāwūd, *Sunan*, 1079; al-Tirmidhī, *Sunan*, 322; al-Nasāʾī, *Sunan*, 2:47; Ibn Māja, *Sunan*, 1133.

87 This is an allusion to 14:5 reminding people of the hereafter.

88 Abū Ṭālib al-Makkī, *Qūt al-qulūb*, 1:67.

of 'seeking'] "not in worldly things, but by visiting a sick person, attending a funeral, learning useful knowledge, or visiting a brother in God عَزَّوَجَلَّ."

In fact, God عَزَّوَجَلَّ calls knowledge "favor" in several places [in the Qurʾān], as, for example, in His words, *and [God] has taught you that which you did not know. And ever has the favor of God upon you been great* [4:113], and *We certainly gave David from Us bounty* [34:10], by which is meant "knowledge."[89] So learning and teaching knowledge on this day is one of the most excellent ways of drawing nearer to God.

Praying [supererogatory] prayers is better than sitting with storytellers. In fact, this was considered a [heterodox] innovation and they used to expel storytellers from the mosque.

Once Ibn ʿUmar رَضِيَ ٱللَّهُ عَنْهُمَا came to the place where he usually sat in the congregational mosque and found a storyteller sitting there. He said to him, "Get up from my place," to which the storyteller replied, "I am not getting up. I sat here and I took this place before you." Ibn ʿUmar then sent for the one who enforces the law and [the storyteller] was made to rise.

If [telling stories] had been a *sunna* practice, then it would not have been permissible to make that man rise from his place, for [the Prophet صَلَّى ٱللَّهُ عَلَيْهِ وَسَلَّمَ] said, "No one should compel his brother to stand up from where he was sitting and then take his place. Rather, move over and make room."[90]

If a man rose to offer Ibn ʿUmar the place where he was sitting, he [Ibn ʿUmar] would not sit until the man sat back down in his place.[91]

It was also related that a storyteller used to sit in the open space in front of the room of ʿĀʾisha رَضِيَ ٱللَّهُ عَنْهَا, so she sent for Ibn ʿUmar and told him, "This person is disturbing me and distracting me in my supererogatory worship." Hearing this, Ibn ʿUmar began beating

---

89 The commentary cites the verse, *And We had certainly given to David and Soloman knowledge* [27:15], as evidence that "favor" and "knowledge" can be synonymous. Al-Zabīdī, *Itḥāf*, 3:278.

90 Al-Bukhārī, *Ṣaḥīḥ*, 911; Muslim, *Ṣaḥīḥ*, 2177. Here al-Ghazālī is referring to the verse that says, *O you who have believed, when you are told, 'space yourselves' in assemblies, then make space; God will make space for you* [58:11].

91 Muslim, *Ṣaḥīḥ*, 2177.

the man on his back until his stick broke and then expelled him from the mosque.[92]

Second is to make goodly preparations for the "noble hour." A well-known narration states, "Verily, on Friday there is an hour during which no Muslim supplicates God عَزَّوَجَلَّ for anything without being given it."[93] And in another version: "No servant who is praying when it arrives…"[94]

Concerning this hour, there is a difference of opinion. Some say it is [before] sunrise, some say it is when the sun nears its meridian, and some [say] that it is at the moment of the call [to prayer].

Some say it is when the *imām* mounts the pulpit and commences the sermon, and others [say] that it is when the people rise for the prayer. Others say it is at the end of the time of *ʿaṣr*, by which I mean the end of its preferred time.

Some have also said that it is when the sun sets, and Fāṭima رَضِيَ اللَّهُ عَنْهَا would observe this time and ask her maidservant to see where the sun was and tell her when it was going down.[95] Then she would begin to supplicate God and ask forgiveness until the sun had completely set. She would tell people that it was the awaited hour and also quote her father صَلَّى اللَّهُ عَلَيْهِ وَسَلَّمَ to that effect.[96]

One of the learned said that this hour is hidden in the day just as the night of power is hidden [in the last ten days of Ramaḍān], in order to encourage those who supplicate God to look for it.

Some of them also say that it moves through the hours of Friday just as the night of power moves [through the nights of Ramaḍān] and this view is the most likely. Therein lies a secret about which it is not fitting to speak when discussing knowledge of conduct (*ʿilm al-muʿāmala*), but the servant should nonetheless believe what [the

---

92 Abū Ṭālib al-Makkī, *Qūt al-qulūb*, 1:68.

93 Al-Nasāʾī, 3:115. The version in al-Bukhārī, *Ṣaḥīḥ*, 935, and Muslim, *Ṣaḥīḥ*, 852, includes the phrase, "and he is standing in prayer."

94 Abū Dāwūd, *Sunan*, 1046; al-Nasāʾī, *Sunan*, 3:114.

95 This occasion likely occurred after the Prophet's death, as during his time Fāṭima and ʿAlī were too poor to have a servant. By this time, Medina had grown and Fāṭima's house, which may not have had windows, was in the city center; out of a scrupulous sense of propriety, she may not have wanted to go out without an apparent purpose, and so we can speculate that she might have sent her maidservant.

96 Ibn Rāhawīh, *Musnad*, 2109; al-Bayhaqī, *Shuʿab al-īmān*, 2716.

Prophet صَلَّى ٱللَّٰهُ عَلَيْهِ وَسَلَّمَ] said, "Verily, during the days of your life, your Lord gives breaths of the spirit, so be open to these breaths."[97] The whole of Friday is one of those days, but the servant should be open to these breaths [during] all his days by the presence of his heart, his constancy in invocations, and by ridding himself of mundane whisperings, that he might be granted some portion of those breaths.

Kaᶜb al-Aḥbār once said, "It is the last hour of Friday, and that is when the sun sets," to which Abū Hurayra said, "How can it be the last hour, when I heard the Messenger of God صَلَّى ٱللَّٰهُ عَلَيْهِ وَسَلَّمَ say, 'A worshiper who meets it while he is in prayer, [God will give him what he asks],' and [sunset] is not a time for the prayer." Kaᶜb replied, "Did the Messenger of God صَلَّى ٱللَّٰهُ عَلَيْهِ وَسَلَّمَ not say, 'Whoever sits, waiting [for] the prayer, is in the prayer'"? Abū Hurayra responded, "He did indeed." Kaᶜb said, "So that is the prayer," at which Abū Hurayra was silent.[98]

Kaᶜb favored [the idea] that this was a mercy from God سُبْحَانَهُ وَتَعَالَىٰ sent to all those who had fulfilled the duties of this day, when they had completed their work.

In short, this is a noble time, as is the time when the *imām* mounts the pulpit, so [servants] should supplicate abundantly during both [times].

Third, on this day it is recommended to invoke blessings on the Messenger of God صَلَّى ٱللَّٰهُ عَلَيْهِ وَسَلَّمَ abundantly, even as he himself said, "Whoever invokes blessings on me on this day eighty times, God will forgive the sins of eighty years." And they asked him, "O Messenger of God! How do we invoke blessings on you?" He answered, "You say: 'O God bless Muḥammad, Your servant, Your Prophet, Your Messenger, the unlettered Prophet,' and this is reckoned as one [invocation of blessings]."[99]

And say,

> O God bless Muḥammad and the people of Muḥammad with a blessing that is pleasing to You and fulfills his right, and give

---

97 Al-Ṭabarānī, *al-Muᶜjam al-kabīr*, 19:233; Ibn ᶜAbd al-Barr, *al-Tamhīd*, 5:339.

98 Abū Dāwūd, *Sunan*, 1036; al-Nasāʾī, *Sunan*, 3:114; Abū Ṭālib al-Makkī, *Qūt al-qulūb*, 1:66.

99 Ibn Shāhīn, *al-Targhīb*, 22; al-Khaṭīb al-Baghdādī, *Tārīkh Baghdād*, 13:463.

> him nearness and raise him to the station of praise, which You have promised him, and reward him on our account what he merits, recompense him with the most excellent recompense You have ever granted a prophet on account of his community. Bless him and all his brethren from among the prophets and the saintly. O most Merciful of the merciful.

You should repeat this seven times, for seven Fridays, for it has been said that one who does so will be vouchsafed his ﷺ intercession.

If someone wishes to add to this, let him add a blessing that has been passed down, and say,

> O God, let the most excellent of Your prayers, most bountiful of Your blessings, the noblest of Your purity, compassion, mercy, and salutations be on Muḥammad, the master of those [You] sent, the *imām* of the pious, the seal of the prophets, and Messenger of the Lord of the worlds, the leader [of those who lead] to what is good, the one who opens the way to goodness, the Prophet of mercy, and master of the community. O God, raise him up to the station of praise by which You bring him ever nearer and cool his eye, [the station] wished for by the first and the last. O God, grant him merit, excellence, honor, proximity, the highest degree, and most exalted abode. O God, answer the prayer of Muḥammad and fulfill his hope, make him the first intercessor, and the first whose intercession is accepted. Make great his evidence, and weighty his scale, and successful his proof, and elevate his degree to the highest of those brought near. O God, gather us in his company, and make us among those who benefit by his intercession, let us live as those who follow his *sunna* and let us pass away as those who are part of his *dīn*, quench our thirsts from his paradisical pond, let us drink from his cup without shame, regret, or doubt, unchanging [in our adherence], neither causing tribulation [to others] nor being tried ourselves. *Āmīn*, O Lord of the worlds![100]

---

100 Ibn Abī ʿAṣim, *al-Ṣalāt ʿalā l-nabī*, 21 and 23.

[When] the servant uses words of blessing, even the best-known one pronounced in the testimony [of the prayer], he will be among those who invoke blessings [on the Prophet ﷺ]. And he should add prayers to this, and ask God's forgiveness, for that too is a preferred practice on this day.[101]

The fourth practice is the recitation of the Qurʾān. [A worshiper] should do this abundantly, especially the recitation of Sūrat al-Kahf [18:1–110]. The following *ḥadīth* was conveyed by Ibn ʿAbbās and Abū Hurayra رضي الله عنه:

> Whoever recites Sūrat al-Kahf on the eve of Friday or during the day on Friday, will be given a light from the place of his recitation [all the way] to Mecca, [will be] forgiven his sins until the following Friday and three days more as well, [and will be] blessed by seventy-thousand angels until [the next] morning, and [will be] protected from illness, stomach ulcers, pleurisy, leprosy, elephantitis, and the tribulations of the Dajjāl.[102]

It is a preferred practice to complete one recitation of the Qurʾān between the eve and day of Friday if one is able, so that he completes it in the two cycles of the supererogatory prayer that precede *fajr* if he recited throughout the night, or in the two cycles that follow *maghrib*, or between the call to prayer [on Friday] and the call (*iqāma*) just before the prayer begins, for in that time is great merit.[103]

Some servants made it their preferred practice to recite [the *sūra*] *Say, "He is God, [who is] One..."* [112:1–4] one thousand times on Friday and it has been said that to recite it in supererogatory prayers of ten or twenty cycles is more excellent than completing the entire Qurʾān.[104]

There are also those who invoke blessings on the Prophet ﷺ one thousand times and repeat "Glory be to God, praise be to God, there is no deity but God, and God is greater," one thousand times.

---

101 Abū Ṭālib al-Makkī, *Qūt al-qulūb*, 1:67

102 Abū Ṭālib al-Makkī, *Qūt al-qulūb*, 1:67; al-Munāwī, *Fayḍ al-qadīr*, 6:198; ʿAbd al-Razzāq, *al-Muṣannaf*, 1:186; al-Dārimī, *Sunan*, 3450; al-Ḥākim al-Nīsābūrī, *al-Mustadrak*, 1:564.

103 Abū Ṭālib al-Makkī, *Qūt al-qulūb*, 1:67.

104 Here and elsewhere al-Ghazālī refers to the *sūras* by their opening words.

It is also good to recite the six [*sūra*s that begin with] glorification on Friday or its eve.[105]

It is not recorded that the Prophet صَلَّى ٱللَّٰهُ عَلَيْهِ وَسَلَّمَ recited specific *sūras* at any other time than on Friday or its eve. For the *maghrib* prayer of Friday eve[106] he would recite, *Say, "O disbelievers..."* [109:1–6] and *Say, "He is God,* [*who is*] *One..."* [112:1–4], and for *ʿishāʾ* he would recite [Sūrat] al-Jumuʿa [62:1–11] followed by al-Munāfiqūn [63:1–11].[107]

It is also related that he used to recite the [latter two *sūras*] in the two cycles of the Friday prayer and for *fajr* on Friday he would recite Sūrat al-Sajda [32:1–30] which comes after Sūra Luqmān [31:1–34] and then *Has there* [*not*] *come upon man a period of time...* [76:1–31].[108]

The fifth concerns [supererogatory] prayers. On entering the mosque on Friday it is preferable for the worshiper not to sit down until he has prayed four cycles in which he recites [the *sūra* beginning] *Say, "He is God,* [*who is*] *One..."* [112:1–4] two hundred times, fifty for each cycle, for it has been transmitted from the Prophet صَلَّى ٱللَّٰهُ عَلَيْهِ وَسَلَّمَ that whoever does this will not die until he has seen his place in paradise or it is shown to another [in a vision].

He should not fail to pray two cycles of greeting on entering the mosque, even if the *imām* has begun the sermon, but he should make them brief as the Prophet صَلَّى ٱللَّٰهُ عَلَيْهِ وَسَلَّمَ enjoined.[109] In a rare naration it is recorded that the Prophet صَلَّى ٱللَّٰهُ عَلَيْهِ وَسَلَّمَ even paused in his sermon for someone who had just entered until he had finished [praying],[110] which is why the scholars of Kufa say, "If the *imām* pauses, he should pray them."[111]

On this day or its eve, it is [also] a recommended practice to pray four cycles in which these four *sūra*s are recited: al-Anʿām [6:1–165],

105 That is, the *sūras* in which the opening verse contains a form of the verb *sabbaḥa* (to glorify); these are al-Ḥadīd (57:1–29), al-Ḥashr (59:1–22), al-Ṣaffa (61:1–14), al-Jumuʿa (62:1–11), al-Taghābun (64:1–18), and al-Aʿlā (87:1–19).

106 That is, sunset on Thursday.

107 Ibn Ḥibbān, *Ṣaḥīḥ*, 1841.

108 Muslim, *Ṣaḥīḥ*, 879.

109 Muslim, *Ṣaḥīḥ*, 875.

110 Ibn Abī Shayba, *al-Muṣannaf*, 5206; al-Dāraquṭnī, *Sunan*, 2:16.

111 It is noted in Abū Ṭālib al-Makkī, *Qūt al-qulūb*, 1:67, that this pause may have been only for this particular case.

al-Kahf [18:1–110], Ṭa Ha [20:1–135], and Yā Sīn [36:1–83]. If he is unable to recite these well, then let him recite [Sūra] Yā Sīn, Sūrat al-Sajda [32:1–30] which follows Sūra Luqmān [31:1–34], Sūrat al-Dukhān [44:1–59], and Sūrat al-Mulk [67:1–30]. He should not fail to recite these four on the eve of Friday, for in this is great merit.

If someone cannot recite these well, then let him recite whatever he can do well instead, and for him, it will be like completing a reading of the entire Qurʾān,[112] and he should also recite Sūrat al-Ikhlāṣ, *Say, "He is God, [who is] One..."* [112:1–4] abundantly.

It is also preferable to pray the prayer of glorification according to the way [it is] described in the section on supererogatory practices, for the Prophet صلى الله عليه وسلم told his uncle al-ʿAbbās to pray this prayer every Friday.[113]

Ibn ʿAbbās رضي الله عنهما did not fail to pray this prayer after the sun had passed its meridian and [he] spoke of its great merit.[114]

The best [act] is for [a worshiper] to spend the time before noon in supererogatory prayer, the time after the Friday prayer until *ʿaṣr* listening to teachings, and the time from *ʿaṣr* until sunset in glorification and asking forgiveness.[115]

Sixth, giving charity on this day is particularly beloved since its merits are multiplied. However, to beg during the *imām*'s sermon is disapproved, because it entails talking over the speech of the *imām*.

Ṣāliḥ b. Muḥammad said, "A poor man was begging on Friday during the *imām*'s sermon and a man sitting next to my father who did not know him gave my father a morsel of food to pass on to the beggar and my father refused."[116]

Ibn Masʿūd said, "When a man begs in the mosque, he does not deserve to be given anything, and when a man begs when the Qurʾān is being recited, do not give him anything."[117]

There are scholars who disapprove of beggars in the mosque who step over people as they move through the mosque begging,

---

112 Abū Ṭālib al-Makkī, *Qūt al-qulūb*, 1:67.

113 Abū Dāwūd, *Sunan*, 1297; Ibn Māja, *Sunan*, 1387.

114 Abū Ṭālib al-Makkī, *Qūt al-qulūb*, 1:67.

115 Abū Ṭālib al-Makkī, *Qūt al-qulūb*, 1:65.

116 Abū Ṭālib al-Makkī, *Qūt al-qulūb*, 1:69.

117 Abū Ṭālib al-Makkī, *Qūt al-qulūb*, 1:69.

but [they do not disapprove] of those who are seated or standing in one place without walking around.

Kaʿb al-Aḥbār said,

> Whoever attends the Friday congregational prayer, then goes out and gives two different things in charity, then returns [to the mosque] and prays two cycles, complete in their bowings, prostrations, and reverence, then says, "O God, verily I ask You by Your name, in the name of God the Merciful, the Compassionate (bismillāh al-Raḥmān al-Raḥīm)" and by Your name, "There is no deity but God, the Living, the Eternal, the One whom neither sleep nor slumber touches" (Lā ilāha illā llāh, huwa al-ḥayyu al-qayyūm al-ladhī lā yaʾkhadhahu sinatun wa-lā nawm)—such a person does not ask God for anything except that he will be given it.[118]

And one of the early Muslims said,

> He who gives food to a poor person on Friday, then sets out early and arrives early at the mosque without doing harm to anyone, and then says, when the *imām* ends the prayer, "In the name of God, the Merciful, the Compassionate, the Living, the Eternal" (bismillāh al-Raḥmān al-Raḥīm al-Ḥayyu al-Qayyūm), I ask that You forgive me, have mercy on me, and deliver me from the fire, then supplicates God for whatever else he needs, his prayer will be answered.[119]

Seventh, [the worshiper] should make Friday a day for the hereafter. He should refrain from all worldly occupations, engage in devotional practices abundantly, and not begin any journeys on that day, for it has been related that the two angels curse the one who begins a journey on Friday eve,[120] while to set out on a journey on Friday after the time of the *fajr* prayer is forbidden except in the case of someone who will be left behind by those with whom he is to travel.

---

118 Abū Ṭālib al-Makkī, *Qūt al-qulūb*, 1:69

119 Abū Ṭālib al-Makkī, *Qūt al-qulūb*, 1:69.

120 A similar saying appears in Ibn Abī Shayba, *al-Muṣannaf*, 5158, and Abū Nuʿaym, *Ḥilya*, 6:75. Muslims traditionally consider that the day begins with the sunset of the night before, so "Friday eve" is Thursday night at sunset.

Some of the early believers disapproved of buying water inside the mosque from water-carriers, either to drink oneself or to give in charity in order that one not be a buyer in the mosque, for it is disapproved of to buy and sell in the mosque. They say, however, that if someone were to give some coins outside the mosque [for water] and then drink it or give it in charity inside, there is no harm.[121]

In sum, on Friday one should increase [his] devotional recitations and other forms of good works. If God most high loves a servant, He will occupy him at the most excellent of times with the most excellent of deeds, and if He hates a servant, He will occupy him at the most excellent of times with the worst of deeds, and the servant's chastisement will be more painful and God's abhorrence greater because he turned away from the blessedness of this time and violated its sanctity.

There are other preferred supplications for Friday which will be mentioned, God most high willing, in *Invocations and Supplications*,[122] and may His blessings be upon every chosen servant.

121 Abū Ṭālib al-Makkī, *Qūt al-qulūb*, 1:69.

122 Book 9 of the *Revival of the Religious Sciences*.

6

Various Questions Which Are Generally Troubling to People and About Which an Aspirant Should Know

These are among the rarer issues taken from books of *fiqh*.

Question [concerning the actions and movements of someone praying and whether or not the prayer is valid.]

EVEN though small actions do not invalidate the prayer, they are nonetheless disapproved of unless there is some necessity. Such is the case of [a worshiper who puts his arm out to] prevent someone from passing [in front of him], or who kills a scorpion that he fears. If this is possible to do with one or two movements [it is permissible], but if it takes three [movements], it is excessive movement and the prayer is ruined. The same holds true for lice and fleas, when someone is being harmed by them and tries to be rid of them, or for someone who needs to scratch himself [because of them] so much that it disturbs his sense of reverence.

Muʿādh would take hold of lice and fleas during the prayer[1] and Ibn ʿUmar would kill lice such that blood was visible on his hand.[2]

And al-Nakhaʿī said, "Let him take and squash [them]. Even if he kills them, that does nothing [to his prayer]."[3]

And Ibn Musayyib said, "Let him take them, squash [them], and cast them off."[4]

Mujāhid said, "In my view, the best thing is to ignore them unless they are causing harm that distracts one from the prayer, in which case one should squash [them] enough so that they do not cause harm, and cast them away."[5]

All this is permitted, but the ideal would be to avoid any extraneous movements, even the smallest, which is why some of them [the *salaf*] would not even brush away a fly; [they would] say, "I do not want to get myself used to that and ruin my prayer, for I have heard that criminals brought before kings bear great injury without moving."

When a person yawns, there is no harm in placing his hand over his mouth—this is best—and if he sneezes, let him praise God عَزَّوَجَلَّ to himself without moving his tongue. If he burps, he should not do so with his head raised to the sky, and if his upper cloth should slip down, he should not try to rearrange it, nor should he do this with the ends of his turban. All this is disapproved of in the prayer unless it is absolutely necessary.

Question [on the ruling about removing sandals for the prayer, and whether or not this ruins the prayer, and whether it is permissible to pray in sandals.]

It is permissable to pray in sandals, even if it is easy to remove them. The license concerning foot coverings (*khuff*) is not because they

1 Ibn Abī Shayba, *al-Muṣannaf*, 7556.
2 Ibn Abī Shayba, *al-Muṣannaf*, 7555, 7560.
3 Ibn Abī Shayba, *al-Muṣannaf*, 7559.
4 Ibn Abī Shayba, *al-Muṣannaf*, 7557.
5 Ibn Abī Shayba, *al-Muṣannaf*, 7563, with wording similar to this.

are difficult to remove, but rather because an unclean substance that might be on them is excused, and sandals are included in the same sense. The Messenger of God ﷺ once prayed wearing sandals, but then removed them [during the prayer] and the people did the same. [When he asked them afterward], "Why did you remove your sandals," they said, "We saw you remove yours so we removed ours." He replied,

> Verily, Gabriel came to me and informed me that there was some impurity on them. When one of you intends to enter the mosque, turn up the soles of your sandals, and if you see any impurity on them, wipe them on the ground and then pray in them.[6]

Someone [even] said [that] the prayer of someone wearing sandals is better because the Prophet ﷺ asked them, "Why did you remove your sandals?" This, however, is an exaggerated view, since he asked them knowing that they had removed their sandals simply in order to emulate him and he wished to explain to them why he had done it.

In fact, ʿAbdallāh b. al-Sāʾib related that the Prophet ﷺ took off his sandals [for the prayer],[7] and [prayed] in both circumstances. Whoever does remove his sandals, however, should not place them to his right or left, for that takes up space and breaks the row [of worshipers]. Rather, he should place them in front of him, and not behind him, so that his heart does not become distracted [by the possibility of their being taken].

This, in fact, may be why someone might consider it better to pray with one's sandals on, to keep one's heart from being distracted by them. There is also a *ḥadīth* related by Abū Hurayra that quotes the Prophet ﷺ as saying, "Whoever prays with his sandals should put them between his feet."[8]

And Abū Hurayra also said to someone else, "Place them between your feet and do not let them bother another Muslim."[9]

6 Abū Dāwūd, *Sunan*, 650.

7 Al-Nasāʾī, 2:176.

8 Abū Dāwūd, *Sunan*, 766.

9 Ibn Abī Shayba, *al-Muṣannaf*, 7980.

As for the Messenger of God صَلَّىٱللَّهُعَلَيْهِوَسَلَّمَ, he placed them to his left when he led the prayer.[10] This is something the *imām* may do, for there is no one standing to his left. The preferred practice, however, is to place them not directly between one's feet, where they might be distracting, but rather just in front of one's feet. This may be the intent of the *ḥadīth*. And Jubayr b. Mutʿim said: "For a man to put his sandals between his feet is a heterodox innovation (*bidʿa*)."[11]

Question [on the ruling about spitting during the prayer. If someone cannot avoid this, how should it be done?]

If someone spits during his prayer, it does not ruin the prayer, for it is scarcely a movement and the sound that results is not reckoned a word, nor does it take the form of letters. Nevertheless it is something disapproved of and one should avoid it [altogether], except that it was permitted by the Messenger of God صَلَّىٱللَّهُعَلَيْهِوَسَلَّمَ. According to one of the Companions, the Messenger of God صَلَّىٱللَّهُعَلَيْهِوَسَلَّمَ once saw that someone had spit on the *qibla* wall and he became extremely angry. He scraped it away using the dried stem of a date cluster in his hand and said, "Bring me some scent," and finally rubbed the remaining mark with saffron. Then he turned to us and said, "Is there any one of you who would like someone to spit in his face?" We answered, "No, none of us." He said, "When one of you begins the prayer, God عَزَّوَجَلَّ is between him and the *qibla*." And in another version,

> God most high is turned toward him, so in no way should one of you spit either in front of him or to his right, but rather to his left or under his left foot. And if the need should suddenly arise, let him spit into his garment inconspicuously, and then, without a lot of movement, wipe that part with another part [of his clothes].[12]

---

10 Abū Dāwūd, *Sunan*, 748; al-Nasāʾī, *Sunan*, 2:74; Ibn Māja, *Sunan*, 1431.

11 Ibn Abī Shayba, *al-Muṣannaf*, 7981.

12 Muslim, *Ṣaḥīḥ*, 3008.

Question [concerning how a follower should stand behind the *imām*.]

Concerning [the way] a person should stand [while] following the *imām*, there is a *sunna* element and an obligatory (*farḍ*) element.

As for the *sunna*: one [man, alone] should stand to the right of and slightly behind the *imām*. One woman [alone] should stand behind the *imām*. If she stands beside him, no harm is done, but she is going against the *sunna*. If there is also a man [following the *imām*], then let the man stand to his right and the woman [stand] behind that man.

One man should not stand alone behind the row [of worshipers]. He should either find a place in the row or pull someone back from the row [to form a row] with him. If he prays standing alone, it remains valid but contains an element [that is] disapproved of.

In respect to the obligatory aspect of following the *imām*, there should be a connection between the row [in which the worshiper stands] and the *imām*. This means some link that shows they are together. If they are in a mosque, that is sufficient, since it was built for that purpose. In that case, there need not be any other connection between them except that [the follower] knows the *imām*'s action. Thus, Abū Hurayra رَضِيَ اللَّهُ عَنْهُ prayed on the roof of the mosque, while following the *imām*.[13]

If the follower is outside the mosque on the road or in a shared open space and there are no structures between him and the mosque, then the distance of "an arrow's furthest flight"[14] away is close enough to be considered connected to the *imām*, as long as the action of one of them [that is, the *imām*] may be conveyed to the other, [the follower]. The condition of a connection is imposed, however, for someone standing in the courtyard of a house to the right or left of the mosque if its doorway opens onto the mosque.[15] In this case,

13 Ibn Abī Shayba, *al-Muṣannaf*, 6215.

14 *Ghalwati sahmin*, literally, "the furthest [that an] arrow [may be shot]." The commentary speculates that this was "three to four hundred yards." Al-Zabīdī, *Itḥāf*, 3:313.

15 That is, the row he is standing in must physically extend into the interior of the mosque; this is different than the case of someone outside or behind the mosque.

the row of worshipers must stretch unobstructed to the threshold of the house and into its courtyard, and the prayer of whoever is in that row and whoever is behind it is valid, but the [prayer of the] one who is in front of [it] is not [valid]. Such is the ruling on [praying in] different buildings; [praying] in a single building with a single space is the same as [praying] in an open space outside.

Question [on the ruling about latecomers.]

For the latecomer [who] joins the last part of the *imām*'s prayer, it will be the beginning of his. He should align himself with the *imām* and then add to that. If he joins the *fajr* prayer for the last cycle, he should pronounce the *qunūt* supplication himself even if he already did so with the *imām*. If he joins the *imām* for some part of the initial standing, he should not busy himself with the opening supplication, but rather begin [directly] with the Fātiḥa [1:1–7] and recite it in a brief fashion. If the *imām* bows before he has completed his recitation of the Fātiḥa, if he can, he should complete [its recitation] [when he] stands up from the bowing. If he cannot, however, then he should [simply] align himself with the *imām* and bow, in which case, his recitation of some portion of the Fātiḥa will suffice for all of it and the obligation [to recite it in total] is lifted because he joined late. If he is reciting a *sūra* [other than the Fātiḥa] and the *imām* bows, he should cease his recitation [and bow].

If [the latecomer] joins the *imām* in the prostration or testimony, he should pronounce the opening *takbīr* and then sit [or prostrate] without pronouncing a second *takbīr*. [However], if [he arrives] when the *imām* is bowing, he should pronounce a second *takbīr* as he bends because that transition is reckoned as his, whereas the other utterances of the *takbīr* belong to the original transitions of the prayer, and [are] not part of imitating [the *imām*].

One who joins the prayer late has not overtaken the bowing unless he is able to come to a complete rest [in the posture of bowing] while the *imām* is still [in that posture]. If he is not able to come to a complete rest until after the *imām* has bowed long enough for all those who were bowing with him [to complete its time and rise up from it], then the latecomer has missed that cycle.

Question [about missing the prayer and praying it in congregation.]

One who has not prayed *ẓuhr* until the time of *ʿaṣr* [should] first pray *ẓuhr* then *ʿaṣr*. If he starts with *ʿaṣr*, it is rewarded, but he will have left what is preferred and risked appearing heterodox.

If, however, he finds an *imām* [praying *ʿaṣr*], he should pray with them and then pray *ẓuhr* afterward, for to pray in congregation takes precedence.

Similarly, if he had prayed by himself in the earliest part of the prayer time and then come upon a congregation, he should pray with the congregation with the intention of praying the prayer of that hour, and God will reckon for him the more perfect of the two, and whether he forms the intention to make up a missed prayer[16] or to pray a supererogatory prayer, it is permissible.

If someone prays in its time in a congregation and then comes upon another congregation, he may join it with the intention of making up a missed prayer, or praying a supererogatory prayer, for there is no reason to pray a second time in congregation. To do that is only to gain the merit of the congregation.

16 That is, some past prayer that was not prayed on time or correctly.

Question [about the ruling of one who sees some impurity on his clothes and whether he should he complete the prayer or repeat it.]

If someone is praying or has prayed and then sees some impurity (*najasa*)[17] on his garments, it is preferable, but not obligatory, to repeat the prayer. If he sees some impurity while in the course of praying, he may cast off that garment and complete the prayer, although it is preferable to repeat it. The basis for this [ruling] is the story of the Messenger of God صَلَّى ٱللَّٰهُ عَلَيْهِ وَسَلَّمَ removing his sandals when Gabriel عَلَيْهِ ٱلسَّلَامُ informed him that there was some impurity on them, for [in that case] he did not repeat the prayer.

Question [about the prostration of forgetfulness.]

If someone omits the first testimony, or the *qunūt* supplication, or the invocation of blessings on the Messenger of God صَلَّى ٱللَّٰهُ عَلَيْهِ وَسَلَّمَ in the first testimony, or negligently makes some action [not in the prayer] that would invalidate the prayer if he had done it intentionally, or if someone is unsure whether he has completed three or four cycles, he should hold to what he is sure of and then make the two prostrations of forgetfulness before pronouncing the closing salutation. And if he forgets [to do these before the closing salutation], then he should complete them afterward, whenever he remembers them, provided it is still close [in time]. But if he made the two prostrations [of forgetfulness], after the closing saluation, and then he became impure [without ablution],[18] his prayer would be invalid. This is because when he [returns] to the prayer, it is as if he had uttered the closing salutation forgetfully in the wrong place, and the prayer was not complete and he is returning to the prayer [without the ablution].

---

17 For the definition of what constitutes an impurity, see *The Mysteries of Purification*, book 3 of the *Revival of the Religious Sciences.*

18 Here the commentary adds, "or he spoke [to someone] intentionally." Al-Zabīdī, *Itḥāf*, 3:314.

This is [also] why the closing salutation is repeated after the prostrations [of forgetfulness].

If, however, he does not remember that the prostration of forgetfulness is due until after he has left the mosque or after a long stretch of time, then it is too late.

Question [on an effective remedy for someone who suffers from whisperings of doubt about the intention to pray.]

Whisperings of doubt when forming the intention to pray may arise either from some mental disorder or from ignorance of the law, for in terms of purpose, following the commandment of God عَزَّوَجَلَّ is like following the commandment of anyone else, and venerating Him is like venerating anyone else. If a scholar entered [the room] where you were, you would stand up for him, and if you were to say, "I intend to rise and stand in veneration for the entrance of the esteemed Zayd, in acknowledgment of his excellence, and I intend to do this in connection to his entrance and turn my face in his direction," you would be deemed foolish. Rather, as soon as you see him, knowing his excellence, the impulse to honor him brings you to your feet, and thus, it is veneration, unless you stood up for some other reason or [just] absentmindedly.

To specify [when forming an intention] that a prayer is "midday, on time, and obligatory" (*ẓuhran, adāʾan, farḍan*) is like specifying that when you stand up [for the respected person], it will be at the moment he enters, with your face turned toward him, only for him, and out of respect, in order for it to be veneration. For if you were to stand with your back toward him, or if you were to wait awhile and then stand up, it would not be veneration.

These attributes, then, must be known and must be the reason [for the action]. They do not need to be present in the soul longer than an instant—no longer, in fact, than it takes to form the phrases which express them, either verbally or in the heart. If someone does not understand what intention for the prayer means in this sense, then it is as if he does not understand what intention is [in itself]. [In reality], there is nothing more to this than the fact that you were called to pray at a given time, and you answered that call and rose [to do so]. So whisperings of doubt [in respect to intention] are pure ignorance. Purpose and knowledge join in the soul in a single state. They are not distinguished as separate by the mind, such that the soul may observe and ponder them.

There is a difference between the actual presence of something in the soul and its being distinguished as separate by the mind. Presence is the opposite of absence and heedlessness, even if this is not something differentiated. Someone who knows, for example, an event (*ḥādith*),[19] knows it by a single act of knowing and in a single instance, but this [single piece of] knowledge includes other knowledge that is present even if [it is] not differentiated. [For example], if someone knows an event, [this assumes] the knowledge of what existence is and what non-existence is, of what "coming before" means and what "coming after" means, of what a span of time is, and how "coming before" pertains to non-existence and "coming after" [pertains] to existence.

All these aspects of knowledge are contained in the knowledge of the event. So if a person who knew the event (if he did not know anything else but that event) were asked, "Do you know what coming before, coming after, and non-existence are? [Do you know that] non-existence comes before and existence comes after, or that time is divided into what came before and what came after?"—and that person said, "No, I know nothing at all about that," he would be lying, for it would contradict his having said, "I know the event."

It is ignorance of these fine points, however, that incites whisperings of doubt, and if the one suffering from this then [tries to] impose on himself, and make present in his heart the fact that the prayer he will pray is also qualified [for example,] as *ẓuhr*, on time, and obligatory—all this in a single state, verbally articulated and in such a way that he might observe what he says, it will simply be impossible for him. Even if only for the sake of rising for a venerable scholar, it would be beyond him.

---

19 Al-Ghazālī uses the term *ḥādith* in its philosophical sense of "something that has come into being" or "contingent." We have opted to translate this as "event," for the sake of simplicity.

So this knowledge [pertaining to the prayer] repels whisperings: following the commandment of God سُبْحَانَهُ وَتَعَالَىٰ in forming intention is like following the commandment of anyone else.

Then, I would add, by way of simplification and license: if someone who is afflicted by whisperings of doubt cannot understand intention without bringing these to mind as separate, discrete elements, and cannot envision in his soul obedience as a single act, and all this is present in his heart while he utters the opening *takbīr*, from beginning to end, such that he does not complete the utterance of the *takbīr* without forming this intention, that will suffice him, and we do not require that he connect all of this together with the beginning of the *takbīr* or the end. That would be too heavy a burden. And if it was something commanded [by the Prophet صَلَّى ٱللَّهُ عَلَيْهِ وَسَلَّمَ], there would have been many questions about it from the first [Muslims], and [at least] one of the Companions would have been afflicted by whisperings of doubt when forming intention. The complete absence of this, [however], is proof that the matter is one of facility. The one afflicted by whisperings should thus be satisfied with whatever way of expressing intention is easiest, until it becomes habitual for him and he is finally rid of [the doubts]. And he should not demand of himself verification concerning this, for to do so will only increase whispering.

We have spoken about this in *al-Fatāwā*,[20] [our book of] legal rulings about aspects of verification concerning differentiating knowledge and purposes in connection with intentions. Since these are things which the learned need to be acquainted with, but which might be harmful for the ordinary person to hear, and [may] only arouse in him whisperings of doubt, we have omitted them here.

---

20 This has been published as *Fatāwī l-Ghazālī*; al-Zabīdī says that al-Ghazālī wrote this book in response to questions sent to him by his companions, colleagues, and students. *Itḥāf*, 3:323.

Question [on the conditions for correctly following the *imām*.]

Someone praying behind the *imām* should not precede him in the bowing, prostrating, rising up from [either of] them, or in any of the other actions [of the prayer], nor should he do these simultaneously with the *imām*. Rather, he should follow him and align [his actions] with those of the *imām*, for this is the meaning of "emulation." If he intentionally performs actions at the same time as the *imām*, his prayer is not invalidated, just as it is not invalidated by his praying right next to the *imām* rather than behind him. If his actions precede those of the *imām*, however, there are two opposing views concerning the validity of his prayer and it is quite possible that it is invalid, [as it is] analogous to the case of someone who prays standing in a place in front of the *imām*. This, in fact, would be the more correct view, since the congregational prayer is founded more on following the *imām* than on the place [someone] stands. Following the [*imām*'s] actions is the more important [of these two elements], because [the condition of] not standing in front of the *imām* is only in order to facilitate following [him] and to complete this emulation [of him], and it is fitting for the one being followed to be in front. There is, then, no real excuse [for someone praying behind the *imām*] to precede him in the actions of the prayer, except forgetfulness, and for this reason the Messenger of God ﷺ was severe in criticizing this when he said, "Does the one who raises his head before the *imām* not fear that God will change it into a donkey's head?"[21]

[Similarly], delaying the performance of one of the fundamental actions until much after the *imām* does not invalidate the prayer. An example of this would be when the *imām* has risen up from the bowing while the follower has not yet begun it. But to be this far behind is disapproved of, and if [the *imām*'s] forehead reaches the ground [in prostration] before the followers have had enough time to bow, then the *imām*'s prayer is invalid, just as it would be

21 Al-Bukhārī, *Ṣaḥīḥ*, 691; Muslim, *Ṣaḥīḥ*, 427.

if he placed his forehead on the ground for the second prostration and the followers have not had enough time to complete the first.

Question [about enjoining what is right, which includes keeping the rows of worshipers straight, and the merit of the congregation and the first row.]

It is the duty of anyone present for the [congregational] prayer to correct a mistake he sees someone else commit in prayer and to point it out as incorrect. If it is done by someone who does not know any better, he should be kind to him and teach him. This includes keeping the rows straight, preventing someone from praying by himself apart from the row, pointing out the error of someone who raises his head up before the *imām* does, and other similiar matters. As the Prophet ﷺ said, "Woe [be] to the learned for the ignorant person he does not teach."[22]

Ibn Masʿūd رضي الله عنه said, "Whoever sees someone praying incorrectly and does not prohibit him from it shares in his error."

And according to Bilāl b. Saʿd, "An error committed secretly harms only the one who commits it, but an error committed openly that goes uncorrected harms everyone."[23]

And in a *ḥadīth* it is stated that Bilāl used to straighten the rows by striking the backs of people's feet with his camel crop.[24]

According to ʿUmar رضي الله عنه, the Prophet said, "Notice who of your brothers are not present for the congregational prayer. If they are ill, visit them, and if they are well, remonstrate them for missing the prayer in congregation." This should not be taken lightly. The early Muslims would go to lengths about this and one of them even

22 Al-Daylamī, *Musnad al-firdaws*, 7141. Al-Munāwī, *Fayḍ al-qadīr*, 9646, explains this *ḥadīth*: "Woe [be] to the learned for the ignorant person [if he does not teach and guide him…], and woe [be] to the ignorant person for the learned man [who tried to teach and guide him, if he refused to be taught or guided]."

23 Abū Nuʿaym, *Ḥilya*, 5:222.

24 ʿAbd al-Razzāq, *al-Muṣannaf*, 2:47.

carried a bier to the door of someone who had stayed away from the congregation to show him that it is the dead, not the living, who may stay away.

When someone enters the mosque, he should head toward the right side of the row. In fact, they used to crowd so much to the right in the time of the Messenger ﷺ that he was told that the left side was being unused and said ﷺ, "Whoever fills the left side will have a twofold reward!"[25]

And when someone does not find a place for himself and there is a boy in the [first row], he should put him in [the row] behind and take that place, provided the boy has not reached puberty.[26]

This concludes what we wished to mention concerning troublesome questions [related to the prayer]. The rules concerning various individual prayers will come in [book 10] *The Arrangement of the Litanies and the Exposition of the Night Vigil*, God most high willing.

25 Ibn Māja, *Sunan*, 1007.

26 Since the prayer is not obligatory until puberty.

7

On Supererogatory Prayer

Know that prayers other than the obligatory [ones] are divided into three categories: those which are *sunna*, those which are recommended (*mustaḥabbāt*), and those which are voluntary (*taṭawwuʿāt*).

By *sunna* we mean what was transmitted of the [supererogatory] prayers that the Messenger of God ﷺ regularly prayed, following [the obligatory prayers], and [also] the morning prayer (*ḍuḥā*), the *witr* prayer, and *tahajjud*. The word *sunna* is an expression meaning "the path that has been followed."

By "recommended" (*mustaḥabb*), we mean what has been characterized as meritorious in recorded tradition, but is not described as being a regular and constant [practice of the Prophet ﷺ]. Examples of these are mentioned in the [section on] the days and nights of the week, or the prayer on leaving the house or entering it.

By "voluntary" (*taṭawwuʿāt*), we mean any [supererogatory] prayer beyond these, [those that are] not mentioned in any text, but are simply prayed by the servant who wishes to commune with God عَزَّوَجَلَّ in the prayer. These are praised in a general way by the law and the one who prays them does so freely since there is no encouragement to a specific prayer, only prayer in general.[1] Indeed, the word *taṭawwuʿ* (voluntary) literally means a "gift."

All three of these categories are called *nawāfil* [lit., "additional"], for these are in addition to the obligatory. We mention terms such as *nāfila*, *sunna*, *mustaḥabb*, and *taṭawwuʿ* only for the sake of definition; there is no harm in someone using them [these terms] in another way, as long as the intention is understood.

Each of these categories has its own degree of merit according to the traditions and sayings that have been transmitted concerning it, how long the Messenger ﷺ observed it as regular practice, and the soundness and authenticity of the traditions themselves. For this reason it has been said: "The *sunna* of congregational practices is more excellent than the *sunna* of individual practice."

The most excellent of the congregational *sunna* practices are the prayer for the two feasts (*ʿīdayn*), the prayer during a solar eclipse (*kusūf*), and the prayer for rain (*istisqāʾ*). The most excellent of the individual *sunna* prayers are *witr*, then the prayer of two cycles before *fajr*, and then the other regular *sunna* associated with daily obligatory prayers which, in turn, differ from one another in merit.

Know that supererogatory prayers may be categorized according to what they are connected to as [1] those connected to external events, such as a solar eclipse or the need for rain, [2] and those connected to certain times, which may be further divided into [2a] those that are repeated daily and nightly, or [2b] those that are repeated weekly or yearly.

In all, then, there are four categories.

Category 1
The eight prayers that are repeated daily and nightly

There are five [prayers] related to the five obligatory prayers. The other three are the morning prayer (*ḍuḥā*), the prayers between the two evening [prayers, i.e., *maghrib* and *ʿishāʾ*], and the prayers in the latter part of the night (*tahajjud*).

---

1 Al-Ṭabarānī, *al-Muʿjam al-awsaṭ*, 245.

The first of the daily and nightly *sunna* are the two cycles before the *fajr* prayer. The Messenger of God ﷺ said of these, "The two cycles [before] *fajr* are better than the world and all it contains."[2]

The time for this begins at the first glimpse of the true dawn, the one that stretches out on the horizon, not the vertical ray of the false dawn. To perceive this with the naked eye is at first difficult, except by learning the stages of the moon, for the conjunction of [the dawn's] rising to the visible stars is known and so it can then be reckoned by the stars. It can also be known by way of the moon on two nights each month: on the twenty-sixth night [when] the moon rises as dawn begins, and on the twelfth night [when] the dawn begins as the moon sets. This is the usual pattern, but variations may occur when [the sun enters] certain astronomical stages, and to explain this would be lengthy.

Learning the stages of the moon, however, is important for an aspirant so that he might know thereby the periods of the night and also the dawn.

The time for the two cycles ends when the time for the obligatory prayer ends; that is, with the appearance of the sun. The *sunna* is to pray them before the obligatory prayer, but if you enter a mosque after the obligatory prayer has begun, you should be occupied only with it, even as the Prophet ﷺ said, "If the [obligatory] prayer has started, there is no other prayer except it."[3]

Then, on completing the obligatory [prayer], you may stand to pray the *sunna*.

The correct view is that they are on time as long as they are done before sunrise, even if they follow the obligatory prayer in its time, while the order between them and the obligatory prayer—praying them first and the obligatory afterward—is *sunna* unless there is a congregation [that might be missed]. In that case, the order is reversed,[4] but the two [supererogatory] cycles remain on time.

The recommended practice is to pray them at home, make them brief, then go to the mosque, pray the two cycles of greeting

---

2 Muslim, *Ṣaḥīḥ*, 725.

3 Muslim, *Ṣaḥīḥ*, 710.

4 Which is to say, the two supererogatory cycles are completed after the obligatory prayers in congregation.

the mosque, then sit without praying any other prayer before the obligatory [prayer]. Between the [beginning of] dawn and sunrise, the most beloved practice is invocation and reflection, limiting [formal worship] to the supererogatory prayer of two cycles at dawn and the obligatory prayer.

The second of the daily *sunna* prayers is connected to *ẓuhr* and consists of six cycles. Of these, the two after the obligatory prayer are considered to be affirmed by consensus while the four cycles before are also *sunna* but with less consensus than the two that follow.

Abū Hurayra related that the Prophet ﷺ said, "Whoever prays four cycles after the sun has passed its meridian and does their recitation, bowing, and prostration well, will have seventy-thousand angels worshiping with him and asking God's forgiveness for him until nightfall."[5]

The Prophet ﷺ regularly prayed four cycles after the sun had passed its meridian and he would lengthen them, saying, "This is a time when the doors of heaven open and I want to have some worship from me ascending [when they do]." This *ḥadīth* was transmitted solely by Abū Ayyūb al-Anṣārī.[6]

Umm Ḥabība, the wife of the Prophet ﷺ, related something similar, that he said, "God will build a dwelling in heaven for whoever prays twelve cycles each day apart from the obligatory: two cycles before *fajr*, four before *ẓuhr* and two after it, two cycles before *ʿaṣr*, and two after *maghrib*."[7]

And Ibn ʿUmar said, "I have preserved from the Messenger of God ﷺ ten cycles [in supererogatory prayer] each day," and then [he] mentioned all that Umm Ḥabība had [said] except the two cycles before *fajr*, adding, "That was an hour when the Messenger of God ﷺ was not visited, but my sister Ḥafṣa told me that he used to pray two cycles in her room and then leave." He also said in this *ḥadīth*, "Two cycles before *ẓuhr* and two cycles after *ʿishāʾ*."[8] Two cycles before *ẓuhr* are thus more affirmed than four.

---

5 Abū Ṭālib al-Makkī, *Qūt al-qulūb*, 1:27.

6 Al-Tirmidhī, *Sunan*, 478; Ibn Ḥanbal, *Musnad*, 5:416.

7 Al-Nasāʾī, 3:262.

8 Al-Bukhārī, *Ṣaḥīḥ*, 1180, 1181.

The time for praying these begins when the sun passes its meridian, which is known when the shadows of standing people begin to lengthen toward the east. When the sun rises, a person's shadow stretches toward the west, then as the sun continues to rise, it retracts from a westward direction, until the sun reaches the meridian, its highest point in the sky, which marks midday, and is the point at which shadows are shortest. Then, as it passes this point, the shadows [again] lengthen. Whenever this lengthening becomes perceptible to the senses, the time of the *ẓuhr* prayer has begun. In actual fact, the sun passes its highest point before that moment; [but] devotional responsibilities are based only on what may be perceived by the senses. The extent of the shadow remaining continues to increase, growing long in the winter but staying short in the summer. Its longest point occurs when the sun reaches the beginning of Capricorn and its shortest point comes when it reaches the beginning of Cancer. These points may be known by feet and measurements.

One of the easiest methods that can be used to ascertain [the meridian] for anyone good at observing [the sky] is to find, at night, the position of the polestar, then place on the ground a square board so that one of its edges is parallel to the [northern] horizon such that if you imagined a line inscribed by a stone falling from the polestar to the board, intersecting the edge of the board closest to it, it would intersect the top edge of the board at a right angle. The point where this line, [B on the diagram] ends [toward the middle of the board] is marked with an O and there a [slender] vertical post is inserted. In the first part of the day, the shadow of this post will fall toward the west side of the board parallel with line A [in the diagram]. Then [as the sun moves toward the west] the shadow will eventually be parallel to line B [in the diagram] at a right angle to both the east and west sides of the board, not bending toward one or the other, and this is when it reaches its highest point [i.e. the meridian]. When the shadow bends toward the eastern side of the board, it indicates that the sun has passed midday.

This is a way of perceiving with the senses the time nearest to the earliest moment [when the sun has passed] its meridian in God's knowledge (*fī ʿilm Allāh*). Then, when the shadow shifts, mark its end point. When the shadow from that mark is equal [in length] to the standing post, the time for the afternoon prayer (*ʿaṣr*) has begun.[9]

This is the extent to which it is good to be acquainted with the science of the meridian.

This is the image [of what has been described].

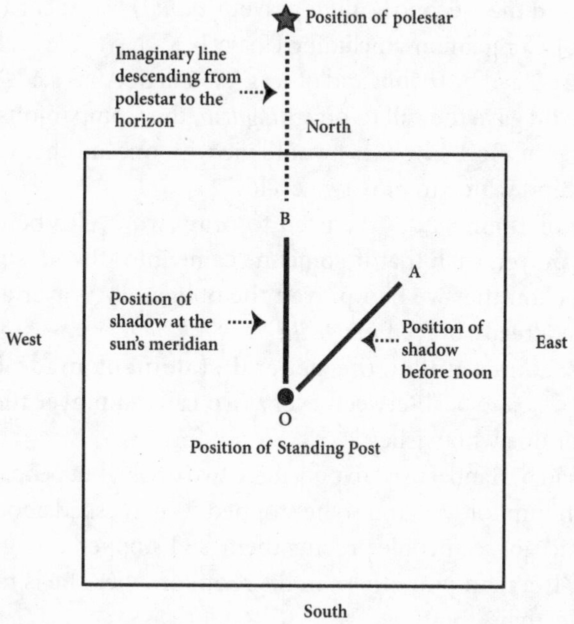

Third: The supererogatory worship connected to the afternoon prayer (*ʿaṣr*) consists of four cycles before the obligatory prayer. It is related from Abū Hurayra رَضِيَ ٱللَّٰهُ عَنْهُ that the Prophet صَلَّىٰ ٱللَّٰهُ عَلَيْهِ وَسَلَّمَ said, "May God have mercy on the servant who prays four cycles before *ʿaṣr*."[10]

To do this in hopes of being included among those for whom the Prophet made supplications is something most assuredly recommended, since the supplications of the Prophet صَلَّىٰ ٱللَّٰهُ عَلَيْهِ وَسَلَّمَ

9 Al-Ghazālī is describing the traditional method of making a sundial. The simple wooden post he suggests is the gnomen, the piece that projects and casts a shadow; in later sundials, it was usually made of steel.

10 Abū Dāwūd, *Sunan*, 1271; al-Tirmidhī, *Sunan*, 430.

are answered. However, he did not pray the four cycles before ʿ*aṣr* as consistently as he did the two cycles before *ẓuhr*.

Fourth: The supererogatory prayer connected to *maghrib* consists of two cycles following the obligatory prayer. About this, there is no disagreement in what has been conveyed.

Praying two cycles before, done rapidly between the call to prayer (*adhān*) and the [second] call to prayer (*iqāma*) was recorded by a number of Companions, including Ubayy b. Kaʿb, ʿAbāda b. al-Ṣāmit, Abū Dharr, Zayd b. Thābit, and others. ʿAbāda or Anas said, "When the muezzin gave the call to pray *maghrib*, the Companions of the Messenger of God ﷺ would vie with one another to find a pillar behind which to pray two cycles."[11]

One of them said, "We used to pray two cycles before the *maghrib* prayer, such that if someone came into [the mosque], he would reckon that we had prayed the obligatory prayer and ask, 'Have you already prayed *maghrib*?'"[12]

This comes under the general statement made by the Prophet ﷺ, "Between every two calls to prayer there is a prayer for one who wishes."[13]

Aḥmad b. Ḥanbal used to pray these two cycles, but people found fault with him for that and so he stopped. When asked about it, he said, "I did not see people praying them, so I stopped doing it." But he said, "If a man prays them in his room or where he is not seen by people, that is best."[14]

The time for the *maghrib* prayer begins when the sun disappears from sight [when seen] in a flat, mountainless, terrain. If there are mountains to the west, however, he should wait until he sees blackness approaching in the east. The Prophet ﷺ said, "When the night approaches from there [indicating the East] and day retreats from there [indicating the West], then it is time for the fasting person to break his fast."[15]

---

11 Al-Bukhārī, *Ṣaḥīḥ*, 625; Muslim, *Ṣaḥīḥ*, 837.

12 Muslim, *Ṣaḥīḥ*, 837.

13 Al-Bukhārī, *Ṣaḥīḥ*, 624; Muslim, *Ṣaḥīḥ*, 838. "Between the two calls" means between the call to prayer (*adhān*) and the call to begin the prayer (*iqāma*).

14 Abū Ṭālib al-Makkī, *Qūt al-qulūb*, 2:147.

15 Al-Bukhārī, *Ṣaḥīḥ*, 1954; Muslim, *Ṣaḥīḥ*, 1101.

For *maghrib* in particular it is preferable to pray it without delay. If you delay it until the redness is completely gone from the west, you have fulfilled the obligation, but it is disliked. Once ʿUmar رَضِيَ ٱللَّٰهُ عَنْهُ delayed praying it until stars had risen and so he freed a slave in expiation, and once Ibn ʿUmar did not pray it until two of the planets had risen and so he freed two slaves in expiation.[16]

Fifth: The regular supererogatory prayers related to *ʿishāʾ* are four cycles after the obligatory. ʿĀʾisha رَضِيَ ٱللَّٰهُ عَنْهَا said, "The Messenger of God صَلَّى ٱللَّٰهُ عَلَيْهِ وَسَلَّمَ would pray four cycles after the last prayer (*ʿishāʾ*) and then go to sleep."[17]

Some scholars hold that, based on the totality of narrations, the number of the *sunna* cycles associated with the [five times of] prayer are seventeen, which is also the number of cycles in all the obligatory prayers: two before *fajr*, four before *ẓuhr* and two after it, four before *ʿaṣr*, two after *maghrib*, and three after the *ʿishāʾ* prayer, these latter being the *witr*.

But when you know the *ḥadīth* that have been conveyed concerning them, there is no sense in [trying] to fix their number, even as the Prophet صَلَّى ٱللَّٰهُ عَلَيْهِ وَسَلَّمَ said, "Prayer is the best worship. Whoever wishes does much, and whoever wishes does little."[18]

The number of these prayers done by every aspirant is a measure of his aspiration toward the good. At the same time, it is evident from what we mentioned that some of these prayers are emphasized more than others and so it is certainly worse to miss these. Moreover, the obligatory prayers are completed by the supererogatory prayers, so anyone who does not [pray] the supererogatory prayers abundantly risks his obligatory prayers not being accepted because there is nothing to rectify their [deficiencies].[19]

---

16 Abū Ṭālib al-Makkī, *Qūt al-qulūb*, 1:26.

17 Abū Dāwūd, *Sunan*, 1303.

18 Ibn Ḥanbal, *Musnad*, 5:178.

19 He is referring to a *ḥadīth* recorded in Abū Dāwūd, *Sunan*, 864; and al-Tirmidhī, *Sunan*, 413: The first thing to be reckoned of people's deeds on the day of resurrection will be the prayer. And our Lord عَزَّ وَجَلَّ will say to the angels—and He knows better—"Look at My servant's prayer. Is it complete or deficient?" If it is complete, it will be written for him completely, and if it is deficient, then [God] will say, "Look to see if My servant has any supererogatory worship." If he does,

Sixth is the *witr* [prayer]. Anas b. Mālik said that the Messenger of God ﷺ prayed three cycles as the *witr*. He would recite in the first *Exalt the name of your Lord, the most high* [87:1–19], in the second, *Say, "O disbelievers"* [109:1–6], and in the third *Say: "He is God, [who is] One..."* [112:1–4].[20]

In another narration: "He ﷺ would pray two more cycles after the *witr* while seated,"[21] or in some versions, "seated cross-legged."[22]

In some narrations it is stated: "When he wished to get into his bed, he would simply shift himself onto it still seated, and then, seated on top [of the covers], he would pray two cycles before lying down, reciting in the first *When the earth is shaken with its [final] earthquake* [99:1–8] and then the *sūra*, *Competition in [worldly] increase diverts you* [102:1–8], or, in another narration, *Say, "O disbelievers"* [109:1–6].[23]

The cycles of the *witr* prayer may be prayed separately or connected—that is, with two closing salutations or with only one.

The Messenger of God ﷺ would pray *witr* with a single cycle, or with three, five, or as many as eleven. There is also a narration that mentions thirteen, and in an unusual *ḥadīth*, seventeen.[24]

These cycles, which have been collectively referred to by the name *witr*, were his night vigil, [also called] *tahajjud*.

The night vigil is a confirmed *sunna* practice whose merit will be mentioned in the book on devotional recitations.[25]

He will say, "Complete My servant's obligatory worship from his supererogatory [worship]," and thus will deeds be taken.

20 Abū Dāwūd, *Sunan*, 1423; al-Tirmidhī, *Sunan*, 460; al-Nasā'ī, *Sunan*, 3:335; Ibn Māja, *Sunan*, 1171.

21 Abū Dāwūd, *Sunan*, 1340; al-Tirmidhī, *Sunan*, 471; Ibn Māja, *Sunan*, 1195.

22 Al-Nasā'ī, 3:224.

23 Abū Ṭālib al-Makkī, *Qūt al-qulūb*, 2:147. Ibn Ḥanbal recorded the Prophet's recitation of these three *sūras* together for the *witr* prayer, but without mention that he did so in bed; Ibn Ḥanbal, *Musnad*, 1:89; al-Bayhaqī, *al-Sunan al-kubrā*, 3:33.

24 Making the *witr* a single, separate cycle is mentioned in al-Bukhārī, *Ṣaḥīḥ*, 995, and in Muslim, *Ṣaḥīḥ*, 749; as three, as noted above; as five in Muslim, *Ṣaḥīḥ*, 373; as seven in Muslim, *Ṣaḥīḥ*, 746; as nine in Muslim, *Ṣaḥīḥ*, 737, and in al-Nasā'ī, *Sunan*, 3:240; as eleven in al-Nasā'ī, *Sunan*, 3:243; as thirteen in Muslim, *Ṣaḥīḥ*, 765, and in al-Nasā'ī, *Sunan*, 3:237; and as seventeen in Ibn al-Mubārak, *Zuhd*, 1273.

25 *The Arrangement of the Litanies and the Exposition of the Night Vigil*, book 10 of the *Revival of the Religious Sciences*.

There is disagreement concerning which [forms of] *witr* are best. It has been said that to do it by a single, isolated cycle is best, for it is true that this was the regular practice of the Prophet ﷺ.

And it has been said that it is better to [pray them] together, so as not to give the appearance of being different [in form] than all the other prayers. This is especially true for the *imām*, since someone might be following him who does not consider a single cycle a prayer.[26]

If they are connected, [the worshiper] should form the intention that all [the cycles] are the *witr*. By contrast, if he is praying a single, separate cycle after the two cycles that follow *ʿishāʾ*, or if he prays it directly following *ʿishāʾ*, he should intend that [it, alone] be the *witr*. This is correct because a condition of the *witr* prayer is that it be odd-numbered in itself and that it make whatever precedes it an odd number, which in the latter case would mean the obligatory cycles of the *ʿishāʾ* prayer.[27]

If one prayed *witr* before the *ʿishāʾ* prayer, it would be invalid in the sense that he would not gain its merit which, according to a narration, is "better that a herd of russet-colored camels."[28] Apart from this, however, a [prayer of] a single cycle is valid [as supererogatory worship]. It is incorrect, however, to pray this before *ʿishāʾ* because it contradicts the consensus of people's practice and also because it would not be preceded by a prayer that it makes *witr*. If one intends to pray *witr* in three [cycles] separated [by the salutation after the first two], then in forming his intention for the two cycles, there is something to consider: if it is to pray the late night prayer (*tahajjud*), or the *sunna* following the *ʿishāʾ* prayer, then it is not part of the *witr*. If he intends [to pray] *witr*, they are not, in themselves, *witr*. Rather, the *witr* is what follows them. It is better for him to form the intention as if he were praying all three connected cycles as *witr*. But *witr* has two meanings:

---

26 The *imām* leads others in the *witr* prayer in Ramaḍān, when it is prayed in congregation at the end of the supererogatory prayers (*tarāwīḥ*) that are prayed during the month.

27 The commentary notes that according to al-Shāfiʿī, the obligatory prayer may be counted as part of the "*witr*." Al-Zabīdī, *Itḥāf*, 3:351.

28 Abū Dāwūd, *Sunan*, 1418; al-Tirmidhī, *Sunan*, 452; Ibn Māja, *Sunan*, 1168. Russet-colored camels were among the most valuable to the Arabs of the time.

One is that it is, in itself, *witr* [ʿodd-numbered'], and the other is that it is structured so as to be made *witr* by what follows it, so that three cycles, collectively, are the *witr*, with the two [first] cycles considered part of the three, and their being "odd" is determined by the third. Thus, if his purpose is to make them *witr* by way of the third cycle, then he would form the intention [of praying] the two as *witr*.

The third cycle is thus *witr* in itself and it also makes the others *witr*, but the two cycles cannot make others *witr* nor are they *witr* in themselves, but are made so by others.

[Finally], *witr* should be the last prayer of the night, so it comes after the late night prayer (*tahajjud*). The special merits of *witr*, and the *tahajjud* and the order between them will be dealt with in the book on the devotional recitations.[29]

Seventh: The morning prayer (*ḍuḥā*). Keeping this as a daily observance is among the most emphasized and meritorious of practices. In what has been transmitted, the maximum number of its cycles is eight.

According to Umm Hānīʾ, the sister of ʿAlī b. Abī Ṭālib رَضِيَ ٱللَّهُ عَنْهُ, "The Prophet صَلَّى ٱللَّهُ عَلَيْهِ وَسَلَّمَ prayed eight cycles for the morning prayer (*ḍuḥā*), making each quite long and beautiful," but no other narration mentions this number.[30]

For her part, ʿĀʾisha رَضِيَ ٱللَّهُ عَنْهَا said, "He would pray four cycles for the morning prayer (*ḍuḥā*) and [sometimes] add more, as God willed."[31] [What she said] does not preclude the possibility that it was more. Rather, what he صَلَّى ٱللَّهُ عَلَيْهِ وَسَلَّمَ regularly prayed was four, no less, and possibly more.

And according to a *ḥadīth* that comes by way of a single chain of transmission, the Prophet صَلَّى ٱللَّهُ عَلَيْهِ وَسَلَّمَ prayed the morning prayer (*ḍuḥā*) with six cycles.[32]

---

29 *The Arrangement of the Litanies and the Exposition of the Night Vigil*, book 10 of the *Revival of the Religious Sciences*.

30 Al-Bukhārī, *Ṣaḥīḥ*, 1103; and Muslim, *Ṣaḥīḥ*, 326, mention that they were beautiful and eight in number, but they are described there as "brief." In Ibn Abī Shayba (*al-Muṣannaf*, 7900), it is mentioned that they were long.

31 Muslim, *Ṣaḥīḥ*, 719.

32 Al-Tirmidhī, *al-Shamāʾil*, 289.

As for the time [of the morning prayer (*ḍuḥā*)], it was related by ʿAlī رَضِيَ ٱللَّهُ عَنْهُ that the Prophet صَلَّى ٱللَّهُ عَلَيْهِ وَسَلَّمَ used to pray *ḍuḥā* in six cycles at two times. When the sun had completely risen he would stand and pray two cycles, this being the beginning of the second devotional recitation [of the day] as is explained later.[33] Then, when the sun had grown bright and reached a quarter of the way across the sky in the east, he would pray four [more cycles].[34]

Thus, the first is when the sun has risen the distance of half a lance. The second is when the sun has risen one-quarter of the way, mirroring the [time for] *ʿaṣr*, when there is one-quarter of the day left. So *ẓuhr* is halfway through the day, the morning prayer (*ḍuḥā*) halfway between the rising of the sun and its meridian, and *ʿaṣr* [is] halfway between the sun's meridian and its setting.

In brief, those [two] are the best times [for *ḍuḥā*], but it may be prayed any time from when the sun is up until before the meridian.

Eighth is worship that enlivens the time between the *maghrib* and *ʿishāʾ* prayers. Prayer at this time is a confirmed *sunna*, and the number of its cycles, based on what has been conveyed of the practice of God's Messenger صَلَّى ٱللَّهُ عَلَيْهِ وَسَلَّمَ, is six.[35]

There is great merit in this prayer and some have said that it is what is meant by the words of God عَزَّ وَجَلَّ, *They arise from* [*their*] *beds* [32:16].[36]

And it was reported that [the Prophet صَلَّى ٱللَّهُ عَلَيْهِ وَسَلَّمَ] said, "Whoever prays between *maghrib* and *ʿishāʾ* … that is truly the prayer of those who turn back to God (*awwābīn*)."[37]

He صَلَّى ٱللَّهُ عَلَيْهِ وَسَلَّمَ also said:

> Whoever remains in the mosque between *maghrib* and *ʿishāʾ*, not speaking except in prayer or recitation of the Qurʾān, truly God will build [him] two palaces in heaven, each of them a journey of one hundred years in breadth, and plant a garden

---

33 In the *Arrangement of the Litanies and the Exposition of the Night Vigil*, book 10 of the *Revival of the Religious Sciences*.

34 Al-Tirmidhī, *Sunan*, 598; al-Nasāʾī, *Sunan*, 2:120; Ibn Māja, *Sunan*, 1161.

35 Al-Tirmidhī, *Sunan*, 435; Ibn Māja, *Sunan*, 1167.

36 Abū Dāwūd, *Sunan*, 1321; al-Tirmidhī, *Sunan*, 3196.

37 Ibn al-Mubārak, *Zuhd*, 1259.

> between them so vast that if all the people on earth were to walk in it, it would still totally envelop them.[38]

The rest of its special merits will be mentioned in the book on devotional recitations,[39] God most high willing.

Category 2

Prayers that occur weekly, [that are] associated with the days and nights of the week, for each day and each night

As for the days, we shall begin with Sunday.

Sunday

Abū Hurayra رَضِيَ ٱللَّهُ عَنْهُ related that the Prophet صَلَّى ٱللَّهُ عَلَيْهِ وَسَلَّمَ said,

> Whoever prays four cycles on Sunday, reciting in each the Fātiḥa [1:1–7] and [the verses beginning] *The Messenger believes...* [2:285] to the end of the *sūra* once, God will write good deeds as numerous as all the Christians, men and women on the earth, the recompense of a prophet, [the reward of] the greater and lesser pilgrimages, one thousand supererogatory prayers for each cycle, and a city of the most fragrant musk in heaven for every letter pronounced.[40]

And according to ʿAlī b. Abī Ṭālib رَضِيَ ٱللَّهُ عَنْهُ, the Prophet صَلَّى ٱللَّهُ عَلَيْهِ وَسَلَّمَ said,

> Affirm God's oneness by abundant prayer on Sunday, for He is the One, glorified is He, without partner. For one who prays four cycles after the obligatory and *sunna* prayers on Sunday, reciting in the first the Fātiḥa [1:1–7] followed by Sūrat al-Sajda

38 Ibn Shāhīn, *al-Targhīb*, 75.

39 *The Arrangement of the Litanies and the Exposition of the Night Vigil*, book 10 of the *Revival of the Religious Sciences.*

40 Abū Ṭālib al-Makkī, *Qūt al-qulūb*, 1:52.

> [which begins] [*This is*] *the revelation of the Book* [32:1–30], and in the second, [recites] the Fātiḥa followed by *Blessed is He in whose hand is dominion* [67:1–30], then sits for the testimony and ends with the salutation, then rises and prays two other cycles, reciting in each one the Fātiḥa followed by Sūrat al-Jumuʿa [62:1–11], and then supplicates God for some need, God will certainly fulfill that need.[41]

Monday

Jābir related that the Messenger of God ﷺ said,

> Whoever prays two cycles on Monday when the sun is up, and recites in each cycle the Fātiḥa [1:1–7] once, the verse of the throne [2:255] once, *Say: "He is God,* [*who is*] *One..."* [112:1–4], and the two *sūra*s of seeking refuge [113:1–5, 114:1–6], once each, and then, after the closing salutation, asks God's forgiveness ten times, and invokes blessings on the Prophet ﷺ ten times—God most high will forgive all that person's sins.[42]

And Anas b. Mālik related that the Prophet ﷺ said,

> Whoever prays twelve cycles on Monday, reciting in each the Fātiḥa [1:1–7] and the verse of the throne [2:255] once and then, upon completing [the prayer] recites *Say: "He is God,* [*who is*] *One..."* [112:1–4] twelve times, and asks forgiveness of God twelve times, will be called on the day of resurrection, "Where is so-and-so, the child of so-and-so, the child of so-and-so?" and that person will stand and be recompensed [directly] from God عَزَّوَجَلَّ. The first thing he will be given in recompense is one thousand robes of honor, a crown will be placed on his head, it will be said to him, "Enter the garden!" and one hundred thousand angels will receive him, each one bearing a gift, and they will take him to visit one thousand gleaming palaces of light.[43]

---

41 Abū Ṭālib al-Makkī, *Qūt al-qulūb*, 1:52.

42 Abū Ṭālib al-Makkī, *Qūt al-qulūb*, 1:27.

43 Abū Ṭālib al-Makkī, *Qūt al-qulūb*, 1:27.

Tuesday

Yazīd al-Raqāshī related that according to Anas b. Mālik, the Prophet ﷺ said,

> Whoever prays thirteen cycles on Tuesday toward midday (or in another narration: "when the day has well advanced"), reciting in each cycle the Fātiḥa [1:1–7] and the verse of the throne [2:255] once, and *Say: "He is God,* [*who is*] *One...*" [112:1–4] thrice, no transgression shall be written for him for seventy days. If he dies during that seventy days, he dies a martyr, and the sins of seventy years will be forgiven him.[44]

Wednesday

Abū Idrīs al-Khawlānī related that according to Muʿādh b. Jabal رضي الله عنه, the Messenger of God said,

> Whoever prays twelve cycles on Wednesday once the day is well advanced, reciting in each cycle the Fātiḥa [1:1–7] and the verse of throne [2:255] once, then *Say: "He is God,* [*who is*] *One...*" [112:1–4], three times and the two *sūra*s of seeking refuge three times each, will be called by an angel at the throne, "O servant of God, begin anew your deeds, for your past sins are forgiven." And God most high protects him from the punishment of the grave and its narrowness and darkness, and protects him from the calamities of the resurrection, and the practice that ascends from him this day is the practice of a prophet.[45]

44 Abū Ṭālib al-Makkī, *Qūt al-qulūb*, 1:27.

45 Abū Ṭālib al-Makkī, *Qūt al-qulūb*, 1:27.

Thursday

ʿIkrima related that according to Ibn ʿAbbās, God's Messenger ﷺ said,

> Whoever prays two cycles on Thursday, between the *ẓuhr* and *ʿaṣr* prayers, and in the first recites the Fātiḥa [1:1–7] once and the verse of the throne [2:255] one hundred times, and in the second the Fātiḥa once and *Say: "He is God,* [*who is*] *One..."* [112:1–4], one hundred times, then invokes blessings upon the Prophet ﷺ one hundred times, God will give the reward of one who fasts Rajab, Shaʿbān, and Ramaḍān, and he will have a recompense comparable to making the pilgrimage, and good deeds will be written for him as numerous as all those who believe in God most high and trust in Him.[46]

Friday

It was related by ʿAlī b. Abī Ṭālib رَضِيَ اللَّهُ عَنْهُ that the Prophet ﷺ said,

> All of Friday is a prayer. There is no faithful servant who rises when the sun is above the horizon the distance of a lance or more and makes the ablution and extends the places washed, then prays the morning prayer of praise (*ḍuḥā*) in two cycles, with faith and reckoning [them for God alone], except that God records for him two hundred good deeds accomplished and erases two hundred bad ones. And if this prayer is prayed in four cycles, God سُبْحَانَهُ will raise his station in heaven four hundredfold; and if in eight cycles, God most high will raise it eight hundredfold and forgive him all his sins; and if in twelve cycles, God will record for him two thousand two hundred good deeds accomplished and erase two thousand two

46 Abū Ṭālib al-Makkī, *Qūt al-qulūb*, 1:28.

hundred bad ones and elevate two thousand two hundredfold his station in heaven.[47]

And it was related by Nāfiʿ b. ʿUmar رَضِيَٱللَّهُعَنْهُمَا that the Prophet صَلَّىٱللَّهُعَلَيْهِوَسَلَّمَ said,

> Whoever enters the mosque on Friday and prays four cycles before the congregational prayer, and recites in each one *Praise be to God* [1:1–7] once and *Say: "He is God,* [*who is*] *One..."* [112:1–4] fifty times will not die until he sees his place in heaven or it is seen by another.[48]

Saturday

It was related by Abū Hurayra رَضِيَٱللَّهُعَنْهُ that the Prophet صَلَّىٱللَّهُعَلَيْهِوَسَلَّمَ said,

> Whoever prays four cycles on Saturday and recites in each one the Fātiḥa [1:1–7] once and *Say: "He is God,* [*who is*] *One..."* [112:1–4] thrice, and then, on finishing [the prayer], recites the verse of the throne [2:255], God will write for him the greater and lesser pilgrimage [completed], and raise up for him for every letter the reward of a year of fasting by day and standing in prayer by night (*qiyām al-layl*). For every letter God عَزَّوَجَلَّ will give him the reward of a martyr, and he will be in the shade of [God's] throne with the prophets and martyrs.[49]

---

47 Abū Ṭālib al-Makkī, *Qūt al-qulūb*, 1:28. The first part of this *ḥadīth* can be found in ʿAbd al-Razzāq, *al-Muṣannaf*, 3:204, and Ibn Abī Shayba, *al-Muṣannaf*, 5471.

48 Abū Ṭālib al-Makkī, *Qūt al-qulūb*, 1:28; al-Dāraquṭnī, *Aṭrāf al-gharāʾib*, 295.

49 Abū Ṭālib al-Makkī, *Qūt al-qulūb*, 1:28.

On the nights

The eve of Sunday[50]

Concerning Sunday night, Anas b. Mālik related that the Prophet صَلَّى ٱللَّٰهُ عَلَيْهِ وَسَلَّمَ said,

> Whoever prays twenty cycles and recites in each one *Praise be to God* [1:1–7] once and *Say: "He is God,* [*who is*] *One..."* [112:1–4] fifty times, then the two *sūra*s of seeking refuge [113:1–5, 114:1–6] once each, then asks forgiveness of God for himself one hundred times, and forgiveness of God for his parents one hundred times, then invokes blessings on the Prophet صَلَّى ٱللَّٰهُ عَلَيْهِ وَسَلَّمَ one hundred times, and disavows his own strength and power,[51] then seeks refuge in God,[52] and then says, "I bear witness that there is no god but God, and I bear witness that Adam is God's chosen and His pure creation, and Abraham is God's dear friend, and Moses is he to whom God spoke directly, and Jesus is God's spirit, and Muḥammad is God's beloved,"—for that person will be a recompense as vast as all those who claim that God has a son and all those who claim that God has no son, and God عَزَّ وَجَلَّ will raise him up on the day of resurrection among those who are safe, and will place him in heaven among the prophets.[53]

---

50 Muslims traditionally consider that the day begins with the sunset of the night before, as indicated in the translation by the use of the word "eve." So the "eve of Sunday" is Saturday night at sunset.

51 That is, by invoking the formula "There is no strength nor power but through God" (lā ḥawla wa-lā quwwata illā bi-llāh). Al-Zabīdī, *Itḥāf*, 3:378.

52 Saying, "I seek refuge in God from Satan, the accursed" (aʿūdhu bi-llāhi min al-shayṭān al-rajīm). Al-Zabīdī, *Itḥāf*, 3:378.

53 Abū Ṭālib al-Makkī, *Qūt al-qulūb*, 1:28.

The eve of Monday

Al-Aʿmash related that, according to Anas, the Prophet ﷺ said,

> Whoever prays four cycles on the eve of Monday and recites in the first, *Praise be to God* [1:1–7] once, and *Say, "He is God, [who is] One"* [112:1–4] ten times, and in the second, *Praise be to God* once, then *Say, "He is God, [who is] One"* twenty times, and in the third, *Praise be to God* once, and *Say, "He is God, [who is] One"* thirty times, and in the fourth, *Praise be to God* once, and *Say, "He is God, [who is] One"* forty times—then ends the prayer with the closing salutation, and recites *Say, "He is God, [who is] One"* seventy-five times and asks forgiveness for himself and his parents seventy-five times, and then supplicates God for what he needs, God will certainly give the supplicant what he asks.

This is called the "prayer of need."[54]

The eve of Tuesday

Whoever prays two cycles and recites in each one the Fātiḥa [1:1–7 once], then *Say, "He is God, [who is] One"* [112:1–4], and the two *sūra*s of taking refuge fifteen times each, and then, after the closing salutation, recites the verse of the throne fifteen times, and asks forgiveness from God most high fifteen times, will have an immense reward and a grand recompense.[55]

And ʿUmar رضي الله عنه related that the Prophet ﷺ said,

> Whoever prays two cycles on the eve of Tuesday, reciting in each one the Fātiḥa [1:1–7] once, then *Indeed, We sent the Qurʾān down* [97:1–5] and *Say, "He is God, [who is] One"* [112:1–4] seven times each, God will deliver [him] from the fire and [that prayer] will be his leader on the day of resurrection and guide him into heaven.

---

54 Abū Ṭālib al-Makkī, *Qūt al-qulūb*, 1:28.

55 Abū Ṭālib al-Makkī, *Qūt al-qulūb*, 1:29.

The eve of Wednesday

Fāṭima رَضِيَ ٱللَّهُ عَنْهَا related that the Prophet صَلَّى ٱللَّهُ عَلَيْهِ وَسَلَّمَ said,

> Whoever prays four cycles on the eve of Wednesday, reciting in the first the Fātiḥa [1:1–7] once, and *Say, "I seek refuge in the Lord of daybreak...* [113:1–5] ten times, and in the second the Fātiḥa once, and *Say, "I seek refuge in the Lord of mankind ...* [114:1–6] ten times, and then, after [finishing the prayer with] the closing salutation, asks forgiveness from God ten times and invokes blessings on Muḥammad صَلَّى ٱللَّهُ عَلَيْهِ وَسَلَّمَ ten times, seventy-thousand angels will descend from every heaven to record his reward until the day of resurrection.[56]

And in another *ḥadīth*,

> [Whoever prays] sixteen cycles, then recites after the Fātiḥa [1:1–7] whatever God wills, and in the last two cycles [recites] the verse of the throne [2:255] thirty times, and in the first two cycles *Say, "He is God, [who is] One"* [112:1–4]. [Whoever prays this] will be granted intercession for ten members of his household destined for the fire.

And Fāṭima رَضِيَ ٱللَّهُ عَنْهَا is reported to have said, God's Messenger صَلَّى ٱللَّهُ عَلَيْهِ وَسَلَّمَ said,

> Whoever prays six cycles in pairs on the eve of Wednesday and recites in each one, following the Fātiḥa [1:1–7], *Say, "O God, Owner of Sovereignty, You give sovereignty to whom You will and You take sovereignty away from whom You will. You honor whom You will and You humble whom You will. In Your hand is [all] good. Indeed, You are over all things competent"* [3:26], and then, on finishing the prayer [petitions God] seventy times saying: "May God reward Muḥammad on our behalf what he merits," God will forgive the sins of seventy years and record for him protection from the fire.[57]

---

56 Abū Ṭālib al-Makkī, *Qūt al-qulūb*, 1:29.

57 Abū Ṭālib al-Makkī, *Qūt al-qulūb*, 1:29.

The eve of Thursday

Abū Hurayra رَضِيَ ٱللَّٰهُ عَنْهُ said that the Prophet صَلَّى ٱللَّٰهُ عَلَيْهِ وَسَلَّمَ said,

> Whoever prays ten cycles on the eve of Thursday between the *maghrib* and *ʿishāʾ* prayers, and recites in each one the Fātiḥa [1:1–7], the verse of the throne [2:255] five times, and *Say, "He is God,* [*who is*] *One"* [112:1–4] five times, and then, on completing the prayer, asks forgiveness from God fifteen times, and asks that the recompense [of this practice] be granted his parents, has fulfilled the right of his parents on him even if he had been recalcitrant toward them, and God will give him what is given to the veracious (*ṣiddiqīn*) and the martyrs.[58]

The eve of Friday

Jābir said,

> The Messenger of God صَلَّى ٱللَّٰهُ عَلَيْهِ وَسَلَّمَ said, whoever prays twelve cycles on the eve of Friday between the *maghrib* and *ʿishāʾ* prayers, reciting in each one the Fātiḥa [1:1–7] once, followed by *Say, "He is God,* [*who is*] *One"* [112:1–4] eleven times, it is comparable to having worshiped God most high for twelve years, fasting by day and standing in prayer by night (*qiyām al-layl*).[59]

And Anas said, the Prophet صَلَّى ٱللَّٰهُ عَلَيْهِ وَسَلَّمَ said,

> Whoever prays the *ʿishāʾ* prayer on the eve of Friday in congregation, and then follows it with the *sunna* of two cycles, and ten cycles after that, reciting in each one *Praise be to God* [1:1–7] and then *Say, "He is God,* [*who is*] *One"* [112:1–4] and the two *sūra*s of seeking refuge [113:1–5 and 114:1–6] once each, and then prays *witr*, and sleeps on his right side facing

---

58 Abū Ṭālib al-Makkī, *Qūt al-qulūb*, 1:29. Al-Zabīdī, *Itḥāf* (2:377) indicates that this saying is also recorded in al-Daylamī, *Musnad al-firdaws*, but we were unable to find it in that work.

59 Abū Ṭālib al-Makkī, *Qūt al-qulūb*, 1:29.

the *qibla*, it is as if he had kept a vigil on the night of power.[60]

And the Prophet ﷺ said, "Increase [the number of your] blessings on me on the glowing night and the dazzling day," [by which he meant] the eve and day of Friday.[61]

The eve of Saturday

Anas said, God's Messenger ﷺ said,

> For whoever prays twelve cycles on the eve of Saturday between the *maghrib* and *ʿishāʾ* prayers, a palace in heaven has been built [for him], and it is as if he had given charity to every faithful man and woman, had become free of Judaism, and it is God's duty to forgive him.[62]

Category 3
Prayers that reoccur yearly

The [prayers that reoccur yearly] are four in number: The prayers of the two feasts, *tarāwīḥ* [in Ramaḍān], the prayer of Rajab, and the prayer at mid-Shaʿbān.

First, the prayer for the two feasts (*ʿīdayn*). These are confirmed *sunna* practices and among the sacred signs of the *dīn*. Concerning them, there are seven matters to be observed.

The first is the *takbīr* recited in threes: "God is greater, God is greater, God is truly greater! Praise be to God in abundance! Glory be to God early and late. There is no deity but God, One, without partner, our *dīn* is wholly for Him, though the disbelievers are averse."[63]

---

60 Abū Ṭālib al-Makkī, *Qūt al-qulūb*, 1:29.

61 Ibn ʿAsākir, *Tārīkh madīnat Dimashq*, 53:309, and al-Bayhaqī, *al-Sunan al-kubrā*, 3:249, with wording similar to this.

62 Abū Ṭālib al-Makkī, *Qūt al-qulūb*, 1:29.

63 'Allāhu akbar, Allāhu akbar, Allāhu akbar kabīran, wa-l-ḥamdu li-llāhi kathīran, wa-subḥān Allāhi bukratan wa-aṣīla; lā ilāha illā-llāhu waḥdahu lā sharīka lahu,

The time [for invocation with] this *takbīr* begins on the eve of the feast of breaking the fast of Ramaḍān [and lasts] until the beginning of the prayer. For the greater feast, it begins after the morning of the day of ʿArafat [and lasts] until the end of the day on the thirteenth [according to] the most complete sayings recorded. This *takbīr* is repeated after the obligatory prayers and [according to some,] after the supererogatory ones as well, but after the obligatory [only] is more strongly confirmed.

The second observance is to rise on the day of the feasts, and bathe and then put on one's best clothes and fragrance, just as we have mentioned for the Friday prayer. For men, a cloak and turban are best. Boys should avoid wearing silk and elderly women should avoid excessive adornment when they go out [to the prayer].

The third observance is to leave [for the prayer] by one route, but to take another returning home, which is what the Prophet ﷺ did.[64] He also commanded that unmarried maidens and women who wear veils come out for the prayer.[65]

Fourth is that it is preferred [to pray this] outside [a mosque], in the desert, except in Mecca and the sacred house [Jerusalem]. If it is a rainy day, however, there is no harm in praying it inside the mosque, and even on a clear day, the *imām* may appoint someone to lead the prayer in a mosque for those too weak [to go out], and [the *imām* can] go with the stronger ones [to the place of prayer], invoking the *takbīr* along the way.

The fifth observance concerns the time. The time for the prayer of the feast day is between sunrise and noon, while the time for the sacrifice starts whenever the sun is fully up and there is time to pray the two cycles and give the twofold sermon [and this time lasts] until the end of the thirteenth day [of the month of Dhū l-Ḥijja].

It is preferable for the prayer of the greater feast to be made as early as possible because of the sacrifice and to delay the prayer of ending the fast [of Ramaḍān] in order to give people enough time to pay the obligatory alms due [at the end of Ramaḍān] before the

---

mukhliṣīna lahu al-dīn, wa-law kariha al-kāfirūn.'

64 Al-Bukhārī, *Ṣaḥīḥ*, 986.

65 Al-Bukhārī, *Ṣaḥīḥ*, 324; Muslim, *Ṣaḥīḥ*, 890.

prayer. This is the *sunna* of God's Messenger ﷺ.[66]

Sixth is the manner of these prayers. People should go out [toward the place of prayer] repeating the *takbīr*, and when the *imām* arrives there, he should neither sit nor pray any supererogatory prayers, even while the people may do so. Then a caller should say, "The prayer is in congregation!" (*al-ṣalātu jāmiʿatun*); the *imām* then leads them in two cycles. In the first, he pronounces the *takbīr*—in addition to the one in the opening and the one preceding the cycle—seven times. Between each two utterances, he says, "Glory be to God, praise be to God, there is no deity but God, God is greater!" and just after the opening *takbīr* he says, *Indeed, I have turned my face toward He who created the heavens and the earth* [6:79] and delays pronouncing the [formula of] seeking refuge until after he has uttered the eighth *takbīr*. Then, after the Fātiḥa [1:1–7], he recites Sūra Qāf [50:1–45] for the first cycle and *The hour has come near* [54:1–55] in the second. [Before starting the second recitation] there are five additional *takbīr*s, not including the one pronounced on standing up [from prostration] nor the one pronounced [to signal] the bowing. Between each two, he should say what we have mentioned above.

[On finishing the prayer], he should give two sermons, sitting down [briefly] between them. And if someone misses the prayer of [either] feast, he may make it up.

Seventh is to sacrifice a ram. The Messenger of God ﷺ sacrificed two very fine rams and did so with his own hands, saying "In the name of God, God is greater. This is for me and for any in my community who are not making the sacrifice."[67]

He ﷺ [also] said, "One who sees the crescent moon of Dhū l-Ḥijja and intends to offer a sacrifice should stop cutting his hair or nails."[68]

Abū Ayyūb al-Anṣārī said, "There was a man in the time of God's Messenger ﷺ who used to sacrifice a ewe for the people of his household and they would eat it and feed others from it."[69]

---

66 Al-Shāfiʿī, *al-Umm*, 2:489; al-Bayhaqī, *al-Sunan al-kubrā*, 3:282.

67 Abū Dāwūd, *Sunan*, 2810; al-Tirmidhī, *Sunan*, 1521.

68 Muslim, *Ṣaḥīḥ*, 1977.

69 Al-Tirmidhī, *Sunan*, 1505; Ibn Māja, *Sunan*, 3147. The preferred sacrifice is a ram.

One may eat from the sacrifice for three days. [Eating the meat] for longer than three days was at first prohibited, but then permitted.[70]

Sufyān al-Thawrī said, "It is preferable to pray twelve cycles after the feast at the end of Ramaḍān and six after the feast of the sacrifice." And he added, "It is part of the *sunna*."[71]

Second are the *tarāwīḥ*.[72] These consist of twenty cycles and the manner of praying them is well-known. They are considered a confirmed *sunna* practice, though not as much as the prayers of the two feasts, and there is a difference of opinion as to whether it is better to pray them in congregation or individually.

The Messenger of God went out [of his room] to pray them in congregation on two or three nights and then did not go out again, saying, "I fear they will be made obligatory on you."[73]

ʿUmar رَضِيَ اللَّهُ عَنْهُ, however, did gather people to pray them in congregation, since revelation had ceased and there was no chance they would become obligatory. It is said that praying them in congregation is better. This is what ʿUmar رَضِيَ اللَّهُ عَنْهُ did and in congregation there is a special merit and blessing—just as there is for the obligatory prayers. Also, one may feel lazy alone but be strengthened by the presence of others.[74]

And it is said that praying them individually is better since, while they are a *sunna*, they are not among the major rites like the prayers for the two feasts. They should, therefore, be considered [on the level] of the morning prayer (*ḍuḥā*) or, [the prayer] of greeting the mosque, neither of which were made congregational by law. No matter how common it is for a group of people to enter the mosque together, they would never pray [the greeting of the mosque] in congregation. In addition, there is the saying of the Prophet صَلَّى اللَّهُ عَلَيْهِ وَسَلَّمَ, "The superiority of voluntary prayer at home to [prayer] in the mosque is like the superiority of an obligatory prayer in the mosque to one at home."[75]

70 Muslim, *Ṣaḥīḥ*, 977.

71 Ibn Abī Shayba, *al-Muṣannaf*, 5799.

72 The supererogatory prayers after the *ʿishāʾ* prayer in Ramaḍān.

73 Al-Bukhārī, *Ṣaḥīḥ*, 924; Muslim, *Ṣaḥīḥ*, 761.

74 Al-Bukhārī, *Ṣaḥīḥ*, 2010.

75 Al-Ṭabarānī, *al-Muʿjam al-kabīr*, 8:46. A *ḥadīth* that expresses the same idea can be found in al-Bukhārī, *Ṣaḥīḥ*, 731, and Muslim, *Ṣaḥīḥ*, 781.

It has [also] been related that he said,

> One prayer in my mosque [in Medina] is better than one hundred [prayers] in other mosques, and one prayer in the sacred mosque [of Mecca] is better than one thousand [prayers] in my mosque—and better than all that is a prayer of two cycles by a man in the corner of his room, which no one knows about except God عَزَّوَجَلَّ.[76]

This is because in doing so, he is safe from the affectation and desire to be seen that might touch someone in congregation. This is what has been said concerning [praying alone].

[The *tarāwīḥ* are] best, however, in congregation.[77] Such was the view of ʿUmar رَضِيَٱللَّهُعَنْهُ and certain supererogatory prayers were made congregational by law, and this prayer warrants being among the principle rites that are apparent.

As for [the question of] wishing to be seen in congregation and feeling lazy when alone, this amounts to saying, "Praying is better than not praying because of laziness and doing so with sincerity is better than doing so in order to be seen."

The view, then, turns between the blessing of the congregation [on one hand] and increasing the strength of one's sincerity and presence of heart when alone. So it is permissable to have some hesitation in weighing the merits of one of them over the other.

Also among the preferred practices is to recite the *qunūt* supplication in the *witr* prayers in the last half of the month of Ramaḍān.

As for the prayer of Rajab, it has been related in a chain of transmission back to the Messenger of God صَلَّىٱللَّهُعَلَيْهِوَسَلَّمَ that he said,

> Whoever fasts on the first Thursday of Rajab, and then, between *maghrib* and *ʿishāʾ*, prays twelve cycles, with a salutation between every two of them; and recites in each the Fātiḥa [1:1–7] once; then *Indeed, We sent the Qurʾān down during the night of decree* [97:1–5] three times; and *Say, "He is God, [who is] One"* [112:1–4]

76 Al-Mundhirī, *al-Targhīb wa-l-tarhīb*, 1:484. The last part of this saying ("One prayer in the sacred mosque...") is recorded in Ibn Abī Shayba, *al-Muṣannaf*, 7716.

77 Al-Nawawī says, "For us, the correct view is that praying the supererogatory prayers in Ramaḍān in congregation is more excellent than alone, and this is also the view of the majority of the scholars..." *al-Majmuʿ*, 4:40.

> twelve times; then, on completing his prayer, he invokes blessings on me seventy times, saying "O God bless Muḥammad, the unlettered Prophet, and bless his people"; then he prostrates, and says in his prostration, seventy times, "glorified and holy, Lord of the angels and the spirit";[78] and then he rises from his prostration and says, "O Lord forgive me and have mercy on me and excuse [my faults] which You know. You are truly the most mighty and kind." He then prostrates a second time and says the same as he said in the first; and then, in prostration, [he] supplicates God for what he needs and it will be provided.

About this prayer, the Prophet ﷺ said,

> Whoever prays this prayer, God will forgive his sins though they be as countless as the bubbles of foam on the sea, the grains of sand, the weight of mountains, and the leaves on the trees, and he will be granted intercession for seven hundred of his household destined for the fire.

This prayer, too, is a preferred practice, and we mention it in this section because it is a yearly prayer, even while its degree, because it was conveyed by a single chain of transmission, is much lower than that of the *tarāwīḥ* [in Ramaḍān] and the prayers of the two feasts. Still, I saw all the people of Jerusalem pray it as a regular practice and they did not excuse its being missed, so I wanted to include it.[79]

The prayer of Shaʿbān: On the eve of the fifteenth of Shaʿbān, one prays one hundred cycles, with salutations between each two, reciting in each cycle the Fātiḥa [1:1–7] followed by *Say, "He is God, [who is] One"* [112:1–4]. If he prefers, it may [also be] in ten cycles, reciting in each one the Fātiḥa one time and then *Say, "He is God, [who is] One"* one hundred times.

This [form, in fact,] has been recorded about a number of [supererogatory] prayers. The early Muslims used to pray this and

---

78 'Subbūḥun quddūsun, rabbu al-malāʾikati wa-l-rūḥ.'

79 There is considerable disagreement about whether there is textual evidence for this prayer; al-Zabīdī, after citing various views, concludes, "This prayer is among the purely voluntary supererogatory prayers; whoever wishes to pray it, let him do so, and whoever does not, let him leave it." Al-Zabīdī, *Itḥāf*, 3:424. That is, he distinguishes it from the *tarāwīḥ*, which is supported by stronger *ḥadīth*.

call it the "prayer of goodness." They would gather to pray it, maybe even in congregation. It has been related that Ḥasan said, "Thirty of the Companions of the Prophet صَلَّى ٱللَّٰهُ عَلَيْهِ وَسَلَّمَ told me that anyone who prays this prayer on this night, God will look on seventy times, and with each look will fulfill seventy of his needs, the least of which is forgiveness."[80]

Category 4
Supererogatory prayers related to events, not times

These are nine in number [and include the following].

The prayer during a solar eclipse; the prayer during a lunar eclipse; the prayer for rain; the prayer of greeting [i.e., on entering] a mosque; the two cycles between the call to prayer (*adhan*) and the call to begin [the prayer] (*iqāma*); the two cycles on leaving the house and returning to it; and some others like these. We speak of those which occur to us at present.

The first is the prayer during an eclipse. The Messenger of God صَلَّى ٱللَّٰهُ عَلَيْهِ وَسَلَّمَ said,

> The sun and the moon are two of God's signs. They do not eclipse because of someone's death or someone's life. If you see this happen, seek refuge in the remembrance of God and in the prayer. He said this after his son, Abraham, passed away, and there was a solar eclipse, and the people began to say that it was because of his death.[81]

On the manner and time [of this prayer]

As for the manner: If there is a solar eclipse, regardless of whether or not it occurs at a time disapproved of for [supererogatory] prayer, a call is made, saying, "The prayer is in congregation" and the *imām*

---

80 Abū Ṭālib al-Makkī, *Qūt al-qulūb*, 1:62.

81 Al-Bukhārī, *Ṣaḥīḥ*, 1043; Muslim, *Ṣaḥīḥ*, 904.

should lead the people in a prayer of two cycles in the mosque. In each of these, there should be two [actual] bowings, the first of which is longer than the second.[82] Furthermore, the recitation should not be [made] aloud. Standing before the first cycle, he should recite the Fātiḥa [1:1–7] and then Sūrat al-Baqara [2:1–286], before the second [bowing specific to this prayer], the Fātiḥa [1:1–7] and Sūrat Āli ʿImrān [3:1–200], before the third [in the second cycle], the Fātiḥa and Sūrat al-Nisāʾ [4:1–176], and before the fourth [also in the second cycle], the Fātiḥa and Sūrat al-Māʾida [5:1–120]. [If he is unable to do this well], then let him recite passages of the same length from whatever part of the Qurʾān he wishes.

If he recites only the Fātiḥa in each standing, that is rewarded, and if he recites only short *sūra*s, that, too, is acceptable, but the object is to make the prayer long enough so as to last until the eclipse has passed.

In the first cycle, [the *imām* and worshipers] invoke the glorification for as long as it takes to recite one hundred verses of the Qurʾān;[83] in the second cycle, the time it takes to recite eighty; in the third, seventy; and in the fourth, fifty. The prostrations should be equal in length to the cycles.

Then, following the prayer, the *imām* should give two sermons, sitting down briefly between them; [these should] urge people to give in charity, free slaves, and repent.

This is also how the prayer for a lunar eclipse should be prayed, except that since these are at night, the recitation should be aloud.

Concerning its time: [this prayer] should begin with the beginning of the eclipse and last until it has passed or—in the case of a solar eclipse—until the sun has set. The time of the prayer for a lunar eclipse, by contrast, ends when the disk of the sun appears inasmuch as it annuls the dominion of the night. It does not end, however, with the setting of the eclipsed moon, for the night in its

---

82 Throughout this translation, we have used the word "cycle" to translate *rakʿa*, meaning a complete cycle of the prayer including standing, bowing (*rukūʿ*), and prostrating. The eclipse prayer, however, has an unusual feature, there are two bowings (*rukuʿayn*) in each cycle.

83 The commentary specifies "for as long it takes to recite one hundred verses… from Sūrat al-Baqara." Al-Zabīdī, *Itḥāf*, 3:428.

totality dominates the moon. And if the moon appears, the prayer should be ended soon. If someone does not join the prayer until the *imām* is bowing for the second time, he has missed that cycle, since the first bowing is what is part of the original [form of the] prayer.

Second is the prayer for rain. When the rivers run dry, the rains cease, or a canal crumbles, it is a preferred practice for the *imām* to instruct the people first to fast for three days, give as much in charity as they can, abandon wrongdoing, and repent from their transgressions. Then, on the fourth day, he should go outside [the city walls] with the people, including the elderly and children, all of whom have bathed, and put on simple and humble garments, and behave in a lowly demeanor, which is to say the opposite [of how they would behave] for the [prayer of the] feast day.

It is said that it is good to bring animals out as well, for they share in the need, even as the Prophet ﷺ said, "Were it not for the nursing babies, the elders bent with age, and the grazing cattle, punishment would rain down on you in torrents."[84]

And if there are non-Muslims under Muslim protection and distinct in their appearance who wish to come out [to the prayer] as well, they should not be prevented.

Then, when all are gathered in a vast outdoor space for prayer (*muṣalla*), a call is made saying, "The prayer is in congregation." The *imām* then prays two cycles in exactly the same manner as for the prayers of the two feasts, followed by two sermons, in which he mostly asks forgiveness,[85] with a brief seated period between the two. Then, in the middle of the second sermon, he should turn his back toward the people, face the *qibla*, and reverse his cloak to symbolize reversing the circumstance [that people are in], even as the Messenger of God ﷺ did,[86] inside out, top to bottom, right to left, and the people should do the same, and at this time all of them should supplicate God silently.

---

84 Al-Ṭabarānī, *al-Muʿjam al-kabīr*, 22:309; al-Bayhaqī, *al-Sunan al-kubrā*, 3:345, with similar wording.

85 That is, asking forgiveness should take the place of the *takbīr* in the sermons of the feast prayers.

86 Al-Bukhārī, *Ṣaḥīḥ*, 1023; Muslim, *Ṣaḥīḥ*, 894.

After this, the *imām* should turn back in their direction and complete the second sermon, but all should leave their cloaks reversed [for the rest of the day].

In the supplication, it is recommended to say,

> O God, You have commanded us to call on You and have promised us an answer, and we have called on You as You have commanded, so answer our prayers as You have promised. O God, grant us forgiveness for the transgressions we have done, and answer our supplications by sending us the water we seek, and the provision that suffices.[87]

There is nothing wrong with also adding supplications for rain following the [obligatory prayers] three days before going out to perform the prayer for rain. For this supplication, too, there are correct manners and internal conditions, such as repentance, the restitution of property or rights wrongfully taken, and others that are mentioned in the book of invocations and supplications.[88]

Third is the funeral prayer, and its form is well-known. The most inclusive supplication [to be said at this time] is what is recorded in the authentic collection on the authority of ʿAwf b. Mālik, who said,

> I saw God's Messenger صَلَّىٱللَّهُعَلَيْهِوَسَلَّمَ pray the funeral prayer and I memorized from his supplication these words: O God forgive him, have mercy on him, pardon him and excuse his sins, ennoble his resting place, make his entrance vast, wash him clean with water, snow, and hail, cleanse him as clean of his sins as a pure white cloth is clean of stain, exchange his worldly abode for one that is better, and his people for those who are better, and his mate for one that is better. Bring him into heaven, and deliver him from the torment of the grave and the torment of the fire.

ʿAwf added, "[when I heard him make this supplication], I wished I had been the one departed!"[89]

87 This supplication is recorded in al-Shāfiʿī, *al-Umm*, 2:546.

88 *Invocations and Supplications*, book 9 of the *Revival of the Religious Sciences*.

89 Muslim, *Ṣaḥīḥ*, 973.

If someone does not join the funeral prayer until the second *takbīr*, he should follow the remaining [elements in] order, pronouncing the *takbīr* with those of the *imām*, and then, when the *imām* pronounces the closing salutation, [the latecomer] should make up the *takbīr* he missed as would one joining [an obligatory prayer] late.[90] This [is correct], for had he tried to rush ahead in pronouncing the missed utterance of the *takbīr*, there would no longer remain any meaning to his following [the *imām*]. Pronouncing the *takbīrāt* is among the outward pillars [of this prayer] and is important enough to take the place of the bowing in other prayers. This is the aspect [of this question] I know and it is possible that there are others.

The narrations recorded about the merits of the funeral prayer and accompanying the funeral procession [to the cemetery] are well known and so we will not spend time recounting them here. How can its merit not be great when it is considered a collective obligation.[91] It is only supererogatory when it is not an individual obligation because others have fulfilled the obligation.[92] By praying it, one attains the merit of a collective obligation. And if it is not an individual obligation, it is because those who undertake to fulfill it collectively remove the burden from others. Thus, it is unlike all other supererogatory prayers, since no other [supererogatory prayer] can remove the responsibility of an obligatory prayer.

It is preferred to seek a large congregation [for this prayer], for the blessing of many who care and [make] supplications and also because it makes it more likely that someone whose prayers are answered will be included among them, in accordance with what Kurayb narrated from Ibn ʿAbbās.

When his son died, he said, "O Kurayb, see how many people have gathered [for the prayer]." Kurayb said, "So I went out and saw that many had assembled, and I told him this." He asked, "Do

---

90 The funeral prayer has no bowing or prostrating, only recitation of the Fātiḥa [1:1–7], invocation of blessings on the Prophet ﷺ, and two supplications of forgiveness, recited silently while standing. Between each of these four elements, the *imām* pronounces the *takbīr* aloud.

91 *Farḍ kifāya* is a legal category which describes worship that, if completed by some members of the community, suffices for the whole community.

92 Although the text makes no mention of how many must be present, the commentary says there are various views ranging from one person to four.

they number forty?" I answered, "Yes." And he said, "Then take him out, for I heard God's Messenger ﷺ say, 'When a Muslim man dies and forty men who associate none with God تعالى pray the funeral prayer for him, God عزوجل will grant them intercession [on the day of judgment] on his behalf.'"[93]

When someone accompanies a funeral procession and reaches the cemetery or enters it, let him begin by saying, "Peace be on you, O people of these abodes, the faithful, the Muslims, may God have mercy on those of us who have gone ahead and those of us who are coming later, for, God willing, we will be meeting you!"[94]

It is also preferred that none leave until the one who has passed away is buried. Then, when the earth is filled in over the departed, one should stand near the grave and say,

> O God, Your servant has been returned to You. Pardon him and have mercy on him. O God, draw the earth away from his sides, open the gates of heaven to his spirit, and accept him with a beautiful acceptance. If he was among those who did good, multiply for him the goodness he did, and if he was a wrongdoer, excuse him his faults.[95]

Fourth is the prayer of greeting the mosque, which is at least two cycles. These are considered an affirmed *sunna* so strong that they are not to be omitted even if the *imām* is giving the sermon on Friday, and the obligation to listen to it is verified.

But if, as soon as he enters the mosque, he prays the obligatory prayer, or makes up a prayer he missed, then the prayer of greeting is considered done and its reward will come to him. It is essential that when one enters the mosque, the first thing one does is worship that is particular to the mosque, out of respect for it. For this reason, entering the mosque without the ablution is disapproved of, and if he enters just to pass through it or sit down, let him say four times, "Glory be to God, praise be to God, there is no deity but God, God

---

93 Muslim, *Ṣaḥīḥ*, 948. The words, "Then take him out," mean "Take his shrouded body out to where the prayer will be held."

94 Muslim, *Ṣaḥīḥ*, 974. ('Al-salāmu ʿalaykum ʿalā ahli al-diyār, min al-muʾminīna wa-l-muslimīn, wa-yarḥamu Allāhu al-mustaqdimīn minnā wa-l-mustaʾkhirīn, wa-innā in shāʾ Allāhu bi-kum lāḥiqūn.')

95 Ibn Abī Shayba, *al-Muṣannaf*, 11827.

is greater." It has been said that this is equal in merit to praying two cycles.[96]

In the teachings of al-Shāfiʿī, رَحِمَهُ ٱللَّهُ, it is not disapproved of to pray the prayer of greeting the mosque at times normally disapproved of for prayer, which are after ʿ*aṣr*, after *fajr*, at the time of the sun's meridian, at sunrise, and at sunset. This is because it has been recorded that the Prophet صَلَّى ٱللَّهُ عَلَيْهِ وَسَلَّمَ prayed two cycles after ʿ*aṣr*, and when it was said to him, "Did you not prohibit us from doing this?" he answered, "These were two cycles I usually pray after *ẓuhr*, but I was too busy with a visiting delegation to pray them."[97] This *ḥadīth* contains two benefits.

One is that the disapproval is limited to a prayer that has no reason [at that time], and among the weakest of these reasons would be to make up a supererogatory prayer. This is because scholars disagree about [whether] supererogatory prayers can be made up. And if a person completes an act like the one that was missed, is it indeed made up? So if disapproval may be overridden by the weakest reason, then it is more true that it is overridden on entering the mosque, which is a strong reason. Thus, it is not disapproved of to pray the funeral prayer whenever it must be done, nor the prayer for an eclipse, nor the prayer for rain, at these times, for all of them have a reason.

The second benefit concerns the question of making up a supererogatory prayer, for the Messenger of God صَلَّى ٱللَّهُ عَلَيْهِ وَسَلَّمَ made up this prayer, and he is our most beautiful model. In addition, ʿĀʾisha رَضِيَ ٱللَّهُ عَنْهَا said, "When the Messenger of God صَلَّى ٱللَّهُ عَلَيْهِ وَسَلَّمَ was not able to rise to worship in the night [*qiyām al-layl*] because of sleep or illness, he prayed twelve cycles by day."[98]

Thus, too, the scholars say, "If someone is praying and misses responding to the call of the muezzin, when he pronounces the closing salutation, let him [utter the responses to the call] then, even if the muezzin has finished." So with this in mind, the words of someone who says, "This is not making something up, this is doing it for the first time" do not make sense. If such were the case,

96 Abū Ṭālib al-Makkī, *Qūt al-qulūb*, 1:23.

97 Al-Bukhārī, *Ṣaḥīḥ*, 1233; Muslim, *Ṣaḥīḥ*, 834.

98 Muslim, *Ṣaḥīḥ*, 746.

then the Prophet ﷺ would not have prayed at a time which is normally disapproved of for supererogatory prayer.

Indeed, anyone who has a regular devotional litany (*wird*) and is prevented from reciting it for some reason, should not, therefore, grant himself license to omit it. Rather, he should make it up at some other time so that his soul does not incline toward ease and comfort. Goodness will come to him for striving against his lower self, and the Prophet ﷺ said, "The most beloved practice to God most high is what is done with consistency, even if it is small."[99] So, in making up a supererogatory practice, his goal should be to not break the consistency of that practice.

It was narrated by ʿĀʾisha رضي الله عنها that the Prophet ﷺ said, "God is angered by someone who worships Him through some form of devotion and then gives it up out of laziness."[100] Let him beware, then, not to be among those to whom this threat applies. This narration confirms that a servant who abandons some worship out of laziness becomes repugnant to God, and also that, had God not been angry with him and had the servant not grown distant from God, laziness would not have overcome him.

Fifth are the two cycles after the ablution. These are recommended inasmuch as the ablution is a means of drawing near to God, its purpose being the prayer, while those occurrences which void the ablution are obstacles. And it may be that [what breaks the ablution] occurs before a prayer, and the effort to make the ablution is wasted. To hasten, then, to pray two cycles fulfills the purpose of the ablution before it is lost. [The merit of this practice is also] known from a *ḥadīth* [narrated by] Bilāl, in which the Prophet ﷺ [is reported to have] said, "I entered heaven and saw Bilāl there, so I asked him, 'How did you get here before me?' He answered, 'I know of nothing except that I never made the ablution without then praying two cycles,'"[101] or words similar to this.

Sixth is two cycles on entering the home and on leaving it. According to Abū Salma, Abū Hurayra رضي الله عنه said, "The Messenger

99 Al-Bukhārī, *Ṣaḥīḥ*, 6464; Muslim, *Ṣaḥīḥ*, 782.

100 Abū Ṭālib al-Makkī, *Qūt al-qulūb*, 1:22, 1:84, with slightly different wording.

101 Al-Tirmidhī, *Sunan*, 3689, and with a similar meaning in al-Bukhārī, *Ṣaḥīḥ*, 1149; and Muslim, *Ṣaḥīḥ*, 2458.

of God ﷺ said, 'Before you leave your home, pray two cycles to keep you from an evil exit, and when you enter your home, pray two cycles to keep you from an evil entrance."[102]

This indicates that every significant event should begin this way [with prayer]. Thus, when one dons the pilgrim's garb (*iḥrām*),[103] or starts a journey,[104] or returns from one and enters the mosque before the home, one should pray two cycles.[105] All this has been recorded as what the Messenger of God ﷺ did. One of the saintly even prayed two cycles whenever he ate a meal, or drank a drink—for everything that happened [in his life].

The beginnings of all matters should be blessed by the remembrance of God عَزَّوَجَلَّ, and these may be of three orders.

[First,] things which are often repeated, like eating and drinking, should begin with, "In the name of God عَزَّوَجَلَّ," even as the Prophet ﷺ said, "Any important matter that does not begin with 'In the name of God, the Merciful and Compassionate' is cut off."[106]

Second are those things that are not frequent, but carry great import, such contracting a marriage, or giving counsel. For such matters as these, it is preferable to begin by praising God, the glorified. One should say, for example, "Praise be to God and may blessings be on the Messenger of God ﷺ. I am marrying you to my daughter," and the one who accepts her should say, "Praise be to God and may blessings be on the Messenger of God. I accept this marriage."[107]

It was also the habit of the Companions رَضِيَٱللَّهُعَنْهُ to begin [writing] a letter, or giving advice or counsel, with praise to God.

The third are things that are not often repeated, but which, when done, have lasting effects. Examples of these would be setting out on a journey, buying a new house, or donning the pilgrim's garb. In

---

102 Al-Bayhaqī, *Shuʿab al-īmān*, 2814.

103 As related in al-Bukhārī, *Ṣaḥīḥ*, 1554.

104 As related in Ibn Abī Shayba, *al-Muṣannaf*, 4919.

105 As related in al-Bukhārī, *Ṣaḥīḥ*, 4418; Muslim, *Ṣaḥīḥ*, 716.

106 With the wording, "Any matter that does not begin with praise to God..." Abū Dāwūd, *Sunan*, 4840; al-Nasāʾī, *Sunan*, 10258; Ibn Māja, *Sunan*, 1894.

107 The commentary notes that it is understood that both of these are preceded by, "In the name of God, the Merciful and Compassionate." Al-Zabīdī, *Itḥāf*, 3:464.

such cases, the preferred practice is to begin by praying two cycles. The least of these would be leaving and returning home—for that, too, is a kind of journey.

Seventh is the prayer for seeking the good (*istikhāra*).[108] If someone is concerned with a particular matter, does not know what its outcome will be, and does not know whether it is best to turn away from it or to go ahead with it, the Messenger of God ﷺ instructed him to pray two cycles. In the first, he should recite the Fātiḥa [1:1–7] and *Say: "O disbelievers..."* [109:1–6] and in the second, the Fātiḥa and *Say, "He is God, [who is] One"* [112:1–4]. When he completes this prayer, he should supplicate God [with these words]:

> O God, I am truly seeking what You choose [for me] in Your knowledge, and what You determine [for me] in Your power, and I ask You for Your immense grace, for You are the One who is able—and I am not—and You are the One who knows—and I do not—and You are the knower of the unseen. O God, if in Your knowledge, You know that this matter is good for me in my *dīn*, my worldly life, and the goal of my life, in the long run and in the short run, then place it within my reach, make it easy for me, then bless me therein. And if in Your knowledge, You know that this matter is bad for me in my *dīn*, my worldly life, and the goal of my life, in the long run and in the short run, then keep me away from it and keep it away from me, and decree for me what is good, whatever it may be. Verily You have power over all things.

This was transmitted by Jābir b. ʿAbdallāh who said, "The Messenger of God ﷺ used to teach us the supplication of seeking the best course in all matters just as he used to teach us *sūra*s from the Qurʾān."[109]

And he ﷺ said, "Whoever is concerned about a certain matter, should pray two cycles, then mention the matter by name,"[110] and supplicate with [the words] we have mentioned.

One of the sages said,

---

108 This prayer is also known as a prayer for guidance.

109 Al-Bukhārī, *Ṣaḥīḥ*, 1162.

110 Ibn Abī Shayba, *al-Muṣannaf*, 30016.

> Whoever is given four things will not be denied four others: whoever is given gratitude will not be denied increase,[111] whoever is given repentance will not be denied acceptance, whoever is given the prayer for seeking the good will not be denied the good, and whoever is given consultation will not be denied what is correct.

Eighth is the prayer of pressing need. If someone finds himself in an oppressive situation or in urgent need of something that will benefit him in his *dīn* or his worldly life, he should pray this prayer. It is related that Wuhayb b. al-Ward said,

This is among the supplications that are not refused: The servant should pray twelve cycles. In each one, he should recite the 'mother of the book' [Fātiḥa 1:1–7], the verse of the throne [2:255], and *Say, "He is God, [who is] One"* [112:1–4]. When he finishes, he should bow down in prostration and say, "Glory be to the One who is clothed in might and by it rules over all; glory be to the One who is enrobed in majesty and by it gives infinitely to all; glory be to the One who in His knowledge has reckoned all; glory be to the One who alone should be glorified; glory be to the One endowed with favor and grace; glory be to the One endowed with generosity and honor; glory be to the One endowed with forbearance! I ask You by the places of honor from Your throne and by the immense mercy of Your book, by Your supreme name, by Your most exalted majesty, and by Your perfect words, which neither the virtuous nor the sinful may trespass, to shower Your blessings upon Muḥammad and his family."

Then he should ask God to fulfill his need, as long as it contains nothing sinful, and he will be answered, God willing.

Wuhayb added, "It has been conveyed to us that he ﷺ said not to teach this supplication to fools, lest they use it to help each other sin against God most high.[112]

This is the prayer that was conveyed from the Messenger of God ﷺ by Ibn Masʿūd.

---

111 This refers to the verse: *And [remember] when your Lord proclaimed, "If you are grateful, I will surely increase you [in favor]; but if you deny, indeed, My punishment is severe"* [14:7].

112 Abū Nuʿaym, *Ḥilya*, 8:158.

Ninth is the prayer of glorification. This prayer has been conveyed in its present form by narrations passed down. It is not limited to any particular time or cause, but it is preferred that a week should not pass without praying it once, or a month without praying it once, for ʿIkrima related from Ibn ʿAbbās that the Prophet ﷺ said to ʿAbbās b. ʿAbd al-Muṭṭalib,

> Shall I not give you, grant you, bestow on you something, which if you practice it, God will forgive your sins, the first and the last, the old ones and new, the accidental and intentional, the secret and open ones? Pray four cycles and in each one recite the Fātiḥa [1:1–7] and a *sūra*. When you finish the recitation [of the *sūra*] of the first cycle, still standing, say "Glory be to God, praise be to God, there is no deity but God, and God is greater" fifteen times. Then bow, and say while bowing [this same invocation] ten times. Then raise your head up from the bowing and say it ten times, then prostrate and say it ten times, raise your head up from prostration and say it ten times, then prostrate a second time and say it ten times, and raise your head up from the second prostration and say it ten times. That makes seventy-five for one cycle, and this is what you should do in all four. If you can, pray this once a day. If you cannot, then once every Friday, and if you cannot, then once a month, and if you cannot, then once a year.[113]

Another narration says to begin the prayer by saying "Glory be to You, O God, and praise be to You, and blessed be Your name, and exalted Your might, and there is no deity but You!" Then repeat the invocation [quoted above] fifteen times before the recitation [of the Fātiḥa [1:1–7] and the *sūra*] and ten times after it, and the rest [as related] in tens but not after the prostration while still seated.[114] This is the better [of the two methods] and was the choice of Ibn al-Mubārak.[115] But the total number of times the glorification is repeated in both versions is three hundred. If this prayer is done

---

113 Abū Dāwūd, *Sunan*, 1297; Ibn Māja, *Sunan*, 1378.

114 That is to say, the invocation is not repeated after the prostrations between the two cycles or after the prostrations that directly precede the testimony.

115 Al-Tirmidhī, *Sunan*, 481.

during the day, it is done with one [closing] salutation,[116] but if at night, then it is prayed with two, since it has been conveyed that night prayers were in two cycles.[117] Finally, it is good if you add "There is no strength nor power except through God, the exalted, the almighty" to the glorification, and this [too] has been conveyed in some of the narrations.[118]

These are the supererogatory prayers that have been passed down.

It is not recommended to pray any of them at times that are disapproved of for prayer, except the greeting of the mosque and what we have said about it.[119] Those that we have set down following our mention of the prayer of greeting—the two cycles after the ablution, the prayer when setting out on a journey, on entering or leaving the house, or for seeking the right course—should [definitely] not [be prayed during times disapproved of for prayer]. The prohibition against praying them in a time that is disapproved of is firm, and the reasons for praying them are weak and not on the order of an eclipse, or seeking rain, or entering a mosque.

I have seen some among the Sufis praying two cycles after the ablution, but at a disapproved of time. This is completely wrong, because the ablution is not the reason for prayer, but rather the prayer is the reason for ablution. He should make the ablution in order to pray, not pray because he has made the ablution. If this were the case, then anyone who needed to make the ablution would do so, and pray, and there would be no meaning left to the notion of disapproval. No one should form the intention to pray two cycles following the ablution as he would for greeting the mosque. Rather, when he makes the ablution, he simply prays two voluntary cycles so that his ablution is not wasted, just as Bilāl used to, as a free voluntary act that happens to follow the ablution.

The *ḥadīth* [narrated by] Bilāl in no way indicates that the ablution was a reason [for praying], like an eclipse, or greeting the mosque is, such that he would form an intention to pray two cycles

---

116 That is, in four cycles in a single prayer.

117 Al-Bukhārī, *Ṣaḥīḥ*, 472; Muslim, *Ṣaḥīḥ*, 749.

118 Abū Ṭālib al-Makkī, *Qūt al-qulūb*, 1:44.

119 That is, the prayer at the eclipses, the funeral prayer, and the prayer for rain.

for it. It is impossible to intend a prayer for the ablution. Rather, in making the ablution, he intends to pray. How is it logical to say, "I am making this ablution because of my prayer," and then say, "I am praying because of my ablution"? Rather, anyone who wants to insure that his ablution is not wasted in a time disapproved of for prayer should simply form the intention of making up a [past] prayer that may have contained a defect for one reason or another. For it is not disapproved of to make up a prayer in a disapproved of time. But as for intending to pray a voluntary prayer [at such a time]—there is simply no way to do this.[120]

In prohibiting the prayer at disapproved of times, there are three important objects.

One is to keep from resembling those who worship the sun.

The second is as protection against the devils who are dispersed [through the land at certain hours], for the Prophet ﷺ said,

> The sun rises and with it [come] Satan's horns. When it rises, it is conjoined to it, and when it is well up in the sky, it separates. Then when it reaches its meridian, it is conjoined to it again, and when it passes the meridian, it separates. And when it nears its setting, it is conjoined to it, but after it sets, it separates.[121]

This, then, prohibits the prayer at these times and gives the reason why.

Third, the travelers on the path of the hereafter do not cease to pray to God at all hours, and to limit oneself to one form [of worship] leads to lassitude. When they are kept from it for a time, it actually increases their energy and attraction for it, because human nature desires what it cannot have. So in leaving these times unused, there is an increase in ardor and anticipation for the time [when prayer is allowed]. Moreover, these times [which are disapproved of for the prayer] are especially recommended for invocations of praise and for asking forgiveness, which is also a way of avoiding lassitude and boredom, and finding relief in going from one type of worship to another. In change and renewal there is delight and enthusiasm, while in keeping to one thing, there is heaviness and

120 This is al-Ghazālī's view; the most common view in the Shāfiʿī school is that a prayer of two cycles after the ablution may be done at times disapproved for prayer.

121 Al-Nasāʾī, *Sunan*, 1:275; Ibn Māja, *Sunan*, 1253.

fatigue. For this same reason, the prayer itself is not only prostration, not only bowing, and not only standing, but rather a worship made up of varied actions and distinct invocations. In going from one of these to another, the heart may experience new delight, while if it were one act continuously, lassitude would quickly set in.

These, then, are some important aspects in prohibiting [the prayer] at disapproved of times, and there are other mysteries [connected to this] which are beyond the power of humans to see: God and His Messenger know best concerning them. The important aspects should not be ignored, except for reasons that [themselves] are important in the law, such as making up an obligatory prayer that was not prayed on time, or praying for rain, or during an eclipse, or in greeting the mosque. For reasons weaker than these, one should not try, in any way, to circumvent the purpose of the prohibition. For us, this is the most correct view, and God most high knows best what is right.

The *Mysteries of the Prayer and Its Important Elements*—
book 4 in the Quarter of Worship from the books of the
Revival of the Religious Sciences—is thus completed
with praise to God and His beautiful accord. May
blessings be on Muḥammad, the master
of those who were sent, and on the
pure people of his family.

This book is followed by
the *Mysteries of Charity*
[book 5 in the Quarter of Worship
from the books of the *Revival of the Religious Sciences*]

Bibliography

Works in Western Languages

al-Ghazālī, Abū Ḥāmid Muḥammad b. Muḥammad. *Fatāwī l-Ghazālī*. Edited by Mahmoud M. Abu Sway. Kuala Lumpur, 1996. Also *al-Fatāwa li-l-Imām Muḥammad b. Muḥammad al-Ghazālī*. Edited by ʿAlī Muṣṭafaʾ al-Ṭassah. Damascus: al-Yamama li-l-Ṭibāʿa wa-l-Nashr wa-l-Tawzīʿ, 2004.

———. *Iḥyāʾ ʿulūm al-dīn*. Jedda: Dār al-Minhāj, 2011.

Translations:

The Arrangement of the Litanies and the Exposition of the Night Vigil: Kitāb tartīb al-awrād fī l-awqāt wa-tafṣīli iḥyāʾi al-layl. Book 10 of *The Revival of the Religious Sciences*. Translated by Muhtar Holland and James Pavlin. Louisville, KY: Fons Vitae, forthcoming.

The Etiquette of the Recitation of the Qurʾān: Kitāb ādāb tilāwat al-Qurʾān. Book 8 of *The Revival of the Religious Sciences*. Translated by James Pavlin. Louisville, KY: Fons Vitae, forthcoming.

Invocations and Supplications: Kitāb al-adhkāri wa-daʿwāt. Book 9 of *The Revival of the Religious Sciences*. Translated by Khalid Williams. Louisville, KY: Fons Vitae, forthcoming.

Inner Dimensions of Islamic Worship (A translation of portions of the first quarter of the *Iḥyāʾ ʿulūm al-dīn*). Translated by Muhtar Holland. Leicestershire: Islamic Foundation, 1983.

The Mysteries of Purification: Kitāb asrār al-ṭahāra. Book 3 of *The Revival of the Religious Sciences*. Translated by M. Fouad Aresmouk and M. Abdurrahman Fitzgerald. Louisville, KY: Fons Vitae, 2017.

Mysteries of Worship. Translated by E. E. Calvery. New Delhi: Kitab Bhavan, 1992.

On Fear and Hope: Kitāb al-khawfi wa-rajāʾ. Book 33 of *The Revival of the Religious Sciences*. Translated by William McKane as *Al-Ghazali's Book of Fear and Hope*. Leiden: Brill, 1965.

The Principles of the Creed: Kitāb Qawāʿid al-ʿaqāʾid. Book 2 of *The Revival of the Religious Sciences*. Translated by Khalid Williams. Louisville, KY: Fons Vitae, 2016.

The Remembrance of Death and the Afterlife. Translated by T. J. Winter. Cambridge: Islamic Texts Society, 1989.

Lings, Martin. *Muhammad: His Life Based on the Earliest Sources*. Cambridge: Islamic Texts Society, 1983.

Works in Arabic

ʿAbd al-Razzāq b. Hammām al-Ṣanʿānī. *al-Muṣannaf*. Edited by Ḥabīb al-Raḥmān al-ʿAẓamī. Beirut: Maktab al-Islāmī, 1983.

Abū Dāwūd, Sulaymān b. al-Ashaʿth al-Sijistānī. *Sunan Abū Dāwūd*. Edited by ʿIzzat ʿAbīd al-Daʿās and ʿĀdil al-Sayyid. Beirut: Dār Ibn Ḥazm, 1997.

Abū Nuʿaym al-Iṣbahānī, Aḥmad b. ʿAbdallāh. *Ḥilyat al-awliyāʾ*. Cairo: Maṭbaʿat al-Saʿāda wa-l-Khānjī, 1357/1938.

———. *Tārīkh Iṣbahān*. Edited by Sayyid Kusrawī Ḥasan. Beirut: Dār al-Kutub al-ʿIlmiyya, 1990.

Abū Ṭālib al-Makkī, Muḥammad b. ʿAlī. *Qūt al-qulūb*. Cairo: al-Maṭbaʿat al-Maymaniyya, 1310/1892.

Abū Yaʿlā, Aḥmad b. ʿAlī. *Musnad Abū Yaʿlā l-Mawṣūlī*. Edited by Ḥusayn Salīm Asad al-Dārānī. Damascus: Dār al-Maʾmūn li-l-Turāth and Dār al-Thaqafa al-ʿArabiyya, 1989.

al-Bayhaqī, Aḥmad b. al-Ḥusayn. *al-Jāmiʿ li-shuʿab al-īmān*. Edited by ʿAbd al-ʿAlī ʿAbd al-Ḥamīd Ḥāmid. Maktaba al-Rushd, Saudi Arabia, 2004.

———. *al-Sunan al-kubrā*. Beirut: Dār al-Maʿrifa, 1356.

al-Bukhārī, Muḥammad b. Ismāʿīl. *Ṣaḥīḥ al-Bukhārī*. Istanbul: n.p. [reprint of Beirut: Dār Ṭūq al-Najāt, 1422/2001].

———. *al-Tārīkh al-kabīr*. Edited by Muṣṭafā ʿAbd al-Qādir ʿAṭā. Beirut: Dār al-Kutub al-ʿIlmiyya, 2008.

al-Dāraquṭnī, ʿAlī b. ʿUmar. *Aṭrāf al-gharāʾib wa-l-afrād min ḥadīth rasūl Allāh*. 5 vols. Beirut: Dār al-Kutub al-ʿIlmiyya, 2008.

———. *Sunan al-Dāraquṭnī*. Edited by ʿAbdallāh Hashim Yamānī. Lebanon: Dār al-Maʿrifa, 1966 [repr.].

al-Dārimī, ʿAbdallāh b. ʿAbd al-Raḥmān. *Musnad al-Dārimī* [*Sunan*]. Edited by Ḥusayn Salīm Asad al-Dārānī. Riyadh: Dār al-Mughnī, 2000.

al-Daylamī, Shīrawayh b. Shahdār. *al-Firdaws bi-maʾthūr al-khiṭṭāb = Musnad al-firdaws*. Edited by Saʿīd b. Basyūnī Zaghlūl. Beirut: Dār al-Kutub al-ʿIlmiyya, 1986.

al-Dīnawarī, Aḥmad b. Marwān b. Muḥammad, *al-Majālisa wa-jawāhir al-ʿilm*. Beirut: Dār Ibn Ḥazm, 2002.

al-Ḥākim al-Nīsābūrī, Muḥammad b. ʿAbdallāh. *al-Mustadrak ʿalā l-Ṣaḥiḥayn*. Hyderabad: Dāʾirat al-Maʿārif al-Niẓāmiyya, 1335/1917 [repr. Beirut: Dār al-Maʿrifa, n.d.].

al-Ḥakīm al-Tirmidhī, Muḥammad b. ʿAlī. *Nawādir al-uṣūl*. Beirut: Dār Ṣādir, n.d. [reprint Cairo, 1293/1876 edition].

al-Haythamī, Nūr al-Dīn. *Bughiyat al-bāḥith ʿan zawāʾid Musnad al-Ḥārith b. Abī Usāma*. Edited by Ḥusayn Aḥmad Ṣāliḥ al-Bākrī. Medina: Markaz Khidma al-Sunna wa-l-Sīra al-Nabawīy, 1992.

Ibn Abī ʿAṣim, *al-Ṣalāt ʿalā l-nabī ṣalla llāhu ʿalayhi wa-ālihi wa-sallam*. Damascus: Dār al-Maʾmūn li-l-Turāth, 1995.

Ibn ʿAbd al-Barr, Yūsuf b. ʿAbdallāh. *al-Tamhīd*. Casablanca: Wizārat al-Awqāf, 1967.

Ibn Abī l-Dunyā, ʿAbdallāh b. Muḥammad al-Qarashī. *al-Maraḍ wa-l-kaffārāt*. Edited by ʿAbd al-Wakīl al-Nadwī. Bombay: Dār al-Salafiyya, 1991.

———. *Mujābū l-daʿwat*. Edited by ʿAbd al-ʿAzīz Amīn. Cairo: Dār al-Risāla, 2005.

———. *al-Riqqa wa-l-bukāʾ*. Edited by Muḥammad Khayr Ramaḍān Yūsuf. Beirut: Dār Ibn al-Jawzī, 1996.

———. *al-Tahajjud wa-qiyyām al-layl*. Edited by Muṣliḥ b. Jazāʾ b. Fadghush al-Ḥārithī. Riyadh: Maktaba al-Rushd, 2000.

———. *al-ʿUqūbāt*. Edited by Muḥammad Khayr Ramaḍān Yūsuf. Beirut: Dār Ibn al-Jawzī, 1998.

Ibn Abī Ḥātim, ʿAbd al-Raḥmān b. Muḥammad b. Idrīs. *Tafsīr al-qurʾān al-ʿaẓīm*. Edited by Asad Muḥammad al-Ṭayyib. Riyadh: Maktabat Nizār Muṣṭafā l-Bāz, 1997.

Ibn Abī Shayba, ʿAbdallāh b. Muḥammad. *al-Muṣannaf*. Edited by Muḥammad ʿAwāmma. Jedda: Dār al-Minhāj, 2006.

Ibn ʿAdī = ʿAbdallāh b. ʿAdī l-Jurjānī. *al-Kāmil fī ḍuʿafāʾ al-rijāl*. Edited by Muḥammad Aḥmad al-Dālī. Beirut: Muʾassasat al-Risāla, 1997.

Ibn ʿAsākir, ʿAlī b. al-Ḥasan. *Tārīkh madīnat Dimashq*. Edited by Muḥibb al-Dīn ʿUmar b. Gharāma al-ʿUmrāwī. Beirut: Dār al-Fikr, 1995.

Ibn Ḥanbal = Aḥmad b. Ḥanbal. *Musnad al-Imām Aḥmad b. Ḥanbal*. Edited by Shuʿayb al-Arnāʾūṭ. Beirut: Muʾassasat al-Risāla, 1995.

———. *al-Zuhd*. Edited by Muḥammad ʿAbd al-Salam Shāhīn. Beirut: Dār al-Kutub al-ʿIlmiyya, 1999.

Ibn Ḥibbān, Abū Hatim Muḥammad al-Tamimi al-Busti. *Ṣaḥīḥ*. Edited by Shuʿayb al-Arnāʾūṭ. Beirut: Muʾassasat al-Risāla, 1993.

Ibn Hishām. *al-Sīrat al-nabawiyya*. Beirut: Dār al-Jīl, 1998.

Ibn al-Jawzī, ʿAbd al-Raḥmān b. ʿAlī. *Ṣifat al-ṣafwa*. Edited by ʿAbd al-Salām Hārūn. Beirut: Muʾassasat al-Kutub al-Thaqāfiyya, 1992.

Ibn Khuzayma, Abū Bakr b. Muḥammad b. Isḥāq al-Nīsābūrī, *Ṣaḥīḥ Ibn Khuzayma*. Edited by Muḥammad Muṣṭafā l-ʿAẓamī. Beirut: al-Maktab al-Islāmī, 2003.

Ibn Māja, Muḥammad b. Yazīd. *Sunan Ibn Māja*. Edited by Muḥammad Fuʾād ʿAbd al-Bāqī. Cairo: Dār Iḥyāʾ al-Kutub al-ʿArabiyya, 1954.

Ibn al-Mubārak, ʿAbdallāh. *Zuhd wa-l-raqāʾiq*. Edited by Ḥabīb al-Raḥmān al-ʿAẓamī. Beirut: Dār al-Kutub al-ʿIlmiyya, n.d.

Ibn Rajab, ʿAbd al-Raḥmān b. Aḥmad al-Baghdādī. *Fatḥ al-bārī fī sharḥ ṣaḥīḥ al-Bukhārī*. Dammam, Saudi Arabia: Dār Ibn al-Jawzī, 1425/2004.

Ibn Saʿd = Muḥammad b. Saʿd al-Baṣrī. *Ṭabaqāt al-kubrā*. Edited by ʿAlī Muḥammad ʿUmar. Cairo: Maktabat al-Khanjī, 2001.

Ibn Rāhawīh, Isḥāq b. Ibrāhīm al-Marūzī. *Musnad Isḥāq b. Rāhawīh*. Edited by ʿAbd al-Ghafūr al-Balūshī. Medina: Maktabat al-Īmān, 1990.

Ibn Shāhīn, ʿUmar b. Aḥmad ʿUthmān. *al-Targhīb fī faḍāʾil al-aʿmāl wa-thawābu dhālik*. Edited by Ṣāliḥ Aḥmad al-Waʿīl. Dammam, Saudi Arabia: Dār Ibn al-Jawzī, 1995.

al-Jazīrī. *Islamic Jurisprudence According to the Four Sunni Schools by ʿAbd al-Rahman al-Jaziri*. Translated by Nancy Roberts. Louisville, KY: Fons Vitae, 2009.

al-Khaṭīb al-Baghdādī, Aḥmad b. ʿAlī. *Tārīkh Baghdād*. Edited by Muṣṭafā ʿAbd al-Qādir ʿAṭā. Beirut: Dār al-Kutub al-ʿIlmiyya, 1997.

al-Lālakāʾī, Hibat Allāh b. al-Ḥasan. *Sharḥ uṣūl iʿtiqād ahl al-sunna*. Edited by Aḥmad Saʿd al-Ghāmidī. Riyadh: Dār Ṭayyiba, 2005.

Mālik, Ibn Anas b. Mālik. *al-Muwaṭṭaʾ*. Edited by Muḥammad Fuʾād ʿAbd al-Bāqī. Cairo: Dār Iḥyāʾ al-Kutub al-ʿArabiyya, n.d.

al-Marūzī, Muḥammad b. Nāṣr. *Taʿẓīm qadri al-ṣalāt*. Edited by Aḥmad Abū l-Majd. Cairo: Dār al-ʿAqīda, 2003.

al-Munāwī, Muḥammad ʿAbd al-Raʾūf b. ʿAlī. *Fayḍ al-qadīr sharḥ al-jāmiʿ al-ṣaghīr*. Beirut: Dār al-Maʿrifa, 1357/[1938].

al-Mundharī, ʿAbd al-ʿAẓīm b. ʿAbd al-Qawī. *al-Targhīb wa-l-tarhīb*. Edited by Muḥyī l-Dīn Mistū, Samīr al-ʿAṭṭār, and Yūsuf Badawī. Damascus: Dār Ibn Kathīr, 1999.

Muslim b. al-Ḥajjāj al-Qushayrī l-Nīsābūrī. *Ṣaḥīḥ Muslim*. Edited by Muḥammad Fuʾād ʿAbd al-Bāqī. Cairo: Dār Iḥyāʾ al-Kutub al-ʿArabiyya, 1954.

al-Nasāʾī, Aḥmad b. Shuʿayb. *Sunan al-Nasāʾī = al-Kubrā*. Cairo: al-Maṭbaʿat al-Maymaniyya, 1312/1894; repr. Beirut: Dār al-Kitāb al-ʿArabī.

al-Nawawī, Yaḥyā b. Sharaf. *al-Majmūʿ sharḥ al-madhhab*. Edited by Maḥmūd Maṭrajī. Beirut: Dār al-Fikr, 1996.

al-Qālī, Abū Ismāʿīl. *Kitāb al-amālī*. Beirut: Dār al-Kutub al-ʿIlmiyya, 2002.

al-Shāfiʿī, Muḥammad b. Idrīs. *Musnad Imām al-Shāfiʿī*. Edited by Ayyūb Abū Khashrīf. Damascus: Dār al-Thaqāfa al-ʿArabī, 2002.

———. *al-Umm*. Edited by Rifʿat Fawzī ʿAbd al-Muṭṭalib. Cairo: Dār al-Wafāʾ, 2001.

al-Sirāj, Muḥammad b. Isḥāq. *Musnad al-sirāj*. Edited by Irshād al-Ḥaqq al-Atharī. Faysalabad, Pakistan: Idrār al-ʿUlūm al-Athariya, 2002.

al-Suhaylī, Abū l-Qāsim ʿAbd al-Raḥmān b. ʿAbdallāh b. Aḥmad. *al-Rawḍ al-unuf*. Beirut: Dār Iḥyāʾ al-Turāth al-ʿArabī, 2000.

al-Suhrawardī, ʿUmar b. Muḥammad b. ʿAbdallāh. *ʿAwārif al-maʿārif*. Edited by Adīb al-Kamdānī and Muḥammad Maḥmūd al-Muṣṭāfa. Mecca: al-Maktabat al-Makkiyya, 2001.

al-Suyūṭī, ʿAbd al-Raḥmān b. Abī Bakr. *al-Durr al-manthūr fī l-tafsīr bi-maʾthur*. Beirut: Dār al-Fikr, 2002.

al-Ṭabarānī, Sulaymān b. Aḥmad. *al-Muʿjam al-awsaṭ*. Edited by Maḥmūd al-Ṭaḥḥān. Riyadh [?]: Maktabat al-Maʿārif, 1985.

———. *al-Muʿjam al-kabīr*. Edited by Ḥamdī ʿAbd al-Majīd al-Salafī. Beirut: Dār Iḥyāʾ al-Turāth al-ʿArabī, n.d.

———. *Musnad al-Shāmiyīn*. Edited by Ḥamdī ʿAbd al-Majīd al-Salafī. Beirut: Muʾassasat al-Risāla, 1989.

al-Ṭabarī, Muḥammad b. Jarīr, *Tafsīr: Jāmiʿ al-bayān ʿan taʾwīl āyā l-qurʾān*. Beirut and Amman: Dār Ibn Ḥazm and Dār al-Aʿlām, 2002.

al-Ṭaḥāwī, Aḥmad b. Muḥammad b. Salāma. *Sharḥ muskhil al-āthār*. Edited by Shuʿayb al-Arnāʾūṭ. Beirut: Muʾassasat al-Risāla, 1994.

al-Ṭawsī, Abū l-Ḥasan Muḥammad b. Aslam. *al-Arbaʿīn*. Edited by Mishʿal b. Bānī l-Jabrīn al-Maṭīrī. Beirut: Dār Ibn Ḥazm, 2000.

al-Tirmidhī, Muḥammad b. ʿĪsā. *al-Shamāʾil al-Muḥammadiyya*. Beirut: Printed by Muḥammad ʿAwwāma, 2001.

———. *Sunan al-Tirmidhī = al-Jāmiʿ al-ṣaḥīḥ*. Edited by Aḥmad Shākir, Muḥammad Fuʾād ʿAbd al-Bāqī, and Ibrāhīm ʿAṭwa. Beirut: Dār Iḥyāʾ al-Turāth al-ʿArabī, n.d. [reprint of Cairo, 1938 edition].

al-Zabīdī, Muḥammad Murtaḍā, *Itḥāf al-sadā l-muttaqīn bi-sharḥ Iḥyāʾ ʿulūm al-dīn*. [Cairo]: al-Maṭbaʿ al-Maymūniyya, 1311/1894.

Index of Qurʾānic Verses

Index of *Ḥadīth*

For this one, if his heart were reverent, his limbs would be as well, 66
Friday is the best day on which the sun rises…, 94

Gabriel عَلَيْهِ السَّلَامُ came to me holding a white mirror…, 93
Give us rest by it, O Bilāl!, 57
God does not look on the prayer of a man whose heart is not present along with his body, 15
God عَزَّوَجَلَّ faces the one praying as long as he does not turn away, 65
God has mercy on the one who rises early…, 99
God has ordained five daily prayers for His servants…, 5
God is angered by someone who worships Him through some form of devotion and then gives it up out of laziness, 170
God عَزَّوَجَلَّ made the Friday prayer obligatory for you…, 92
God most high says, 'My servant is not delivered from My punishment except by completing what I have made obligatory on him,' 77
God puts a seal on the heart of whoever does not attend three [consecutive] Friday congregational prayers…, 92
God عَزَّوَجَلَّ says in one of the scriptures, 'Verily, My houses on earth are the mosques…, 19
[God sees him in] his standing, his bowing, his prostration, and his sitting, 66
God will build a dwelling in heaven…, 139

The hand of the most merciful is upon the head of the caller to prayer…, 4
Hell is kindled every day before noon…, 94
He [Muḥammad] would pray four cycles for the morning prayer (*ḍuḥā*) and [sometimes] add more…, 146

I considered asking someone to lead the prayer…, 9
I entered heaven and saw Bilāl there…, 170
I fear they will be made obligatory on you, 160
If Friday is safe, the week is safe, 94
If his heart were reverent, his limbs would be as well, 16
I forgot to tell you to put a cloth over the cooking pots in the room…, 53
If someone passing in front of a person praying knew the gravity of that action…, 105
If someone prays *ʿishāʾ* [in congregation]…, 10
If someone's prayer does not prohibit him from immorality and wrongdoing…, 15, 40
If [the *imām*] prays perfectly…, 80
If the [obligatory] prayer has started, there is no other prayer except it, 138
If the servant rises to pray…, 58
I have divided the prayer between Me and My servant…, 64
I have never seen a prayer as brief and at the same time, [as] complete as that of the Messenger of God صَلَّى ٱللَّهُ عَلَيْهِ وَسَلَّمَ, 87–88

I humble myself to my Lord عَزَّوَجَلَّ that He might not hate me, 54
The *imām* is a guarantor and the muezzin is someone given a trust, 80
The *imām* is one to be trusted. When he bows, bow; when he prostrates, prostrate, 80
Increase [the number of your] blessings on me…, 157
In the last days, there will be people from this community who go to the mosque…, 19
I saw God's Messenger صَلَّى ٱللَّٰهُ عَلَيْهِ وَسَلَّمَ pray the funeral prayer…, 166
Is there anyone who calls on Me that I might answer?…, 1
It is all right for someone to make the ablution for the Friday prayer, but to bathe is better, 100
It is better for a man to be ashes in the wind than pass in front of someone praying, 105
It is better to wait forty years than to pass in front of someone praying, 105

Lā ilāha illā llāh is My citadel…, 61–62
Let whoever comes to the Friday congregational [prayer] take a bath…, 99–100
Let whoever is present at the Friday congregation, men and women, [first] take a bath, 100

May God have mercy on the servant who prays four cycles before the afternoon prayer, 141
The Messenger of God صَلَّى ٱللَّٰهُ عَلَيْهِ وَسَلَّمَ once prayed wearing sandals…, 124
The Messenger of God صَلَّى ٱللَّٰهُ عَلَيْهِ وَسَلَّمَ once saw that someone had spit on the *qibla* wall and he became extremely angry…, 125
The Messenger of God صَلَّى ٱللَّٰهُ عَلَيْهِ وَسَلَّمَ prayed three cycles as the *witr*, 144
The Messenger of God prohibited *sadl* in the prayer…, 31 n.26
The Messenger of God صَلَّى ٱللَّٰهُ عَلَيْهِ وَسَلَّمَ sacrificed two very fine rams…, 159
The Messenger of God صَلَّى ٱللَّٰهُ عَلَيْهِ وَسَلَّمَ used to converse with us and we with him, but when the time of prayer arrived…, 50
The Messenger of God صَلَّى ٱللَّٰهُ عَلَيْهِ وَسَلَّمَ used to teach us the supplication of seeking the best course…, 172
The Messenger of God صَلَّى ٱللَّٰهُ عَلَيْهِ وَسَلَّمَ was giving the sermon on Friday when he saw a man stepping over people…, 104
The Messenger of God صَلَّى ٱللَّٰهُ عَلَيْهِ وَسَلَّمَ would pray four cycles after the last evening prayer and then go to sleep, 143
The most beloved practice to God most high is what is done with consistency, even if it is small, 170
The muezzin should leave enough time between the call to prayer…, 84
A Muslim is someone from whose tongue and hand the Muslims are safe, 60

No one should compel his brother to stand up from where he was sitting…, 113
No one should wish for death…, 53 n.24

The Prophet ﷺ used to pray two cycles [of supererogatory prayers] after the Friday prayer…, 111

Recite distinctly, in a slow, measured voice…, 65
The right of pre-emption [in inheritance] applies to…, 40

The servant does not draw nearer to God by anything more excellent than a prostration done in secret, 12
The servant gains nothing from the prayer except that of which he is mindful, 40
A servant may pray, yet there will not be written for him even one-sixth…, 43–44
The servant may pray at the end of its time and he does not miss it, but…, 82
A servant will pray and yet not even one-half…, 75
Setting out for the Friday prayer in the first hour is like sacrificing a camel…, 102
Seven things [which occur] in the prayer are from Satan…, 33
Shall I not give you…, 174
The sun and the moon are two of God's signs…, 163
The sun rises…, 176
The superiority of voluntary prayer at home to [prayer] in the mosque…, 160

Take as a muezzin someone who does not take compensation for giving the call to prayer, 83
Take this back to Abū Jahm, for it distracted me in my prayer…, 54
That is a devil named Khanzab. If you sense him, seek refuge in God, 33 n.35
[The one praying] should block [the passerby]…, 105
The Prophet ﷺ was asked about turning away in the prayer…, 33 n.35
There are those who stand in prayer and get nothing from it except weariness and distress, 40
There are three things that, if people knew their true value, they would…, 103
There is no prayer for someone who lives next to the mosque except in the mosque, 18
There will come a time when people will talk, in the mosque…, 111–112
This is a time when the doors of heaven open…, 139
The two cycles [before] *fajr* are better than the world and all it contains, 138
Two men from my people may stand, and bow, and prostrate in the same prayer…, 8

Ubayy was right, 110

Verily, during the days of your life, your Lord gives breaths of the spirit…, 115
Verily, on Friday there is an hour during which no Muslim supplicates God عَزَّوَجَلَّ for anything without being given it, 114
Verily God and His angels bless those who wear a turban on the day of the Friday congregation, 102

Index of People and Places

Subject Index